We're Going Home

Single and 65, the author adopts
a teenage girl and her brother from Siberia

★ ★ ★

C.C. LeBlanc

Going Home: Single and 65, the author adopts a teenage girl and her brother from Siberia
© Copyright 2021 by C.C. LeBlanc
C.C. LeBlanc, Naples, FL

ISBN: 978-1-953114-29-7

Published by EA Books Publishing, a division of Living Parables of Central Florida, Inc. a 501c3

Table of Contents

Dedication

To my precious children, Kristina and Anton,
I dedicate this book to you.
You entered my heart three days after we met.
You gave me a reason to get up each morning.
Because of you I became a mother, later a grandmother.
I have loved you and will continue to love you for an eternity.
I thank you for being part of my life,
Mama C.C.

Acknowledgements

To Sir John and to my Earth angels,

Without Sir John, this beautiful story would not have been possible.

His continued love and loyal support during the process of the adoption and beyond should be a story of its own.

Sir John's love and loyalty and his unflinching support were gifts of immeasurable value. During the two-and-one-half years it took to be able to say to my children, "We're going home," he was the archangel of all the earth angels involved in this process.

He and his wife, Laura, introduced me to the Wise family who had just adopted two Russian children. The epiphany was instant. This was the beginning of this incredible journey, a journey filled with love and dedication to successfully adopt my beautiful children, Kristina and Anton.

You are gone now Sir John and Laura, and I miss you. I am immensely grateful to you. I feel so privileged to have had you and so many friends who supported my efforts through the so many challenges my children and I faced. From the bottom of my heart, I thank each of you. You have all helped make this beautiful story a reality.

Valerie and Murray Wise

Lidia my Russian-speaking friend from Belarus

Reverend Patterson and the members of the Naples United Church of Christ

My family in Québec, especially my brother Roger who kept mom and my family informed and my niece Sylvie who was most supportive

Polina Morris

Liz Mossman

Judy Graham

My long-time friend Sol Mester who spent one week with us as a Russian translator

Jamie Knight, Murray Wise's secretary who, while I was in Krasnoyarsk, was an invaluable help collecting documents requested by the Siberian court.

Fran Nelms

Vice Admiral (retired) Rex Rectanus.

Johanne Couture

John Zetzman and later his wife Phyllis

The Stonebridge Golf and Country Club Community

Naren and Dr. Renate Chevli,

My cousins from Montreal, especially Louise

Neta LeBlanc, her family, Karen F. and Joanne G.

Jerry Knox

Mrs. Louie, INS in Miami

My Montreal long-time friend Claudette Sergerie

And so many others.

Acknowledgements

To: Mel Park, Ph.D.,

We met mid-December 2018. Since then, we have been happily intertwined in each other's lives.

Where or how could I find the right words to convey my total appreciation and gratitude for your support and help Mel? You accepted the massive responsibility to guide me to prepare this beautiful story for publication.

Your patience, your tolerance, knowledge, and desire to help me were unconditional. Starting in December 2020 through the publication process, we worked together for hours, almost every day to prepare the manuscript to meet the requirement of the publishing company. Without your help, I would still be struggling with Microsoft Word . . .

Thank you from the bottom of my heart, Mel.

To my Pelican Bay Writers Group,

Without you, my friends of the Pelican Bay Writers Group, this book would still be on the workbench.

For the last several years, I so appreciated the constructive criticisms, from each one of you during your membership in the writers group. You started helping me from the time I joined you. You were the thread that encouraged me, propelled me further and further until I reached the end of my story. I had always considered myself a poor writer. I am still not an outstanding writer but with your help, guidance and, yes, your indispensable criticisms and suggestions, I improved, and today, I am proud to be able to publish this wonderful story, *We're Going Home*, a story very dear to my heart.

Thank you.

To my family,

Before there was me, there were my parents. With their encouragement and their trust, I was able to flourish. Number two of a family of seven, I was given additional responsibilities at a very young age by becoming my mom's right hand.

The support and love of my parents and of my four brothers gave me a strong sense of values, and the security of family closeness. I am so thankful to have experienced the extraordinary love my four brothers and I shared. You are deeply locked into my heart. Thank you.

In 1955, when I was just fifteen years-old, a great opportunity came my way thanks to Uncle Charley and his wife, Gen, and thanks to my parents, who had the wisdom to accept their invitation.

This invitation was first intended to benefit my older sister. Early that summer, she was misdiagnosed with tuberculosis and spent three months in a sanatorium in Roberval, Qc. Was this a twist of fate or a miracle that her misfortune opened the door for me to take her place and spend one high school year in upper New York State to learn English?

Without the knowledge of the English language, my life would have taken a very different path. The adoption and this story, *We're Going Home*, would not have happened.

All my life, I have cherished the memories of my time spent with uncle Charley, aunt Gen, their son, Chuck, his wife Neta, daughter Joanne, their nine grandchildren as well as their niece, Sandy Prenoveau Buckley, who became my earth angel during the school year 1955-56. She and all her friends and teachers made me feel welcomed and loved.

I thank you all from the bottom of my heart.

A Story to Tell

WE ALL HAVE A story to tell. Mine started August 31, 2003, and it ended May 11, 2005, the day we arrived in Naples, Florida as a family. What is written is what I saw, what I experienced and what I felt, expressed as truthfully as I can. The names of several people and some institutions have been changed to protect their privacy.

For as long as I can remember, I have been interested in people in general, but more so if they came from a different part of the world than I. In the 1940s and 1950s, the several small towns in Québec Province, Canada where I grew up, everyone was similar—all white, all Catholic, except in Grand'Mère where there were several protestants. We were taught that to engage in conversation with Protestants would be a mortal sin. My first exposure to black people was in school, and that was only through photographs. The nuns who taught us collected money for the Catholic missions in Africa. For every quarter we gave, we received a picture of a black child who needed our help. Then, in 1955, when I was almost sixteen, I went to high school in Plattsburgh, New York to learn English. That is when I saw a real black person for the first time. From that moment on, I became fascinated with anyone who looked different than me or who came from a far-away country.

But it is when I moved to Montreal in 1961, at age twenty-two, that my curiosity took flight. First, with my cousin's help, I rented a room from a pleasant older Jewish woman who mostly spoke Yiddish. To me then, her speech sounded very strange and harsh in my ears. At work, I sat next to a woman who spoke French with a mixture of Parisian and Québec accents. When asked where she came from, she answered, "Oh! I was born in Egypt. My parents moved here when I was eight years old."

She went on to share how her parents used their family's gold jewelry to pay their way out of Egypt. Wow! How did they accomplish that? I wanted to know more.

One of my coworkers, who became a close friend, told me she had been dating a Jewish man whom she was going to marry. She added, "I will convert to Judaism. My parents are furious. They are very catholic you know, and I am their only child."

To my surprise, I was invited to her wedding. For the first time, I saw a very different but beautiful wedding ceremony, followed by a lavish celebration. At that time, according to my church, if I had died that day, I would have been in deep trouble when I arrived at the Pearly Gates of Heaven. It was forbidden to even speak to a Protestant, much less a Jew.

I have continued to be fascinated with people's color, features, and accents. I find beauty and value in people of every race and every color. More recently, I became curious to know the details of how some of my international friends' parents or grandparents came to the United States. Most did not know, or they had very few recollections. In fact, most were sorry they did not take the time to sit down with their parents and grandparents to learn the details of how they came to America, the story of their roots in this country.

James and Nora became close acquaintances. They had escaped Czechoslovakia and first moved to Canada. Later they placed their names in the United States lottery and won permanent green cards to move to the U.S.

James remembered their escape from his country some thirty years earlier. He shared that Nora, who was a trusted employee in one of the larger banks in their city, obtained, with the help of a powerful customer, a visa and traveling papers for her and for her husband. While both Nora and James had talked about leaving their country, Nora did not share her exact plans with her husband until the last minute, much less sharing her plans to escape with any family members or friends, for fear that her ambitious secret would leak out.

James recounted, "One evening, Nora told me, 'James pack light, we're leaving in the morning.' "

He talked about how he wanted to run to his mom's home to hug her one last time.

"I could not bear leaving the family I loved and the only land I had ever known albeit one that offered so little. Our departure was so sudden."

With emotions, tears, his voice almost mute, he spoke about the torment he felt at each of the seven or eight check points on the long train ride to freedom.

"Nora and I were so afraid of getting caught. The train was filled with people just like us, all trying to escape. At each checkpoint many were captured. They were taken off the train by ruthless, cold-blooded guards. Who knows what happened to them?"

James spoke about how sick to his stomach he was and how his heart dropped to his feet at the Austrian border, the final checkpoint before reaching freedom. He started sobbing, remembering his emotions,

"The imposing, puffed up, and stone-faced guard took our papers. He looked at them for several minutes. Then he raised his eyes, looked at Nora intensely, turned toward me, his eyes locked on mine, trying to determine if we were lying, if we were escaping. Nora and I prayed with all our might. After what appeared to be an eternity, the guard returned our papers and said with an indignant voice, 'Get out of here. Go, go quickly before I change my mind.' "

James broke down and sobbed while reliving the events of that day.

Then there is the story of Corina's grandmother who came to the United States in the late 1920s. Corina shared the following with me.

"When I was a young girl, grandma spoke so many times about the precious little house in Romania she and grandpa lived in, right up to the time they immigrated to the US. When my husband and I visited Romania recently, I was determined to find that precious little house.

After questioning some villagers, my husband and I followed their directions, walked up the hill and there it was, grandma's little house. With courage and much anticipation, I knocked on the door. A man opened it.

"My name is Corina. Many years ago, my grandparents owned this house before they moved to the United States." The elderly gentleman graciously invited us in. The little house was exactly as grandma described it. The stone chimney on the right, the staircase on the left, the grape vine wrapped around the porch in the back yard, and the little garden filled with newly grown vegetables. Tears of beautiful memories and emotions filled me up, so grateful I was to be in the very little house where my beloved grandparents had lived. I felt they were right there with me."

These are very small segments of so many other precious tales. While listening to these two stories, I was able to make a movie in my mind and follow the events just as if I were there. If we could hear the stories of those who immigrated to our shores, they would reveal the strength, the determination, the character, the courage, and the fabric each one was made of. Their stories would reveal how each person trusted themselves enough to take the chance to overcome difficult, if not impossible and dangerous obstacles along the way. These brave individuals would rather leave their possessions, their families, even take the risk of dying to cross the oceans, or to find their way over the borders to reach the land of the free. Each story deserves to be written, to be passed on for all the generations that follow.

Sadly, many have no idea how their ancestors arrived in the United States. At best, they have heard some adult conversations about it when they were young. With the grandparents and the parents' passing, future generations have forever lost these precious stories.

I invite you to join me to experience the intense true story of the adoption of my children. I invite you to live it as we lived it, to feel my emotions and the emotions of my children, to cry with us. Come along, fly with me, walk with me, be with me as though it were your story. You will laugh, you will cry. In the end, it will touch your heart in a very special way.

What was it that possessed me to make this bold decision? What could have possibly triggered my emotions to the point I overlooked the enormous challenges ahead? Was I in need of a meaningful purpose for my life? Did I feel for an instant, for a moment, for a period of time, so invincible that I could, alone, handle, manage, or accomplish this most difficult task? Why did I not sober up and stop before embarking on a blind adventure? Why did I choose to give up my comfortable lifestyle to take on a responsibility way over my head? While some friends thought I was venturing upon a beautiful, purposeful cause, some thought I was insane, completely out of my mind.

"C.C., before you embark on such a journey, you should get some counseling."

The bigger questions for me were: What makes people do what they do? What influences or experiences did they have in their lives that triggered their desires, their way of thinking, their ambitions? Or perhaps one could ask: What is missing in peoples' lives that drives them to change course? Do they sense an emptiness deep down in their soul? Or is it the legacy they want to leave behind after they're gone?

There are days when I still question the reasons why I made this daring decision to singlehandedly adopt two children when I was already sixty-five years old. The answer has many facets, but for sure it has forever changed the way I live. It has forever changed my priorities. This decision has turned my life upside down. What has become important and what has been pushed aside have been completely reprioritized. Once I embarked full speed ahead, with a heart filled with love, there was no chance, no possibility of going back. I reached the point of no return when I fell in love with my two children, Kristina and Anton, three days after we met.

This emotionally charged roller coaster story is filled with deep love, unsustainable pain, indestructible determination and immeasurable joy. Its sense of high purpose has made it all worthwhile. This book tells the accurate story of how my children came to the United States. It is the story of their roots in America. It is the story they will pass on to their descendants. My hope is that this book will inspire some of you to consider a similar journey, to give hope to a child when hope is lost, to give that child love when love has died.

1.

Inspiration

Coincidence is God's way to remain anonymous.
Horace Walpole[1]

ALL AROUND THE WORLD, New Year's 2003 celebrations had come and gone. The Auld Lang Syne was sung, the champagne bottles had popped, and the toasts were exchanged.

It had already been sixteen years since my retirement March 31, 1987. My working career had had a surprising longevity of thirty-one years. But retiring at age forty-seven was an exceptional gift.

My working life started in the small town of Roberval, Québec Province, Canada in 1956. I was then in the mid-teenage years of sixteen. A college education was rarely offered to young girls at that time. The general opinion was girls were meant to get married and have babies. Being born number two of seven children, I had an older sister, four younger brothers and a younger sister. The boys would have a chance to go to college, rarely would the girls.

My thoughts were that if I worked hard, if I were responsible and honest, if I asked my managers to teach me complicated tasks, if I improved my knowledge by taking evening classes, if I read serious books, and if I listened to older people, I would learn some of what I missed by not going to college, and I would have a better chance to succeed. At that young age, I did not quite understand what success really meant. How is a successful person defined? Growing up, I had two new dresses a year, one at Christmas and one at Easter. For me, at that time, success may have meant having three or four new dresses a year.

In the course of my life, I evaluated every opportunity that came along. When I thought these opportunities would enhance my life, I remembered the words, "Fear is a reaction; courage is a decision." I would brave my fears, jump in and work as hard as I could to succeed.

Since my retirement, March 1987, at age forty-seven, my life had been full of "busyness," but my soul was missing a true purpose. I needed something genuinely meaningful to justify the easy living I enjoyed for so many years. My energy was spent doing special things for some members of my family, volunteering, playing tennis, going to lectures, learning about investments, going to lunches, reading, taking classes at Florida Gulf Coast University, dating, organizing cocktail parties, charity balls, buying real estate, traveling, and more. But each night as I went to sleep, I felt an emptiness. There was a missing part. I wondered when I would find this missing link. . . .

"When will I find the meaningful something that will fill my heart, fill my soul and fill my life?"

I could not imagine continuing this easy lifestyle without sharing, without giving . . . but to whom and to what?

I prayed to God, I prayed to my angels, I asked the universe, "Why was I given such an opportunity to retire at forty-seven? What do I need to do? What do you expect of me now? How do I share some of what I have received?" I pleaded so many times, "Don't wait too long, God, I'm getting old."

I truly believed nothing is free. No one gets such a huge break in life without having to reciprocate, to do something meaningful for someone, for the world, whatever that might be. These were many of the questions I so often asked myself.

Whether it is a myth or a truth, not only do I believe in God, I also believe in angels. Not only do I believe in angels, I know

I have one on each shoulder at all times. They are my friends, they protect me, they give me advice when no one is around, they are my sounding board. When God is busy, my angels take over, or at least I like to think so. It may sound childish, but it is very comforting to think I am not alone.

With the everyday activities or the everyday busyness taking me into so many directions, I developed a few profound friendships, many fingertip friends, and many more acquaintances. Two of my dearest friends were Laura and John W. I first met Laura in 1991 at a Naples Philharmonic board meeting for the "Auction on Stage Fundraiser." We met a few more times at the Naples Town Hall discussion groups and at some social gatherings. One day, Laura said, "C.C., we keep running in to each other, we must have something in common. Let's have lunch."

We did. A few days later Laura introduced me to her husband, John. The three of us began a long and beautiful relationship. They were fifteen and sixteen years older than I. Laura and I participated in many women's social events together. John and I played tennis in a foursome once or twice a week. Most Sundays, we attended the service at The Naples United Church of Christ. The Sunday service was always a very special bonding time for us. I often sat between the two of them.

Laura's parents were from Scandinavia. Her dad was a physician, her mother stayed at home with their four children. Laura had obtained a pilot's license. She, however, worked as an airline stewardess. John, born in 1923 just outside London England, was the son of Salvation Army officers. John was quite an entrepreneur. At twelve years old, he started selling manure door to door as fertilizer. He had made an offer to a farmer to use the manure piled up by the barn. The farmer was delighted to get rid of it. As such, John never paid a dime for his product. He was so successful; he soon hired young boys to help him sell his precious product. John immigrated to the United States at age twenty-six to join his sister. He had $250 in his pocket. Shortly after he arrived, he met Laura at a reception and just three weeks later, he asked her to marry him. His business sense led him to start a dry-cleaning company. Its success propelled him to join those who have achieved the "American Dream."

John was the most charitable, the most elegant and the most proper gentleman I had ever met. In my eyes, he was the perfect picture of an English gentleman, with old fashion chivalry. I thought of him as a "Sir," a title that seemed to be a perfect fit for him. One day after our double's tennis game, I ask our good friends and opponents, Trudy and Dr. Gerard, "Would you join me in elevating our friend from John to Sir John."

They agreed. So, "Sir John" he became. Little by little, many of his friends started addressing him as such.

On Sunday, August 31, 2003, Sir John said, "C.C., after the church service, Laura and I want to introduce you to a couple who adopted two Russian children."

"I would be delighted to meet this couple and say hello to the children."

At the end of the service, Sir John said, "C.C., the couple we want to introduce to you is standing against the wall over there. The children arrived from Russia just three days ago. They are very shy and cannot speak English."

I turned toward the wall. My eyes focused on this beautiful sight: a well-dressed man, a well-dressed woman, a blond boy holding onto the dad's trousers, and a blond girl holding onto the mom's dress. My whole body froze in place. I could not move. I became oblivious to my surroundings. I could not hear nor see the people around me. This foursome, this picture, this vision became all that I saw. I stayed completely focused on this beautiful sight for several minutes, mesmerized, paralyzed. As this image was sinking into my heart, into my soul, I suddenly felt gentle vibrations in my toes. The vibrations moved upward through my body ever so slowly. I felt an incredible tranquility. By the time the vibrations reached my chest, I was in sort of a trance, hypnotized by this beautiful vision. A feeling of total peace overpowered me, the same feeling of peace I had experienced once before, when I was thirty, at another turning point in my life.

"This is it! This is what I am going to do. I found it. This is what I've been searching for so long. I will adopt. I will adopt two children. I will share what I have. Yes, I will give two children a chance for a better life."

Sir John had been trying to get my attention. He touched my arm, "C.C., what happened? I've been calling you. Did you not hear me?"

"Oh! Sir John, something magical just happened, something . . . well something incredibly beautiful, something almost indescribable. I just received the answer to my prayers. Sir John, I cannot say in words how happy I feel. Like this couple, I want to adopt two children. I want to give two children a chance for a better life. For sixteen years, I've asked God and the universe what I could do to repay my debt. I have it now! I found my answer."

"C.C., are you sure you want to do this? Would it not be too much of an undertaking at your age?"

"Yes, Sir John, I'm sure this is what I want. That's what I want to do. I feel it in my heart. This is the sign I've been waiting for. Let's go meet this couple, I have to find out how to proceed."

Her name was Valerie, his, Murray, their twin children, David and Diana were seven. We agreed to rendezvous at their home, at 4 p.m., September 2.

On that Tuesday, at 4 p.m. sharp, I was ringing their doorbell. They were most gracious. They shared their experiences as well as the pictures and videos they took in Russia. They explained the process and gave me the name of the adoption agency they had used, Adoption Over-Seas. As I was leaving, filled with hope, Murray said, "C.C., please call us at any time. We will be here to help and guide you during this process."

My energy level was over the roof. I had a new purpose, a new passion. From this point on, I will devote my time to make this quest a reality.

2.

The Mission is On

To succeed in your mission, you must have
single-minded devotion to your goal.
A.P.J. Abdul Kalam[2]

INSIDE THE BEAUTIFUL WHITE United Church of Christ, I accepted, without hesitation, the spiritual invitation revealed to me. My quest to give back for my good fortune was defined clearly and overwhelmingly. With intense joy, I silently thought, *This is it! I feel it! I will adopt two children and give them a chance for a better life. This endeavor will completely fulfill the desire I held for so many years to give back a little of what I have received.* I promised myself to make every effort possible to bring this endeavor to fruition.

The office of Adoption Over-Seas was located in Texas. Wednesday, September 3, 2003, I checked the time. It was 9 a.m. in Texas. As I was reaching for the receiver the phone rang.

"Hello!"

"Good morning C.C. This is Murray. C.C., would you consider adopting a fifteen-year- old boy from my children's orphanage?"

"Hum! . . . Gee . . . A fifteen-year-old . . . b . . . "

"C.C., before you answer, I need to ask, are you an American citizen?"

"No, I'm a Canadian citizen here on a permanent green card."

"Well C.C., I hate to tell you, but before you can adopt, you will have to become a U.S. citizen. To make things more challenging for you, a few weeks ago, the *New York Times* stated, 'It takes an average of twenty-three months for green card holders to become U.S. citizens.' "

"Twenty-three months?" I exclaimed. "I don't have twenty-three months! I'll be sixty-four in November! I can't wait that long! There must be a way around this. Thank you, Murray, I will keep you informed."

"Impossible!" I voiced out loud. "There must be a mistake. I came to this country on a green card in 1976. I've been a good citizen, paid my taxes, never collected a government check, nor committed any crime, well . . . just annoying little ones like . . . speeding and parking tickets. . . . I bet every city that caught me speeding was happy to collect the fine.

"Wait a minute! I remember applying for citizenship a long time ago! The government cashed my check, but I never heard back. At the time I thought, 'Perhaps I'm not supposed to be an American.' But now, several years later, the scenario has changed. I must be a U.S. citizen to adopt, and it has to happen quickly."

I picked the phone to call the adoption agency.

"Adoption Over-Seas, Gen speaking?"

"Hello. My name is C.C. LeBlanc from Naples, Florida. Yesterday, I met Valerie, Murray and their two adopted Russian children. I was very impressed with their story and would like to follow their lead. They referred me to your agency."

"Congratulations C.C. Adopting is the most generous gift you can give a child. By doing so, you will save the lives of two children. Ed, my partner, and I will guide you through the process."

"Gen, I am a Canadian citizen, here on a green card since 1976."

"Well, C.C., before you can adopt a child, you must become an American citizen. The United States will not let you adopt as a Canadian citizen or a citizen of any other country."

"Gen, I was told it takes twenty-three months. Is this correct?"

"That's about right."

"I will find a way to accelerate the process. I can't wait twenty-three months. Citizenship will be priority number one. Please tell me how to proceed for the adoption."

"Our program, CampKidHope, brings children ages five to twelve to the U.S. to be hosted by families interested in adopting. Our next CampKidHope will be held in Tampa, Florida toward the end of December. We will host an informative meeting in Tampa on October 27. We recommend you attend. I will send you the paperwork needed to reserve your seat."

"Wonderful!"

"After the meeting, if you decide to host a child for the two-week period, you will be asked to fill out a questionnaire and choose the gender and age of the child or children you would like to host. After you spend time with your children, you can decide if you wish to pursue an adoption."

The conversation continued with names, addresses, etc. She added, "The packet will be in the mail this very day."

I called Sir John right away to share the news.

"The good news first: The hosting packet is on its way. The bad news . . . I cannot adopt on a green card. It could take twenty-three months to get my U.S. citizenship. I don't have twenty-three months . . . ."

"Well Kiddo, you better get on the ball, even better, you better get that ball rolling fast!"

"I'll find a way, Sir John. I'll ask my angels to work on it 24/7."

"C.C., I'll go on the internet right away to find the forms you need to apply for your citizenship. I'll bring them to you ASAP."

"That's wonderful Sir John. You are the first Earth angel to help me with this project. Thank you so much."

As soon we hung up, I sat in my comfortable chair. Out loud I said, "Angels! Wake up! I need your inspiration right now! How do I begin? Whom do I know? Who can help me? In twenty-three months, I'll be just about sixty-six years old! It will still take several more months before an adoption can be granted. I'll be almost seventy years old . . . much too old . . . Sorry angels, but no can do. I cannot wait this long. This citizenship has to be granted and granted soon. You must help me find a way . . . I beg of you."

I continued to sit quietly, thinking, praying, and hoping to get an inspiration, a way to establish a plan of action to accelerate the process. But how?

"The application forms would be easy. I'll answer the questions and write a check in the amount of the fee. But government moves slower than frozen molasses. I'd need to find a way to put a little fire in somebody's behind. Or better still, touch someone's heart. But whose heart? And how? I must come up with a plan."

My stomach needed attention. It was already noon. Perhaps a revealing thought would come while I was eating. After lunch, I walked to my desk, opened the bottom left drawer, picked up the beautiful, now decrepit, address book I'd received as a gift for my fiftieth birthday. *In it,* I thought, *I may find the name of someone who can guide me through the citizenship process.* I flipped the pages one at the time . . . M, N, O, P, still nothing sprung up, Q, R, my eyes stopped on the name Rex. I exclaimed, "Rex, my friend Vice Admiral Rex R. If anyone can help, he can."

Vice Admiral (retired) Rex R. served his country during the Second World War. He was assigned to serve in the Pacific on a minesweeper, which he later commanded. Then, he became an Intelligence Officer and performed duties in the Persian Gulf in the early 1950s. Subsequently, he was Assistant Naval Attaché to the Soviet Union in the early 1960s, at the height of the Cold War. He served as Intelligence Officer for Admiral Elmo Zumwalt in Viet Nam in the late 1960s. He was then advanced to the rank of Rear Admiral and appointed the Director of Naval Intelligence in 1973. He retired in 1976 at the rank of Vice Admiral. After a second career in banking, he relocated to Fort Myers Beach, Florida, and continued to be very active in organizations associated with his naval profession and other passionate interests. Rex and I often met at social gatherings of Who's Who International, an organization of professional singles founded in the early 1970s by Conrad Hilton, of the Hilton Hotels, and some of his friends.

I shared with Rex what had transpired in the last several days and the decision I had made.

"Well C.C., that is quite a decision at your age. What sort of help are you looking for?"

"Because of your connections in Washington, I thought you may be able to find someone who could help me obtain my U.S. citizenship sooner than the average twenty-three months."

"All this is very noble C.C. Your heart is in the right place. I'll need a day or so to think whom I can recommend. But before I do C.C., I would like you to write me an email and share your thought processes as to how you came to make such a bold decision."

"Okay, Rex. I'll start working on that email today. It will be a good exercise for my own understanding of this major decision. Thank you, Rex."

It was now mid-afternoon. The doorbell rang. Sir John handed me the citizenship application forms. He asked, "How is it going C.C? What have you found out so far?"

I briefed him. He left saying, "Knowing you C.C., you'll find a way. Let me know if I can help you. You know my telephone number."

I thought, *As if I did not! Sir John's telephone number was carved into my brain.*

This had been an intense day. I needed a break. I put on some comfortable shoes, grabbed a visor and sunglasses and left for a walk on the beach. The fresh air will clear my brain, I thought. I'll get back to work when I return.

Back home, the citizenship application won first priority. My goal was that Tuesday, September 9, 2003, one week after meeting Valerie and Murray, I would have gathered and fulfilled the application requirements for citizenship. The envelope already addressed to the INS Service Center, Mesquite, Texas, will be sent FedEx. Next on the priority list was to write the memo to my friend Vice Admiral Rex.

3.

Rex and Citizenship

*You are never too old to set another goal
or to dream another dream.*
Les Brown[3]

DEAR REX,

Thank you in advance for whatever help you can offer. Here are some thoughts regarding my decision to adopt two children.

As you know, retirement came at a very young age for me. I never understood why I was given this unimaginable gift. Why me?

As we have discussed in the past, I grew up number two in a wonderful family of seven children. Money was tight; I did not go to college. The cost of higher education was reserved for "the boys," my four brothers. I did the best I could to increase my knowledge by taking college classes whenever I could, read books or magazines I could learn from, etc.

Regardless of how hard I worked during the thirty-one-year span of my career, retiring at age forty-seven had never entered my mind. When that opportunity arrived, I felt I had a debt to pay. Yes, a debt to pay for the privilege of retiring so young with enough financial security to enjoy a comfortable lifestyle for the rest of my life. Since my retirement, in March 1987, I prayed, asked, and waited to receive an inspiration for something worthy that would fulfill my self-imposed obligation of giving back some of what I had received.

When I was much younger, especially between the ages of twenty-eight and thirty-two, I experienced strong maternal instincts. I seriously considered having a child as a single woman. In the late seventies, early eighties, perhaps more so in Québec Province, that was taboo, a big NO-NO for a single woman to have a child outside of marriage. I would have lost my job and be frowned upon by society in general. Later, I thought about adopting, but that notion did not germinate because there was no daddy. I felt that having my own baby or adopting someone else's child would have only fulfilled my own maternal instincts. I thought about it long and hard, but in the end, I felt it was important for any child to have both a mom and a dad. I did not want to pursue motherhood for my own selfish reasons.

Now, twenty-five-plus years later, in the twenty-first century, society is much more emancipated, in some ways to my chagrin. Women can choose to have children married or not. A very large percentage of children are raised by one parent or even by grandparents. I will be a single parent, but I'm old enough to be a grandparent, so I qualify for both. Hahaha!

Rex, what happened last Sunday after the church service, when I first glanced at the couple standing against the wall with their newly adopted Russian children, was an extraordinary moment. For several minutes, I had no control over what was happening to my whole being. Call it God, call it the positive forces of the universe, call it an epiphany as some friends have suggested, I felt so very strongly this was the signal I've been asking for during the past sixteen years. Adopting and giving a chance for a better life to two children, in exchange for the privilege of retiring so young, was the most-worthy cause I could imagine. It was a beautiful and a positive moment that overwhelmed me with joy.

Rex, I heard there are over one million children in Russian orphanages. The statistics say these orphanages receive at least one hundred thousand children every year. Some children may be there temporarily, until their parents are able to provide for them. Most stay until they are eighteen years old, then they must leave. Once they are on their own, they have not much to look forward to. Rex, *children do not ask to be born, they just are. In my view, the abandonment of children is one of the biggest crimes in our society and it is poorly addressed.*

Someone may ask, why not adopt a child from the US? In the US, the law gives one year to a parent to reclaim his or her child. The thought of giving back the child into whom I had poured all my love and energy is unthinkable. Adopting from Russia eliminates this concern.

Why adopt at my age? As you know Rex, my life has been lived outside of the box. My timing is never in line with the rest of society. The inspiration in church Sunday was the catalyst. Giving two orphans a chance for a better life, a better future, is perhaps the best deed or act of love I can do. My mom is in excellent health at eighty-nine. Dad lived to eighty-two even though he was a heavy smoker. I believe I will live long enough to bring my future children to adulthood. I've had a wonderful life, a great childhood, a successful career, and lots of traveling. I have had my fill of parties and black-tie affairs to last me a lifetime. I have had meaningful relationships, but I am still single. From my humble beginnings to now, I am satisfied with my accomplishments. I've reached much more than I ever thought possible. I feel ready to fulfill this mission and unleash all the love that has been bottled up within me. I understand the challenges will be enormous, but I am strong and feel that with the help of God, my spiritual angels, and some Earth angels, I will be able to handle whatever comes my way.

Do I have fears? Of course, I do. Fear of not being an adequate mother, fear my health may not last, even though it is excellent now, fear for the challenging teenage years, fear of whether, once in America, I will adapt to the children, and they to me, and fear of some unknown factors. But I cannot live my life in fear of something. I cannot let fear prevent me from doing something good. Fear is a negative word, a negative thought one must learn to overcome. In the past, whenever I overcame my fears, I was rewarded with positive and wonderful experiences.

Why two children instead of just one? Because of my age, when I'm gone, they will have each other. I will ask for siblings with the same mom and dad. This adoption is not as much for me to become a mama as it is for me to give a chance to two children to have a better life, a better future in America.

Dear Rex, I hope this memo will satisfy your curiosity regarding the reasons why I want to adopt two children. I truly appreciate your willingness to help me reach citizenship sooner than later.

Much love,

C.C., 09-5-2003

Rex replied the next day.

Dear C.C.,

Go for it! You obviously have given this some thought and have allayed my concerns of "fad-ism" to your credit.

Porter Goss is your state representative in Washington. He is a friend of mine. You may mention my name when you write him a letter. In the meantime, I will write him a note to inform him.

Since time is of some criticality, I still would offer the suggestion that you find the name of the best Immigration Naturalization Service or "INS type" attorney, locally or preferably in Miami or Washington DC, and get a road map with objectives and milestones vs. time. Sometimes bureaucratic obstacles need to be recognized at the beginning. Only a competent attorney can speak to the "real world of Murphy's Law!"

Warm regards, Rex

It had been one week since my life took a new direction. Sir John had said then, "You better get the ball rolling and rolling fast."

Well, I felt the ball was on track. I was moving ahead. Much was accomplished in the last few days. My next focus was to write a letter to The Honorable Porter Goss, my Congressman in the House of Representatives. But before I did, I looked for the cancelled check sent long ago with my first application for citizenship.

I opened the old file cabinet. The top drawer was filled with must-keep bank account statements. Where do I begin? Which bank? What year? I decided to start with the 1995 statements and go backwards. I was looking for one transaction only, a check made to: Immigration and Naturalization Services. I flipped the pages of each register, looking at each and every line, 1995, 1994, 1993 . . . nothing.

I wondered if I should continue with the 1992 register or skip to the year 1996. I chose to go as far back as 1990 before reverting to 1996. I flipped the pages for January 1992, for February, then March . . . and *voilà* . . . my eyes stopped on check 341, March 8, 1992. "There it is!" I exclaimed, "Immigration and Naturalization Services, $90." I took the bank statement out of the file folder and found the cancelled check attached to it. Printed on the back was the following, "Pay to the order of any Federal Reserve Bank or Branch General Depository for credit to the Treasurer of the United States, March 17, 1992."

Finding this check felt like finding a rare prize, a trophy, a well-deserved reward for all the work done so far. I now had concrete proof a previous application for citizenship had been filed. The government cashed the check but never contacted me. With this cancelled check as ammunition, I felt ready to write a letter to the Honorable Porter Goss to ask for his help.

I ended my letter this way,

"Congressman, there are two young children who need a mama badly. They are waiting for her in a Russian orphanage. Please help me be that mama. I'm almost sixty-four years old. Your help will be your gift of love to these children and a dream come true for me."

I wrote a similar letter to the representative of the INS hoping to touch someone's heart.

I telephoned and made an appointment with Porter Goss's secretary, Sylvia, for September 9, 2003, at 2:00 p.m., to hand deliver the letter to Congressman Goss's office. I felt a face-to-face meeting with Representative Goss's secretary would be more powerful. It is easy to say "No" to a piece of paper, but more delicate to say "No" while looking into the eyes of a person, especially for a cause as noble as this one.

On September 20, several days after my visit with Sylvia, I wrote her the following letter to inform her of the progress being made.

Dear Sylvia,

First, I want to thank you for giving me the opportunity to meet with you. Our meeting was valuable.

The suggestion you made to ask the INS to find the original application, dated March 1992, is excellent. If it cannot be found, the canceled check should be proof that it was sent. The FedEx tracking number confirmed delivery of the new application sent September 9th.

I will be meeting with Mary S. this week. Mary is a former neighbor and friend of Congressman Goss. I am hoping she will intercede for me with the Congressman. The name of Vice Admiral Rex R. is in the body of my letter to Congressman Goss dated 9-7-2003. All of us working together may help accelerate the process of citizenship.

It was most enjoyable to speak a little Spanish with you. I'm looking forward to our next visit.

Respectfully yours, C.C. LeBlanc

4.

Preparing to Host

Desire is the starting point in all achievement,
not a hope, not a wish, but a keen pulsating desire,
which transcends everything.
Napoleon Hill[4]

A YEAR EARLIER, SEPTEMBER 2002, at a Who's Who International cocktail reception, I had spoken with an acquaintance named Candy. She asked, "C.C., have you ever thought of adopting a child?"

"I don't think I could as a single woman, especially at this stage of my life."

Just one year later, Candy and I met again. This time a different story was taking place. I shared with her the incredible revelation I felt on that special Sunday, August 31. I added, "Candy, I felt touched by an angel or some Holy Spirit or by an awesome inspiration. After meeting with Valerie and Murray two days later, I decided to pursue the adoption of two children from Russia."

"Oh C.C.! I've been wanting to do this for so long. Could I join you? Could we do this together?"

"Yes, of course. It would be wonderful. We would be a team!"

I invited Candy to meet at my home the next day. We discussed our partnership and called Gen of Adoption Over-Seas.

No surprise, Gen was most happy to welcome Candy to join the many host families. She added, "The introduction meeting for the adoption process will be held at the Holiday Inn, in Tampa, Florida, October 27, 2003, at 7:00 p.m. We will inform the attendees about our CampKidHope program and guide you as to how you can participate as host parents."

We promised to attend. Candy and I met a few more times to discuss our plans. We were excited at the thought of combining our efforts to support each other in the care of the children.

At the Tampa meeting, we were introduced to a mixture of couples and single women between the ages of thirty-five and fifty-five. Gen, from Adoption Over-Seas, gave a very emotional talk about the rewards of adopting children. I sensed she was hoping to touch our hearts and even touch a cord of guilt for "enjoying such a good life, while children all over the world were abandoned in orphanages." With tears rolling down her cheeks, her voice trembling with emotion and barely audible, she convinced most of us to sign up. This was her business. She was selling her product. The product was children. I thought her emotional display was . . . well . . . you guessed it . . . a bit dramatic.

After the presentation, Candy was even more convinced she wanted to adopt. Her heart had definitely been touched. Gen did not need to persuade me. My heart had already been tapped. So certain we would pursue an adoption, Candy and I had already filled out the application forms mailed to us earlier. We attached our checks for $200 to the forms and handed them to Gen.

The application required us to describe the children we hoped to adopt. Candy chose a girl twelve years of age. My choices were twins, boy/girl, or twins, two girls, or a brother and a sister between the ages of eight and eleven. I thought twins would be easier. They would both go to the same school, be in the same grade, and have the same homework.

CampKidHope would be held in Tampa, Florida. We lived in Naples, Florida, approximately three driving hours away. Following the meeting, Candy and I decided to find a hotel in

Tampa for the night. In the morning, we would start the process of securing two efficiency apartments to host our children for the two-week period. Their arrival was expected to be December 25, 2003.

The next day, after an extensive search in the telephone directory, we drove to the extended-stay hotel we had found to physically view the site and to meet with the manager. She suggested we each have a two-bedroom efficiency unit kitty corner from each other. We asked, "What will the cost per night be?"

She answered, "I am so impressed with what you're doing, I want to help you a little. I will charge you the price of a one-bedroom efficiency at $79 per night, instead of $129 for a two-bedroom."

We were amazed and touched. This young manager took it upon herself to reduce the rate of our suites. I felt she wanted to contribute to our project in her own special way. The goodness of people is everywhere. As we thanked her and left, she added, "I can't wait to meet your children."

We returned to Naples, happy and comfortable with our partnership. We looked forward to meeting our, yet unknown, dear little ones at the end of December.

October 30, 2003

I emailed Gen and Ted at Adoption Over-Seas to inform them we had secured our dwelling to host our children and hired Elena, a fifteen-year-old Russian girl, to help us with translation. Elena would be with us until January 3, 2004, the end of her Christmas vacation. I met this young lady through Lidia, a dear friend, originally from Belarus, who shared an apartment with Elena's "*babushka*" [grandmother]. I ended my email by writing, "At the meeting, you said, 'God has a child for each one of you.' Well Gen, God must have two children for me, one for each arm."

My mind never strayed from pursuing the U.S. citizenship needed to embark on this mission. I felt I had exhausted all possibilities to accelerate the process. Now, I had to be a little patient and let the system do its job. Patience is in very short supply in my being. My mother used to say I was like *une soupe au lait*, a boiling milk soup. I boil quickly. Lack of patience is my biggest flaw. Waiting for something to happen is unproductive, boring and stressful. In the meantime, I would pray to whomever could hear me for a compatible match between my children and me. At almost age sixty-four, this is the one and only time I could consider such an undertaking. I promised myself to practice patience for the next few weeks. I would take the time to prepare myself mentally. I would visualize loving my future children without the slightest idea of whom they would be.

December 10, 2003, 9:30 a.m., an email arrived from Andrea, of Adoption Over-Seas.

The children we have assigned to your family are from a group of nineteen children coming from the Krasnoyarsk region of Siberia. The following siblings have been assigned to your family.

Name: Kristina Bajenova S.

Birth: xx/xx/1992

Gender: Female

Name: Anton Bajenov S.

Birth: xx/xx/1995

Gender: Male

A medical report and pictures for these children have not yet been received. We will forward this information as it comes.

This was exciting news. Kristina was eleven-and-one-half, her brother Anton, eight. I immediately called Sylvia, Congressmen Porter Goss's secretary, to share the good news and to ask if she could obtain an update on my citizenship status. A few days later a letter from Congressman Goss arrived. Attached to it was the following correspondence from the INS:

12-15-2003, 3:08 p.m. Ms. LeBlanc called asking for an update. Please let me know if you have the file. Sylvia

The INS reply:

12-15-2003 3:41 p.m. I've been chasing this down through archives. The Texas Service Center has no access to Miss LeBlanc's N-400 filed from 1992. If Miss LeBlanc wishes to pursue this matter, you will have to contact the congressional liaison at the Texas Service Center, or she may discuss this with the adjudicating officer at the time of her interview for her currently filed N-400 (the application form for citizenship).

Regarding her present N-400, dated September 16, 2003, it is the long-standing policy of the Service that all applications be processed in chronological order by date of receipt. The only exceptions to this rule are for extreme emergent humanitarian reasons or for reasons in the interest of the United States. The applicant's request for expeditious handling does not appear to meet these criteria. For the most part, application processing is well under two years. Her current N-400 is just about ninety days old. Our records indicate it is within normal processing time. With this in mind, it will probably be about a year before she is interviewed.

Please let me know if I can be of any further assistance.

Signed by [the name was crossed out]

Congressional Liaison Specialist

You can just imagine! I screamed,

"One year from now would take us to December 16, 2004. And that's only for the interview appointment for citizenship! That's too long a wait! Then my name would be added to the waiting list for the next swearing-in ceremony, which takes place only four times a year. Then I would have to go through another slow-as-frozen-molasses process with both the Russian and the American Governments to approve the adoption of my children. This is not acceptable! I have to find another way!"

Even though I didn't know my children to be, I knew they were waiting in an orphanage, somewhere in the Krasnoyarsk Region of Siberia. Frustrated and with a strong voice, "God! Angels! Whomever! Where are you? Please help me! What do I do next?"

After several arrival date changes for the children, December 28, 2003 was confirmed. All host parents were asked to be at the Tampa International Airport by 8:00 p.m., and to look for an Adoption Over-Seas sign near the airport entrance to the Marriott Hotel.

On December 28, Candy and I met at Costco to buy all the non-perishables for our two weeks with our children. Perishables would be purchased in Tampa. We packed the trunks of each of our cars. While Candy drove back to her home to pick up her Cocker Spaniel, which she referred to as "the stupid dog" I drove to pick up Elena, our Russian translator.

We felt good, ready, able and willing to fulfill our commitment.

5.

Children's Arrival, December 28, 2003

Cherish your visions and your dreams,
as they are the children of your soul,
the blueprints of your ultimate achievements.
Napoleon Hill[5]

THE DAY I DECIDED to host two Russian children, I made a promise to God, to myself and to the children I had yet to meet.

"If the children and I form a bond, I will pursue their adoption. If we do not, I will give them the best two weeks of their lives."

This day, December 28, 2003, the moment so waited for was finally here. I hoped with all my heart it would be the start of a new life for all three of us and the beginning of a new family in America for Kristina and Anton.

Shortly after 8 p.m., Candy, Elena and I arrived at the Tampa International Airport in my big old 1993 Cadillac Fleetwood. I drove right to the main entrance of the Airport Marriott Hotel. After explaining to the young bellman the reason we were there, I asked, "Young man, could you keep our car by the curbside until we return with the children?"

He agreed with enthusiasm adding, "I myself was adopted as a young child. I am happy to do this for you."

With the car secured, we entered the airport terminal carrying a gift for each of our children. For my children, it was two teddy bears with the year 2003 printed on the bottom of one foot. As we entered the terminal, I felt a mixture of excitement and nervousness. My heart was beating rapidly. Approximately one hundred feet from the terminal entrance, we noticed an accumulation of people. As we approached, Candy asked someone, "Is this where we are to wait for the Russian children?"

"Yes, they should arrive in about one hour."

If only you could have been there. The meeting area at the airport was already a sight to behold. Children, parents, grandparents, aunts, uncles and cousins were already waiting for the precious Russian children they would host. There were balloons, flowers, stuffed animals, toys and more. People were arriving from different parts of the airport with more flowers, more balloons and more toys. The positive energy was through the roof. The chatter was happy. We could feel excitement and laughter from all directions. It was so invigorating. It was one of those moments in time one would never forget.

One helium balloon with a long string made its way to the high ceiling. After several tries by several people to bring it down, an attendant with a hook at the end of a long pole succeeded. The crowd exploded with cheers and applause. It was entertainment at its best for this very special occasion. All of a sudden we heard, "Hush! Hush!"

Gen appeared with a happy smile and said, "The children will be here in few minutes. They are very tired after traveling for thirty-one hours. Each parent will be introduced to his or her respective child. Once you've greeted your child, please wait for more instructions before you leave the airport."

Someone exclaimed, "They're coming! They're turning the corner! Look! Over there!"

Guided by their Russian caregivers, the children walked military style, two by two, following one another. For the first time, we could set eyes on our precious children. The chatter stopped.

All became quiet as we watched the children, dressed in Adidas jogging suits, come toward us in complete silence. They looked pale, tired, scared. Candy touched my arm and said, "I see mine. She's right there, she's tall, blond and blue eyed."

I could not quite recognize Kristina and Anton in the group. The picture the agency sent was a poorly executed photocopy. But as I stretched my neck to look at each child, I said, "Candy, look at the fifth row. I think I recognize Kristina. My children are siblings. The sister is older. She has dark hair, his is lighter. I'm almost sure."

Can you understand the trepidation, the fear, the doubt I felt in my heart and soul? While the energy and the anticipation were incredibly positive, a part of me wanted to run away. Fear, fear of not being adequate for the monumental commitment I was about to make. Throughout my life, I fulfilled my commitments to the best of my abilities. Would I have the capacity, the wisdom to fulfill this one—by far, the most important one of my life?

The host families were now in almost complete silence as each one concentrated on the child they would soon be introduced to. Gen made another announcement. "Host parents, your children are here! (Applause) They are very tired. Remember, they have been traveling for thirty-one hours. Oleg, the bilingual Russian representative, has a matching list of parents and children. He will call the name of the host parents for each child. You are to greet your child quickly then move back to give room for the next parents. The Russian adults accompanying the children will be introduced to you tomorrow. Please wait until the last child has been united with his host parents for more instruction."

Oleg called the name of the host parents for the first child, then the second, then Candy was called to meet Misha. I watched her as she greeted the young girl she hoped would be her daughter. Two more names were called, then mine.

"C.C. LeBlanc."

My heart was beating out of my body. When I arrived in front of Kristina, I knelt down to be at her height. I looked at her and smiled with the warmest, most engaging smile I could produce.

"C.C., this is Kristina, Kristina this is C.C."

Oleg said a few words to Kristina. I kept smiling and welcomed her in the English language, a language she could not understand. Kristina had a faint smile but before I had a chance to hug her, she moved next to me and put one arm around my shoulders. It seemed she was rehearsed to move quickly to give room for her brother to be introduced. Anton was a little stiffer, a little frozen. He looked scared. I hugged him and gave him his teddy bear, then I turned to hug Kristina and to give her hers. Together we moved back to where Candice, Misha and Elena were standing.

A soon as we joined them, Kristina started to cry, then sobbed uncontrollably. A fountain of tears was flowing down her cheeks while her brother looked on speechless with the saddest little face. I put my arms around Kristina, tried to console her. Elena spoke with her. She tried to let her know she was safe, but to no avail. She continued to cry profusely for several minutes. I reached for Anton's hand to bring him close to his sister for assurance. I kept one arm around Kristina's shoulders, smiling, trying to make her feel safe. Slowly, the tears became less of a torrent then gradually stopped.

When each child was introduced to his or her host parents, Gen made the following announcements.

"Tomorrow morning, you must buy clothes for your children. Once you dress your children with new clothes, you are to wash the ones they are now wearing. The clothes the children travelled with must be returned to Russia when your child leaves the U.S."

She continued, "We will meet at the Presbyterian church recreation hall at 9:00 a.m. every day except weekends and holidays. Tomorrow, after your shopping spree, you must arrive at the church by 11:30 a.m. There, you will meet Tatiana, our official Russian translator. She will assist you with whatever you need. For emergencies, please call the number listed in your application packet. Take good care of the children we have entrusted to you. You may go to your home now. Thank you and good night."

The six of us walked back to the hotel entrance. I held my children's hands, one on each side. The car was waiting at the curb. Elena, Kristina, Anton and Misha sat in the back seat. Candice sat in the front seat with me. I thanked the attendant and gave him a nice tip. We left to return to our hotel.

6.

Hosting the Children Begins

Adoption is not about finding children for families,
it's about finding families for children
Joyce Maguire Pavao[6]

HOW EXCITING! OUR TWO weeks together had just begun.
I slowly drove away from the hotel looking for the airport exit.
For the life of me I could not find my way out of the airport area,
much less back to our hotel. We had to stop a few times to ask for
directions. There was no GPS at that time, at least I did not own
one, and the Tampa airport was new territory for me. Candy was
of no help. It was her first time at this airport. Finally, we reached
the highway.

All of a sudden, I heard Elena say, "C.C., Anton feels car sick!"

"OK Elena, I'll take the next exit."

I aimed the car directly at the closest exit. Right there was
a convenience store. Kristina untied Anton's safety belt just in
time. He got out of the car quickly and did what he had to do. I
took his hand and walked him around a little. In the meantime,
Candy went inside the store to ask for directions and to buy a
club soda for Anton. By the time we arrived at our hotel, it was
well past midnight.

With the help of Elena, I asked the children if they would like to take a bath or a shower that night or wait till morning. Kristina preferred to wait till morning. I offered them a banana and a glass of milk, which they took. I hugged and tucked them both in the same bed, thinking they would feel safer. They both held their teddy bears tightly and fell asleep right away. During the night, I looked into their bedroom a couple of times. Each time, they were both peacefully sound asleep.

The next morning, I was determined to let my children sleep as long as they were able. If we were late, so be it. These children need to rest. Candy left for her shopping spree with Misha around 9:00 a.m. Elena stayed with me. When my children woke up, Kristina asked to take a bath. I helped her fill the tub. She took her brother into the bathroom and helped him with his bath first. Without changing the water, she stepped into the tub to take hers. I asked Elena to explain to Kristina it is OK in America to change the bath water for each person.

We had a healthy breakfast, and then left for our shopping spree. I was impressed with the type of clothes both children were attracted to. Kristina liked soft colors. She would take the pants or the T-shirt from the rack, put them in front of her and wait for my nod of approval. Anton did the same. He was attracted to black and beige. They were so excited. They had never seen such a big store with so much variety. What a treat it was to have their own clothes and brand-new sport shoes.

By noontime, we were ready to drive to the Presbyterian church. Back on the expressway, we drove for perhaps fifteen minutes when Elena said, "C.C.! Anton just lost his breakfast in your car!"

"Oh no! The poor thing, he must feel horrified!"

Just ahead was an exit. I took it and drove to the nearest service station. I parked the car near a row of trees, got out of the car, ran to his side, and unbuckled him to let him out, saying and repeating several times,

"It's OK. Don't worry. Don't worry dearest little one; all will be fine."

I realized he could not understand my words. I hoped the tone of my voice would console him. I looked at Kristina. She appeared embarrassed and scared. She didn't move. She probably thought they would be punished. I asked Elena to tell the children not to worry, all would be OK. What I really wanted to say was, "What a mess! What a horrible mess! Did I need this right now?" I ran to the service station for help while Elena stayed with the children.

"Sir, would you have a bucket of water, some old rags, and two large garbage bags? I have two Russian children in the car who do not speak English. One of them was sick . . . I need to clean the back of my car right away."

The man was very helpful. He gave me all I needed and pointed to a water hose I could use. Most of the expelled breakfast ended up on the removable carpet, which could be rinsed and eventually washed in a commercial washing machine. I cleaned the best I could. We resumed our drive.

I asked, "Elena, could you sit in the back with Kristina, I will keep Anton distracted in the front."

I hugged Anton, and I repeated a few times, "It's OK my dearest little one, all is well."

We finally arrived at our destination. As we entered the room, the children ran to see their friends, while Gen walked briskly toward me.

"You're very late C.C. Where in the world were you? I was about to send the police after you. What happened?"

I explained and sternly added, "You do not have to worry about me, Gen. I am safe. Nothing will happen to these children under my watch."

I slowly walked away from Gen to join Candy and Elena. Gen returned later to ask if I had met Boris. No, I had not. I followed her.

Boris was the director of my children's orphanage, a strong, 5'8" handsome man with penetrating eyes. We shook hands, smiled, but could not speak without a translator. Tatiana came to our rescue. Tatiana was a physician in Russia before she immigrated to the U.S. We talked about Russia, Canada and the U.S. Boris shared the information that the orphanage was in the small village of Dzerzhinsk in Central Siberia. Several caregivers took care of fifty children who attended the village school.

At 4:30 p.m., all families were dismissed until 9:00 a.m. the next day. When we arrived at our hotel, the children wanted to swim. Into the pool we went. Misha and Kristina knew how to swim a little, Anton did not. I jumped in the pool while Candy sat watching. Like most children, they loved the water, a heated pool at that. Anton had to either hold on to Kristina, to me or to the edge of the pool. I tried to teach him to swim but he was like a worm, he could not be still, so I taught him how to jump in my arm from the edge of the pool. He hesitated for a long time. He wanted to jump but fear held him back. Several times, he moved to the edge of the pool, then moved back. Once he succeeded to overcome his fear, he jumped several times and loved it. Kristina and Misha were having a blast while I got completely exhausted.

Every day at the camp, the children had different activities such as a trip to The Teddy Bear Factory store, a Santa Claus visit to deliver presents that the parents had bought, a visit to the aquarium, another to the zoo, to a bowling alley and, one day, a clown came to the church to entertain them. Several days were spent at the church hall doing crafts or just playing games. A variety of fruits was available at will, and a healthy lunch was served each day. On weekends the host parents entertained their children on their own.

Each day, when we returned to our hotel, we swam, cooked dinner, played games, did crafts, looked at the maps in the large *National Geographic Atlas of the World* I had brought, went for ice cream, walked to the park and played with the "stupid dog."

New Year's Eve 2004, we had a special dinner with candles. We each made a toast in our respective language, in English, Russian and French. We entertained ourselves for a while, then Candy announced,

"Tomorrow, C.C. and I invite you to celebrate your first American New Year's Day at Busch Gardens."

Elena explained that Busch Gardens was a little bit like Disney World. Even in Siberia, the words "Disney World" sparked some attention. The children were all smiles.

New Year's Day 2004 at Busch Gardens was a spectacular day. For our children, it was filled with new discoveries at every corner. When they saw the Gwazi Roller Coaster, the girls wanted to try it. We got in line. Candice chose to sit aside. Anton looked at it very attentively. He was hesitant. As much as he wanted to be brave, fear kept him reluctant. We reached the embarkation deck. He had to make a decision. He stepped forward then stepped backward a few times. In the end he braved it. So, on board we went.

Misha sat alone. Elena and Kristina were together. I sat with Anton. Once the ride started, I could not stop laughing watching Anton turn white, scared out of his wits. I had to hold on to his little body as hard as I could to prevent him from slipping under the security bar. Since he had been car sick, my imagination created a wild picture, visualizing the food in his stomach flying out of his mouth, hitting the people behind us smack in the face. There was nothing we could do but wait till the ride was over. With the help of Elena, I asked him if he would like to try it again. His answer was a definitive "*Nyet.*" In fact, he said he didn't want to go on these crazy rides ever again.

Throughout the day, the *Wows!* and *Ahs! Look over here! Look over there!* were constant. Anton figured out how to get animal food out of the dispenser without inserting a coin. He came running to us with a face full of pride. He extended one hand and pointed to his find with the other. His eyes and his funny big smile, missing a few baby teeth, showed genuine happiness. Even though Kristina and Misha were more reserved, I could see the joy and excitement in everything they touched and saw. Just to see them so happy was a gift to my eyes and to my ears. The memories of this day are forever carved in my mind.

7.

Falling in Love

The day you came into my life, I knew what my purpose was.
To love and protect you with everything I have.
Proudmummy.com[7]

FROM THE TIME THE children arrived, December 28, my mind was going through its own struggles. By December 31, I had become very attached to Kristina and Anton. Kristina, at age eleven-and-a-half, was a little more guarded. I sensed she was evaluating every move I made. She entered my heart slowly, gradually, a little more each day, as I was also evaluating my feelings toward her. Anton came into my heart all at once when all of a sudden, he ran into my arms and gave me a hug that completely penetrated my being. Within just a few days, both children became locked into my heart where they will reside for the rest of my life.

It seemed foreign, almost alarming, for me to fall in love with two children from a foreign culture and a foreign language I could not speak. How could this be? We had just met three days earlier. These children came from twelve time zones away, on the other side of the planet. How could I fall in love so quickly? The promise I made was now squarely facing me, "Be careful what you ask for, you may just get it," was pounding in my brain. I was scared. I trembled at the enormity of this responsibility. *What do I do now?*

Meditate? Pray? Ask for guidance? The thought; *Have I reached the point of no return?* was foremost in my mind. *Can that be? So soon? Or can I run away from this commitment?*

New Year's Day 2004 had been a beautiful day. Sleep time had arrived, all was quiet again. As is the norm for me, I woke up in the middle of the night for a bathroom visit. After taking a look in the children's bedroom, I sat on the edge of my bed and whispered,

"God, what am I to do with these children?"

The message or the intuition came right away as though God had been waiting for this question.

"These are your children. You are to take care of them."

"Oh God! This is an overwhelming thought . . . I can't . . . I can't think about this right now . . . I'm going back to sleep God, good night."

The next night, I asked again.

"God, please be serious, what am I to do with these children?"

The intuition was the same.

"These are your children. You are to take care of them."

"God, I don't know if I can . . . I'm not sure I can . . . I'm afraid . . . It's . . . well, it's . . . it's a very big responsibility . . . It frightens me . . . I have to think about it more . . . I'm going back to sleep now. Good night."

On the third night,

"God, in case you made a mistake, I ask you again. What am I to do with these children?"

"These are your children. You are to take care of them."

"OK, OK God, You win. I will. I will take care of them. But *You* must help me. I cannot do this alone. I'm going back to sleep now. Good night, God."

I woke up reflecting on the heavy commitment I had just made. Before hosting the children, the commitment I made to God, to myself and to the children I was looking forward to meeting was, "If the children and I bond, I will adopt them. If we don't, I will give them the best two weeks of their lives."

During those first three days, I felt the children and I had bonded. Then God and I made a deal. When I said, "OK, OK, I will," I made a vow. I accepted the responsibility. At that moment, I reached the point of no return. I could not go back on my promise. In my heart, Kristina and Anton were my children. My focus from now on will be to make it a reality and to bring my children home. The commitment was now sacred. I felt nervous. I questioned over and over, "Will I be able to overcome the tremendous challenges ahead?" All my life, I pushed ahead in the face of adversities, but this time I felt scared, scared of the unknown. This was an enormous responsibility to fulfill all by myself, even though all through my life, I felt strong and invincible. Not that I succeeded every time, but I often said to myself, "C.C. LeBlanc can accomplish anything she sets her mind to." I could not see myself defeated until I had at least a chance to try. This time it was different, it involved two beautiful children.

Kristina and Anton entered my being as small embryos. They both lodged deep in my heart instead of deep in my tummy. I knew with time my attachment to them would grow stronger and stronger, just as it does in a normal pregnancy. I knew deep in my soul I was given a clear mandate, a mandate that started some five months before, inspired by Valerie, Murray and their newly adopted children. Now, I must be strong, I must trust myself and trust the universe. I must trust God will send help. I shall pursue this mandate with all my strength, all my determination and make it a reality as quickly as possible.

After being dismissed from camp, we went on a shopping spree. Kristina and Elena shopped for girly things. Anton needed my help in the boys' department. All of a sudden, Kristina came running to me, started pulling on my clothes trying to drag me somewhere saying,

"Pleeese, CeeCee, Bitny Speeeese, C.C. Plceese CeeCee, Bitny Speeeese."

Not understanding, I asked,

"Elena, what in the world is she saying? I have no idea what she's talking about?"

"C.C., she wants a poster of Britney Spears."

"For the life of me, Elena, who is Britney Spears?"

Elena's face went blank. Her jaw dropped. Her eyes filled with question marks, not comprehending that there was someone on this planet who did not know of Britney Spears.

"C.C., Britney Spears is a very popular pop singer. Kristina wants to take a poster of her to Russia."

"Let's first see the poster," I replied.

Kristina ran back to the poster section. By the time we arrived, she had pulled Britney out of the bin. I looked at it. I saw a pretty young girl in a very provocative pose. Her very short shorts were already half removed from her sexy body and I thought,

"This poster will not travel twelve time zones to my child's orphanage on my dime. This is a NO, NO."

I asked Elena to explain to Kristina that I could not send her back with this poster, that it would be inappropriate to do so, and to ask Kristina how she knows of Britney Spears. Here is Kristina's answer, translated: "We listen to MTV all the time in our orphanage. We know all the American singers."

What is remarkable and totally unexpected is that this type of trashy material made its way to such a remote part of the world and that the orphanage allowed this type of program to be viewed by their children. I was told some MTV programs were translated into Russian.

Elena's Christmas vacation was over. This was an opportunity for the children to visit the town they would live in. Early Saturday morning we drove to Naples. Elena's parents and younger brother, Eric, met us at my condo in the Grosvenor highrise in Pelican Bay. We went to the beach. It was my children's first time putting their feet in saltwater. Kristina wasted no time to collect shells with Elena. Anton built a castle in the sand with Eric. Later in the afternoon, my dear friend Renate, an OB-GYN, came to say hello. She immediately approved of the children.

Later in the afternoon, my wonderful friend, Lidia, an immigrant from Belarus, arrived.

Lidia was well educated, maternal and loving. She came to the United States on a three-month visa at age fifty-three. She lived in Naples for the next ten years. Within two months of working for a large hotel, she was promoted to manager of her department. For many years, Lidia tricycled to and from work every morning and every and night. I once asked her,

"Lidia, are you not afraid to tricycle alone to your home late at night?"

She answered, "I made friends with the police. They follow me home to make sure I'm safe."

Whatever amount of money was left after paying her expenses, she sent to Belarus for the education of her younger daughter. Often times, she also sent money to her brother in Ukraine.

To know Lidia is to love Lidia. Everybody loved her. When she smiled, several gold teeth were visible. She was charismatic with an inviting twinkle in her eyes. She never complained about her lot in life. As stressful as it was to be here, she counted her blessings. One could see a loving woman who had an abundance of warmth and kindness to share. Her knowledge of both English and Russian was instrumental in helping us with translation during and after the process of the adoption.

Kristina had already had a telephone conversation with Lidia while we were in Tampa. She already felt comfortable with her. As soon as the concierge of my building called to announce Lidia's arrival, Kristina ran to the elevator to greet her.

During her visit, I asked Lidia if she could ask the children if they would like to come live in America and have me as their mama.

When Lidia posed the question, Kristina put her head down as though to think it through, then looked up at Lidia and said, "*Da.*"

Lidia asked the same question of Anton. His response was, "But I have a mama."

Obviously for Anton, he was not prepared for this question. He was not ready to relinquish his loyalty to his mama even though he had not seen her for over three years. Kristina was older. Perhaps she understood their situation better and the advantages of coming to the U.S. I respected both answers.

Sunday, January 4, we went to the United Church of Christ to meet my dear friends Sir John and his wife, Laura, and to say hello to Murray, Valerie and their adopted Russian twins, David and Diana. To our surprise, the four Russian children froze when they were introduced. As soon as they took a quick look at each other, their gazes moved in a different direction as to avoid each other's eyes. They were fidgeting, seemingly uncomfortable in each other's presence. To everyone's surprise, they did not exchange a word. Many years later, we learned that David and Diana were deathly afraid of being returned to Russia.

We returned to Tampa in the afternoon. Early in the evening, Sol, a dear friend whose Russian parents immigrated to Montreal when he was a child, arrived. He had driven from Birmingham, Alabama to help with translation. His room was down the hall from ours. He participated in all our activities. Anton was especially happy to be able to relate to a man who spoke his language and who had electronic gadgets . . . and gadgets he had.

From the time the children arrived, Gen from Adoption Over-Seas, had asked me several times if I intended to adopt Kristina and Anton. Monday the 5th, while the children were busy with their program, I informed her that, yes, I intended to pursue the adoption. A meeting was arranged for the next day with Boris, the director of my children's orphanage and Tatiana, the official Russian translator.

8.

Asking Permission

*What makes you a man is
not the ability to make a child;
it's the courage to raise one.*
Barrack Obama[8]

ON TUESDAY, JANUARY 6TH, Boris, Tatiana, the Russian translator, my friend Sol and I sat at a table. As I looked around, I could feel a lot of anticipation and nervousness on everyone's face. I felt like a young man facing his future father-in-law asking for his daughter's hand. Yes, I was anxious but determined. The goal was, first, to inform Boris of my desire to adopt Kristina and Anton. Second, to convince him my intentions were well thought out. Third, ask for his support.

I started, "Boris, when I decided to host Kristina and Anton for this camp, I promised myself I would pursue the adoption if the children and I bonded. Within just a few days, the three of us felt very comfortable with each other. I believe we have bonded. My love for them and my desire to adopt them is real. In my heart they are already my children."

I stopped talking for a few seconds to let these thoughts sink in.

"Boris, would you give me permission to adopt Kristina and Anton and support my efforts during the adoption process?"

Boris started by saying, "When we left Russia, Kristina said she didn't want to be adopted, she just wanted to come to see America. Perhaps she'll change her mind."

Looking straight into Boris's eyes, I replied, "When we visited my condo in Naples, Lidia, my Belarus friend, asked Kristina if she would like to live in America and have me as her mama. After a few seconds of silence, Kristina answered, '*Da.*' "

Boris looked pleasantly surprised. He asked me numerous questions such as why I wanted to adopt children at my age, especially as a single woman, how I grew up, what my parents were like, how many children in my family, what my role was in my family, what was my education, what was my career, how I would care for the children, how would I discipline the children, what kind of home would they live in, would they have their own bedrooms, could I afford to send them to college, how financially secure was I, would I allow them to keep their language, what was my involvement with religion, would the children have medical insurance, etc. With the extra time required for translation, the interview went on for at least two hours. I answered all the questions truthfully, but I wondered why Boris was so concerned about college for the children or my financial abilities. The Russian government had little to offer orphaned children, if anything.

Finally, he said, "C.C., you have answered my questions. I feel you are making a serious and sincere offer. I will support your request. You will never have problems with Kristina, but Anton will be much more difficult. He will need a lot of discipline. Kristina likes to sing and dance. Anton enjoys cars and trucks."

"Thank you, Boris, for trusting me. I will do everything in my power to give them a mother's love, a safe home and a college education of their choice. I will teach them the values I learned from my parents as I was growing up." I paused a few seconds, then I asked, "Boris, could Kristina join our meeting? I would like to ask her in your presence." He agreed.

Kristina joined us. She sat next to Boris, across from me. Sol, who had been listening silently and intently since the start of the interview, was now focusing on Kristina. He was witnessing the starting point of something bigger than anything he had been part of in his life. He was witnessing the first brick, the beginning of the foundation that would culminate in the creation of a new family, a family uniting two Russian children and a Canadian woman, all living in the United States of America.

The adults at the table were very serious, a bit emotional, anticipating the next move. My heart was beating fast. I was searching for the right words, words that would be comforting for Kristina. I started very softly, pausing between each segment to give Tatiana time to translate.

"Kristina, during the few days we've been together, you and your brother have conquered my heart. I love you and I love Anton very, very much. Kristina, I want to ask you a very serious question. Your answer could change your life and your brother's life forever. If you do not feel ready to answer now, or if you want to think about it for a while, I will understand."

Everyone at our table was focusing on Kristina in complete silence. The tension was high. We couldn't hear a person breathe. Kristina kept her eyes locked on mine. She was very serious. She controlled her nervousness very well.

I continued, "Kristina, would you accept my invitation to come live in America with Anton and have me as your mama?"

While Tatiana translated the question, no one dared move. All eyes were on Kristina. She stared at me for a few seconds. She then turned her head toward Boris. She stared at him with question marks in her eyes. She maintained her gaze on Boris, searching for direction. Boris nodded his approval. She looked at him a little longer; perhaps to be sure she understood his nod correctly. She then turned toward me, stared into my eyes as if to try to read the sincerity of my offer. Her long silence became uncomfortable for everyone.

I started speaking, "Kristina, I truly love you and Anton. It would an honor if you accept me as your second mama and live here in America with me. We would form a family of three people.

We would love and care for each other. I will love, protect and take care of you and Anton. You will love and take care of Anton and me, and Anton will love and take care of you and me. We will work together to be a happy family." Her eyes were laser beamed on mine while Tatiana was translating. After a few more seconds of silence, she said, *"Da."*

"Kristina, I am so happy you said yes. Would you like to ask me some questions?" She thought for a few seconds then replied, *"Nyet."*

This was truly a beautiful and a very emotional moment. Boris and Tatiana had moist eyes. Sol had a few tears rolling down his cheeks. I felt very emotional and humbled by her answer.

I regained my composure and suggested, "Boris, could we invite Anton to join us? I would like to ask him the same question in front of you."

Anton sat next to his sister. I looked at him as tenderly as I could. I asked my angels to guide my words. With the help of Tatiana, I asked him,

"Anton, since you and Kristina arrived in America, I've become very attached to you and I love you and Kristina very much. I asked Boris first, then I asked Kristina, now I will ask you.

"Anton, would you accept my invitation to come live in America with Kristina, and have me as your mama?"

He turned white, his jaw dropped, he stared at the table and completely froze. I quickly looked at everyone, Sol was sobbing. Tatiana and Boris's eyes were filling up.

I softly said, "This child is not ready to give an answer. He needs more time. Perhaps the two children will discuss this offer together and come to a decision later. Let's send them back to play."

The meeting ended. A few minutes later, a man, not part of our camp, entered the room with a young boy. Within seconds Anton ran to this boy. It was obvious they knew each other. A little while later, I looked around the room and noticed Anton and this boy were sitting on the floor in a corner of the room talking up a storm. I asked Gen if she knew who he was.

"Yes, he comes from your children's orphanage. He was adopted by that man and his wife just a few months ago."

Her words were music to my ears. This full-of-energy young boy looked so happy. I hoped he would discuss his wonderful new life with Anton and convince him to say, "*DA!*"

9.

Departure

I hide my tears when I say your names, but the pain
in my heart is still the same. Although I smile and seem carefree,
there is no one who misses you more than me!
Toni Kane[9]

WHILE I HAD BEEN in Naples with the children the prior weekend, a letter from the Immigration and Naturalization Service
(INS) had arrived informing me that the FBI office in Miami had
scheduled me for finger printing on January 8 at 1:00 p.m. Had
the children and I not come to Naples, I would have missed the
letter and the appointment. Who knows how much that would
have delayed the process? Candice volunteered to be responsible
for my children for that day.

Sol insisted, "C.C., Miami is a five-hour drive from Tampa, a
ten-hour round trip. I will drive with you."

We left at 6:30 a.m., 280 miles each way. We started our drive
back to our Tampa hotel as soon as the fingerprints were completed. We arrived at 7 p.m.

The next day, January 9th, just after breakfast, Candy
announced, "C.C., it's not working out with Misha. She left my
room last night. A single woman offered to adopt her. She took
Misha to her home. There's no point for me to stay any longer. I'm
all packed. I'm leaving. I'll see you in Naples."

"I'm sorry to hear that, Candice. Let's talk about it later. We'll need to meet to settle our bills. I'll call you when I'm back in Naples."

Friday was the last day of camp. One could sense high emotions, nervousness and agitation on the part of the children, and on the part of most parents, as these wonderful two weeks were coming to an end. All children, except two, received offers to be adopted. The lucky children knew their return to Russia would be temporary, just long enough for both governments to process the documents and for the Russian courts to grant the parents their petitions to adopt.

Saturday after breakfast, Sol, who helped so much with translation, said an emotional goodbye to the children to return to his home in Birmingham, Alabama. The children and I were on our own. We spent the afternoon shopping for luggage, packing clothes, toys and the very large stuffed animal Kristina received from Santa Claus. Each child was allowed only one small bag to take back to Russia. No matter how hard we would try to squeeze "Mr. Big Bear" into the allowed luggage, it would not fit. A solution had to be found. On Friday, I made the following offer to the director of my children's orphanage,

"Boris, if I give you a piece of luggage as a gift, would you let Kristina put her large stuffed animal in it to travel to Russia?"

"*Da.*"

I felt I was bribing him. Was I? Is this how bribery starts?

The last full day for the host families and their children was Sunday, January 10, 2004. Candice's little girl, Misha, was reassigned to a new host mama who invited everyone for a Sunday brunch at her beach condo in Clearwater, Florida. It was a very cold and windy day. Anton dressed himself in a long-sleeved cotton shirt and his Adidas jacket. Kristina came out of her bedroom with only a lightweight, short-sleeved, pink T-shirt. With gestures I tried to tell her it was very cold outside. I put my arm out of the window.

"Brrrrrrr! Brrrrrrr! It's cold . . . you need a jacket my love . . . ."

I dangled two different ones in front of her. She absolutely and irrevocably refused to wear a long-sleeved shirt or to even bring a jacket. As much as I tried to persuade her, she would not budge. So, I thought, *So be it; she will have to live with the consequences of her decision.*

As soon as we got out of the car in Clearwater, Kristina squeezed her arms to her chest. The forty-mile-per-hour cold wind from the Gulf of Mexico was strong enough to cut a skinny dog in half. The frigid, hurricane-like wind reduced our efforts to walk forward to the entrance door. For every step forward, the wind pushed us back half a step. We needed to bend forward to create less resistance. Kristina kept her arms folded, trying to retain whatever heat her body could produce. Once in the apartment, she disappeared into the room where all the children had gathered. She quickly borrowed a jacket then came back to sit on my lap.

I pulled on the sleeve of her borrowed jacket and said, "What's this Kristina? Huh! What is this you're wearing, dearest little one?"

Even though she did not understand my words, she understood what I was communicating. She sheepishly smiled, shook her head from side to side while Boris was looking on. I smiled and raised my eyebrows. When I shared this event with my dear *tante* Lucienne in Montreal, she said, "This little girl has a mind of her own."

I replied, "I like people with character."

What I really thought was, for the first time since we met, Kristina was testing me.

We returned to our hotel room later in the afternoon. I suggested we call Lidia, my Belarus, Russian-speaking friend. Both children were excited to speak with her and to say goodbye. Before hanging up, Lidia and I exchanged a few words. What I heard was music to my ears.

"C.C., the children told me they had a great time. They wished they could stay. When I said to Anton, 'I hope to see you again,' he answered, 'You will, because C.C. wants to adopt us.' "

The sound of these words warmed my heart. Anton's answer was positive. Kristina and the young boy from his orphanage, with whom he had had a long conversation at the church hall during CampKidHope, must have convinced him.

On Monday, January 11, all parents had to be at the airport by 11 a.m. We had breakfast early, finished packing our bags and carried what was left of the food into the car. Anton had more fun than God with the luggage trolley. He was pushing it, riding it, hanging on to the high bars, as any typical young boy would do . . . or would they? Kristina was holding on to my arm in silence. She was withdrawn, pensive, she looked extremely sad. I wished we could have been able to communicate better. I tried to tell her I would pursue the adoption as fast as I could. That I would succeed in bringing her back to America. Her sadness and her whole body language tore me apart.

Anton was basically the same Anton, happy and funny. At the airport, he was very busy being curious about what was going on with each child and with each family. He watched with intensity those who were sobbing. As I looked around, the boys seemed to be more controlled than the girls. Several boys were clustered on the floor playing cards. There was one little girl who was hanging on to her host mama crying, sobbing and screaming. I asked Tatiana what was going on.

"Oh C.C., this little girl has some serious bipolar disorder problems. No one offered to adopt her. She is hysterically screaming, 'Don't leave me . . . . I want to stay with you . . . . I love you . . . . Please don't let me go . . . . I don't want to go back . . . . Please keep me with you . . . . I love you . . . . Please . . .' "

As I am writing these words, I have tears in my eyes remembering this little girl's desperation and her unstoppable sobbing. As she was pulled away from the host mama by a caregiver, she continued to scream and to fight, trying to go back to the host mama. Instead, she was dragged toward the lineup, where she remained under the grip of the caregiver until they disappeared. This poor little girl! One could only wonder what would happen to her once she returned to the orphanage.

Misha and her new host mother came to join us. Misha would decide later if she wanted to be adopted by her new host mama. The adoption offer would be her only chance to come to America. She would be too old for a second chance.

To distract our children, we bought them hamburgers, French fries and ice cream. Kristina remained silent. Her mood did not change. Again, I wished we could have been able to communicate. I wanted so much to comfort her, to tell her I loved her and that I would pursue the adoption as fast as I could. I wanted to ask her to pray God to guide us in the pursuit of the adoption, but I did not even know if God or angels were a part of her life. The only thing I was left with was to hug her in a way that she could feel the love I had for her, that she could sense my sincerity, that she could believe I meant what I said and to believe I would go to her country and bring her and her brother back to America.

The whole scene at the airport was gut wrenching. It tore me apart. It broke my heart just as it must have broken the hearts of every host parent. I felt I had to be stoic. I had to maintain my composure. I had to show a positive front for my children. If they saw me cry it may have caused them more pain, at least for Kristina. There would be time for me to cry later.

The final announcement came.

"Parents, you may take a minute or two to say goodbye to your children."

The three of us hugged. We hugged as tight as we could for as long as the time allowed. I almost started to sob. Kristina and Anton were my children. How could I let them go? When would I see them again? Would I ever see them again? I held my tears. The last call came, first in Russian then in English.

"It's now time for the children to line up."

Holding hands, we walked together until I had to let them go. We quickly had one last hug before they crossed to the other side of the rope.

I stood there and watched as they walked away, two by two, following the other children. Kristina turned around a few times.

I could now see the tears running down her cheeks, tears she had held back so successfully earlier. As they both disappeared, I walked to the ladies' room. It was time for me to let my own tears flow out. And flow out they did. I sobbed until my supply of tears was exhausted.

During the three-hour drive back to Naples, I reviewed what had just happened during the last two weeks. In just a few days, my life took a turn never expected before meeting Valerie and Murray. While I felt happy with the outcome, I realized I was physically and mentally drained. The beautiful and deep emotional experiences of the last two weeks were without parallel. I understood the consequences of my commitment were enormous. In some strange way, I felt I was given this responsibility by forces I could not quite comprehend. I accepted the challenge and I was determined to fulfill it to the best of my abilities. I sensed God, my angels and the positive forces of the universe were all with me. My intuition led me to believe that somehow, if help is needed, help would be provided along the way.

Kristina and Anton entered my heart permanently on January 3, 2004. That night I made a commitment to God, to myself and to my children: "Yes, I will pursue their adoption. At that moment, they became embryos in my heart. This will be my first and only pregnancy. I will love and cherish my two children for the duration of the gestation, in this case, until the Russian court releases them to my care. Until that day, they will grow in my thoughts, in my heart and in my soul." I welcomed the challenge. I was hooked. I was uplifted by the thought of changing both the course of my life as well as the course of these two beautiful children's lives.

By the time I entered my condo I was depleted. I had given my all. I needed a couple of C.C. Days, days of complete R & R (rest and relaxation). I unplugged the telephone, did nothing other than sleep, eat a little, read, meditate and watch some insignificant TV programs. The purpose of a C.C. Day was to bring both body and mind to complete tranquility to replenish the energy needed to undertake whatever life would bring next.

10.

Citizenship, a Priority

Often when we lose hope and think this is the end,
God smiles from above and says,
"Relax . . . it's just a bend, not the end!
Aanchal Jain[10]

DURING MY TWO DAYS of rest, I carried my children in my heart. I prayed for guidance as I prepared for the months ahead. My prevailing thoughts were to be unrelenting in my quest to obtain my U.S. citizenship, and that, with the shortest delay possible.

I will send letters with pictures of my children to whomever. I will drive to Miami's immigration office to beg for an earlier interview until I'm sworn in as a citizen of the United States of America. If only I could touch someone's heart. If only one person, at the immigration office, yes, only one person could see the beauty in my actions. If only one person could understand. I'm asking for help not for myself, but for my children who have been living in an orphanage in Siberia for the last four years.

If only one person could perceive and feel the love I have to give, perhaps that person would help me get an early citizenship interview. Out loud I blurted, "God, please listen up! I'm determined to achieve this goal in whatever legal way I can. Will *You* help me?"

Now, it was time to share the good news with my mom and siblings who lived in Québec City, Canada. With the letter I sent,

I included several pictures of my children and ended with, "I will need courage and patience. But I also hope to create a positive environment, give my children the tools to have a successful life and, most of all, give them all the love I hold in my heart. Years come and go. Each brings new turns and twists. Do I dare say that maternity has no age!"

Below is the response from my eighty-nine-year-old mom, translated from the French.

Dear Cécile,

A few days ago, I received your letter, which included the pictures of the children you want to adopt. I am not surprised. My "antennas" had already informed me of your decision when you announced you were going to host two Russian children with the intent to adopt them.

It is comprehensible that living alone in the United States, you want to prepare for your old age by adopting children who will become your family.

My best wishes are with you in this project, which I hope will fulfill you. Do not forget that children, as intelligent as they may be, do not always answer to the expectations of their parents, even if the parents do their very best.

If you succeed, and I wish it for you, be assured that I will accept them as part of our family and that I will be happy to meet them.

Your gesture will give these two children the chance to pursue a better life when compared to the life they now have. They look charming in the pictures you sent.

I hope all is well, and that your shoulder break is not too painful. As for me, except for getting older, which is not a disease, I am doing well.

My best regards to Laura and John,

Love and hugs, Maman

I replied to my mom on February 12, 2004.

Dear Maman,

Your letter of January 30th warmed my heart. I thank you. Your intuition has not left you with your advancing age. You have guessed correctly.

Adopting two children represents a heavy project with unknown consequences. I feel ready to embark on this adventure. I understand difficulties will present themselves along the way. At the same time, I will experience profound happiness as I watch them grow into their respective lives using their God-given talents. In their country, Anton's future would be the armed forces at best and, for Kristina, working in manufacturing or even, perhaps, being taken by the Mafia as a sex slave, a frequent occurrence in Russia.

Maman, adopting two children to prepare for my old age never crossed my mind. Instead, my desire has always been to do something of great importance to repay my debt for the privilege of retiring at a very young age. I will keep you informed as events take place.

Love and hugs to you, Cécile.

Earlier in January, with Sylvia's help, I had asked the INS to inform me of the status of my citizenship application. They told me (remember) that it would be a year before I could even hope for an interview. This was totally unacceptable. The children and I could not wait that long. I had to take action.

"I will maneuver and tap dance around each obstacle until I reach my next goal. The goal is citizenship."

On January 17, I wrote to the INS Homeland Security Office in Mesquite, Texas, to inform their office that my fingerprints had been taken, as scheduled, at the FBI office in Miami on January 8. I ended my letter this way.

"To be able to adopt, I must first become a United Sates citizen. My children, Kristina and Anton, (pictures included) are waiting in an orphanage in Siberia. Your help will be your gift of love and compassion for two children desperate to have a family in America. I thank you for whatever help you can give us."

On January 22, a document from Homeland Security arrived.

"We cannot find your file. Please provide your alien number."

I complied. In the envelope, I included a memo that ended by pleading for their help to expedite my citizenship request in the name of my children.

On February 18, 2004, with Lidia's help as a translator, I wrote a letter to Boris, the director of the orphanage, to give him an update on the progression of my citizenship. I included a letter to Anton. I asked Anton if he could send me a drawing instead of writing a letter. I asked Anton to discuss with Kristina if there was something special they would like to learn when they come to America. For example, they may want to learn to play the piano or the violin, ride a bicycle, play soccer, or tennis or take swimming lessons, etc. Everything is possible in America.

I added, "Both of you are always in my heart. I miss and love you very much."

11.

Birth Certificate

Perseverance is not a long race;
it is many short races one after the other.
Walter Elliot[11]

WHILE WAITING TO BE sworn in as a citizen, I continued
gathering needed documents to prepare my adoption dossier. On
February 26, 2004, I mailed a letter to the Government of Québec
Province, Canada requesting a copy of my birth certificate. It
arrived two weeks later with the name "Cécile Marie LeBlanc."

"What! Cécile Marie LeBlanc! Impossible! My birth certificate has always been Marie Cécile LeBlanc."

I immediately called the Québec Government Office to clarify
this issue. As is the case when one calls a government office, one
is never at the right department, nor speaking to the right person. My call was transferred to four different telephone exten-
sions before I was able to reach Madame Sylvie Sauvé who agreed
to speak with me. I asked why my name was reversed on my
birth certificate. Madame Sauvé explained it this way.

"In the beginning of time, in French Québec, all Catholic girls
were baptized starting with the name Marie, in honor of the
Blessed Virgin Mary. At that time, the birth record of each baby
was kept in the archives of the various, mostly Catholic, churches.
When the Québec government took over the registration of all

54

their citizens, all churches in Québec Province transferred their archives to us. When the names were entered in our computers, there were columns upon columns of girls' name starting with Marie, such as Marie Cécile, Marie Johanne, Marie Claudette, etc. To simplify our records, the Québec Government decided to put Marie as the middle name. Your name became Cécile Marie."

"Madame Sauvé, can my name be reversed back to the original one of Marie Cécile?"

"That would be most difficult Madame LeBlanc."

"Madame Sauvé, this change, made without my knowledge, will cause me some serious complications. I am in the process of adopting two Russian children. All the legal documents for the adoption have been filed under Marie Cécile for both the Russian Government and the United States Government."

"Unfortunately, Madame LeBlanc, I do not have the authority to reverse your name. You will have to speak to Madame Morneau. She will be in the office tomorrow."

"Could you give me her direct extension number?"

"Hum . . . it's . . . you must know . . . it's against our policy Madame LeBlanc . . . hum . . . well . . . I like your story. I'll give it to you but please don't tell anyone. You can call the same number and ask for extension 1004."

A few day later, after much arm-twisting, I convinced Madame Morneau to re-register my name in the original format of Marie Cécile. A new birth certificate arrived several days later.

On March 20, I wrote a letter to the INS in Mesquite, Texas pleading with them to help resolve the inaction and delays.

Recently, I called the INS Customer Service number to inquire about the status of my application to become a U.S. citizen. The person answering the call informed me the FBI had cleared my fingerprints taken Jan. 8, 2004. She suggested I visit the Immigration Office at 7880 Biscayne Blvd in Miami, Florida for further information.

After making an appointment via the internet for March 10, at 11:00 a.m., I drove to the above address. After a few hours wait, the

*young lady at the window, who spoke only in Spanish, informed me
I was in the wrong office. She suggested I visit the following address:
77 SE 5th Street. The representative there informed me my file was
still in Mesquite, Texas. She added,*

*"Yes, your fingerprints have cleared, but since 9-11, further FBI
checks are required for each applicant." There was nothing further
she could do until my file was received in Miami. She suggested I
write to your office.*

*I am in the process of adopting two foreign-born children who
have been living in an orphanage in Siberia since May 2000. These
siblings are twelve and eight-and-one-half years old. I cannot start
the adoption process until I become a U.S. citizen. Can you help me
accelerate the process? Time is of the essence. I will be sixty-five
years old in November. I am asking for your help, not for myself,
but for two children desperately waiting to be adopted and come to
America. Please find it in your heart to help us.*

Respectfully, C.C. LeBlanc

On March 16, I called the FBI office in Naples to review the
status of my background check. I was referred to a Washington
office, then to another one in West Virginia. I could not talk to
anyone, so I left a pleading message to give me an update on the
status of their investigation.

On March 18, desperate to obtain my United States citizenship,
and wanting to reach anyone who would help me, I wrote a letter
to our First Lady, Laura Bush. I explained in a poignant manner
the purpose of my letter, hoping to touch someone's heart. I did
not think Mrs. Bush would ever see my letter. Instead, I thought
her staff would handle my request. I ended my letter this way:

*Mrs. Bush, I ask for your help in the name of my two children,
Kristina, age twelve, and Anton, age nine. They are siblings living
in an orphanage in Siberia since May 2000. They are waiting for me
to bring them home here to America. Included are photocopies of
pictures taken at CampKidHope, a two-week cultural visit held in*

Tampa, Florida, to introduce older children to prospective adoptive
parents. Please Mrs. Bush, could you find it in your heart to help us.

Wanting to make sure Congressman Goss's secretary, Sylvia,
would not forget us, I wrote her to remind her of my efforts and
update her on my progress.

A few days later, I wrote a letter to Boris, the director of my
children's orphanage to keep him informed of whatever progress
there was. I wanted so much to make it possible for my children
to start school in the United States in August 2004. I even asked
Boris if the Russian Government would let them come here on a
visa before the adoption was finalized. I told him I was working
to obtain medical insurance for Kristina and Anton. I extended
an invitation for his daughter, the same age as Kristina, to stay
with us and go to school here for one year. I found out later that it
was wishful thinking on my part. The Russian government would
never allow the children to come to America unaccompanied.

For Kristina's twelfth birthday, April 29, I posted a package
which included two small binoculars, a level three children's book,
one small Russian/English dictionary, two packages of hair decorations from Lidia, three wide headbands, a wide-angle picture of
the Naples sunset, a birthday poster and a watch for Kristina. I
included a special poster I made for Anton. I also included a picture of the cast of the play "Alice in Pelican Land," based on Alice
in Wonderland, where I played The Red Queen. I thought Kristina
would enjoy knowing I like to act, as she participated in several
acting roles in her orphanage. Finally, I included a letter to tell
them both how much I missed them and how hard I was working
to prepare for their arrival.

On April 13, a document from the INS arrived announcing
my interview for citizenship had been scheduled at the Miami
Office for August 7, 2004.

"Finally! I'm on the schedule. Someone has heard my pleas."

After a Google search, I found that the next swearing-in ceremony for citizenship was scheduled for August 10. That only gave

the government agency three days, from August 7 to August 10, to put my name on the swearing-in list. Not very likely . . . bureaucracy moves slowly. The following ceremony would be held in mid-December.

"I'm almost there. This is definitely progress. But I can't take the chance on whether or not my name will be part of the August ceremony. I must find a way to be interviewed sooner to insure I'm part of that ceremony."

Now, my new challenge was to devote all my energy to obtaining an interview/appointment early enough so my name could be added to the August list. Waiting for the December date would mean another four months delay before I could start the adoption process. I was energized by the following thought. "If I become a U.S. citizen on August 10, 2004, my children could be home before the end of December. We could celebrate our first Christmas together. What an invigorating possibility!"

One more time, I was filled with hope, anticipation and excitement. But deep in my soul fear of yet another delay was looming. I rejected those thoughts.

"I must not bring any negativity into my being. I must stay positive, fill my heart with all the positive energies the universe can send my way."

I called Sir John to share the good news. So happy he was, he immediately drove to my home to hand me a small book of questions and answers on the United States history, government, etc. Part of the interview included a verbal quiz, based on this little book, written for potential new U.S. citizens.

"It's happening . . . I'm on my way. Thank you, God."

12.

Citizenship Quest Continues

If there is no struggle,
there is no progress.
Frederick Douglas[12]

REENERGIZED BY THE POSSIBILITY of bringing my children to America before the end of the year, I embarked on a new mission. The mission was to find a way to be part of the swearing in ceremony scheduled for August 10.

I contacted Sylvia, Congressman Porter Goss's secretary, to ask if she could arrange for an earlier interview. Sylvia wrote the following to the INS.

Miss LeBlanc has received an appointment for an N400 interview on 08/07/2004. The swearing-in ceremony is scheduled three days later. Ms. LeBlanc is waiting for her naturalization to adopt two children from Russia. She is asking to be placed on a waiting list for an earlier interview. Should there be a cancellation, could her name be substituted? Is this possible?

The answer came quickly.

Sylvia,

The only cases that we expedite are active duty military personnel with deployment orders and American Embassy employees.

Unfortunately, this case appears not to comply with the criteria for an expeditious processing.

Congressional Liaison Office,
Miami Citizenship Office

Feelings of despair were entering my soul.

"Can't anybody understand? This request is for the benefit of two future American children now living in a Siberian orphanage. Doesn't anybody have a heart? Can't they feel the anguish? Maybe not. I must continue to fight. As Churchill said, 'Never, Never, Never give up.'"

A few days later, I called Sylvia to ask if she could arrange an appointment with the INS in Miami.

"I would like to make a request for an earlier interview, face-to-face, with someone of authority."

Sylvia succeeded in arranging an interview. On May 5, 2004, I left my condo at 5:00 a.m. for the two-and-one-half hour drive to the United State Citizenship and Immigration Services on Biscayne Ave. in Miami. At 7:30 a.m., I took my place in line on a long wooden bench outside the building. The scene was a new one for me. I was one of three white people sitting on the bench. It felt more like I was on a trip to Central or South America, or the Middle East, Africa, India or even Pakistan. More people kept coming. Some were large families including grandparents and young children. I could sense anxiety and stress in their eyes and in their faces. I admired them in having found the courage to go through so many hoops to fight for their dream of living in America. They were here for the same reason I was: to obtain U.S. citizenship, to be part of the land of the free. I now understand what it feels like being a minority among a crowd. I also felt empathy for these immigrants. Life must have been very difficult in their countries, just as it was for my children in Siberia.

The doors opened at 8 a.m. After a security check, each person was given a number, then directed to enter a large room with chairs set up theater-style facing large TV monitors near the ceiling. After a two-hour wait, my number popped up on the screen. I walked to window #24. I soon realized the representative, Mrs. Valdez, barely spoke English. I ventured to explain in Spanish, a third language I speak to some extent, the reason for this visit.

"Mrs. Valdez, I'm in the process of adopting two Russian children. First, I must become a U.S. citizen. The interview for citizenship is scheduled for August 7th . . . "

Mrs. Valdez interrupted me and said in Spanish, "If you're adopting children, I'm not the right person for this question. You must see Mrs. Louie whose office is on the fifth floor just around the corner. Show this pass to the security officer. He will direct you to her office."

With exasperation and trepidation, but with a glimmer of hope, I arrived at the reception desk.

"May I speak with Mrs. Louie?"

"She will be with you in just a few minutes."

I waited, standing. When Mrs. Louie arrived, she extended her hand and asked me to follow her. On the way to her office, I asked, "Mrs. Louie, do you speak French?"

"Yes, I do."

"Are you from Haiti?"

"Yes I am."

"I'm from Québec, from the French language. I visited your country several years ago."

"I have many relatives in Québec, Miss LeBlanc. I'm looking forward to visiting them on my next vacation."

Once in her office, she pointed to a chair. I sat. With a smile, she asked, "What can I do for you, Miss LeBlanc?"

Sitting on the edge of the chair, I bent forward. Holding back tears, I locked my eyes on hers and said, "Mrs. Louie, a few minutes ago, I spoke with Mrs. Valdez on the first floor. She referred me to you. I'm a Canadian citizen here on a green card since 1976. I am in the process of adopting two Russian children from Siberia. I must first become a U.S. citizen. An appointment for a citizenship interview is scheduled for August 7. The next swearing-in ceremony will take place August 10, only three days later. I'm concerned there will not be enough time to add my name to that list. Could you help me obtain an earlier inter...."

Her eyes were blank ... empty ... there was nothing coming back. I could sense she was not receptive to what I was saying ... She was not with me in thought nor spirit. I stopped talking. I felt desperate. I quickly regrouped and said, "Mrs. Louie, you're not the right person either, are you?"

"No, I'm not Miss LeBlanc. I will only work with you when you are ready to adopt your children. My office determines the acceptability of both the parents and the children. Your children's papers for the U.S. Consulate in Moscow will come through my office."

Now, tears were filling my eyes. I felt sorry for myself. I had left Naples at 5 a.m. to arrive on time for an 8:30 a.m. appointment, only to hit a dead end. With pleading eyes and a shaky voice, I asked, "Mrs. Louie, I'm almost sixty-four years old. I must bring my children home soon. They are waiting for me in an orphanage in Siberia. Can you help me find someone who can make this happen?"

Mrs. Louie was a pretty Black woman. She was stoic and very professional. One could feel kindness in her face and in her eyes. I sensed she felt my desperation, my anguish.

"Wait here Miss LeBlanc, I'll see what I can do."

She returned a short while later, "Follow me."

On the way I prayed, "God, you asked me to take care of these children, now you must help. You must make it happen. I need your help now!"

We arrived at a large impressive office with a sitting area. I was introduced to Mr. Jones, who invited both Mrs. Louie and me to sit. It was obvious I was disturbing the gentleman. He appeared to be cold, distant, uninterested. In an unfriendly, impatient tone he said, "What can I do for you Miss LeBlanc?"

I repeated what I had already shared with Mrs. Louie. I ended by saying, "Mr. Jones, could you assist me in arranging for an earlier interview so I could be part of the August 10 swearing-in ceremony?"

"What makes you think the United States will accept you as a citizen, Miss LeBlanc?"

What an arrogant man! I wanted to jump in his face, grab him by the tie, and spit the words, "You despicable jerk!" But I needed him. I needed him for the sake of my children. I swallowed. With a soft voice and pleading eyes, I answered, "Mr. Jones, I have no guarantee the United States will accept me, but I have been a good resident of this country since 1976. I believe the interviewer will see that I and my two children will be a positive addition to the fabric of these Untied States."

"Well Ms. LeBlanc, I don't know how or if I will be able to do anything for you. I'm being transferred to Philadelphia next week."

Again, I became emotional. I felt tears filling my eyes. Mrs. Louie's presence helped me stay strong. I continued, "Mr. Jones, all I'm asking is for an earlier interview, so my name can be on the list along with those who will be sworn-in at the August 10th ceremony. Could you see it in your heart to find the person who can accomplish this? Could you find it in your heart Mr. Jones, to help me for the love of two children who are waiting in a Siberian orphanage?"

I kept my pleading eyes, filled with tears, focused on his for as long as it took for him to reply.

"Ms. LeBlanc, I don't know if anything can be done. If you'll excuse me, I have another appointment."

Mrs. Louie and I left his office. We walked in silence to the elevator. She gave me a hug and said, "Miss LeBlanc, I'll talk to Mr. Jones."

"Thank you, Mrs. Louie. You are a wonderful woman."

The almost three-hour drive back to Naples felt longer than usual. All I could think about was the arrogant and heartless Mr. Jones. I felt disheartened. I was trying so hard to bring my children home. Meeting this Mr. Jones was like meeting a person without a soul. I wondered if he truly understood the value of the enormous commitment I was pursuing. I prayed to whomever could hear me, then I told myself, "Even in the most noble causes, there are numerous challenges one has to overcome before success can be achieved. I thought about the many struggles Gandhi and Martin Luther King, Jr., had to face. I must not get discouraged, tomorrow is another day, let's see what it brings."

13.

Citizenship

The difference between a successful person
and others is not a lack strength, not a lack
of knowledge, but rather a lack in will.
Vince Lombardi, Jr.[13]

M RS. LOUIE HAD DISPLAYED a kindness and a sympathy toward me, and I felt she would do the same for any parents of to-be-adopted children. She became an Earth angel for me the day we met. A few days later, I wrote a letter to thank her. I was hoping that she would be successful in convincing Mr. Jones to help us.

On June 3, at 9 a.m., the phone rang.

"May I speak to Marie Cécile LeBlanc?"

"Speaking."

"Miss LeBlanc, my name is Mrs. Cortez. I'm with the INS office in Miami."

So surprised was I, I almost dropped the phone. Not knowing what to say I blurted, "Oh! Mrs. Cortez, I'm so glad you called!" (I had never met Mrs. Cortez.)

"Miss LeBlanc, why do you want to accelerate your citizenship?"

I repeated the reasons, you the reader, already know, then added, "Mrs. Cortez, could you find a way to help us?"

In a soft voice she said, "I can't promise you anything Miss LeBlanc, but one way or the other, you will hear from us by next Tuesday, June 8."

"Thank you so much Mrs. Cortez . . . for whatever you can do."

I hung up the phone and flopped on the nearest chair saying out loud, "Am I just dreaming? Is this call for real? Is something really happening?"

I whispered, "Thank you God."

I called Sir John and my good friend Dan Recer to share the good news. Then I enthusiastically emailed everyone on my list.

On Monday, June 7, an envelope from the INS Miami arrived in the mail. I opened it quickly.

It said, "Please present yourself at the INS office in Miami on June the 10, at 10:30 a.m. Please fill out the enclosed forms, bring two pictures of the size shown on the application and be prepared to answer questions on the history of the United States."

"It's here! I exclaimed with joy. I was given an appointment to the INS office for June the 10th at 10:30 a.m. and asked to bring two pictures of the size shown on the application form and to be ready to answer questions on American history.

"Wow!" I exclaimed. My heart was racing. "Is this it? Am I dreaming? Did the letter say the word 'interview'? Yes, yes, scanning the letter . . . there it is! The word 'interview' is right in front of my eyes! In just a couple of days . . . June 10th. How wonderful, my name will on the schedule. I will be sworn as an American citizen in two months, at the August 10th ceremony."

I called Sir John right away. He was as excited as I was. I had kept Sir John informed on every detail after our bi-weekly tennis games. Both he and his wife, Laura, were my number-one supporters. In addition, Sir John was my best friend and adviser. After speaking with Sir John, I called Dan Recer who said in a euphoric tone, "C.C., I think they will swear you in on June the 10th!"

"Oh Dan, that would be incredible! I can't imagine that! They'll just give me an interview so I can be sworn in August 10th."

"Why would they ask you to bring two pictures, C.C.?"

"Could it be to prepare the citizenship certificate for August 10th?"

"I don't know, but whatever it is C.C., it's good news. Is there anyone going with you?"

"No, I'll just drive myself just as I've done in the past."

"C.C., I think someone should go with you. How about I pick you up at 7:30 a.m.?"

"Dan, are you sure you want to drive all the way to Miami and back?"

"For you C.C., absolutely!"

"Great! That's wonderful Dan. Thank you. I'll be at the door at 7:30 a.m."

On June 10th, at 7:30 a.m. sharp, we started our drive straight east on I-75. The rising sun facing us was brutally blinding. Dan did not seem bothered by it. He was so excited to be part of whatever would happen today. Dan was a U.S. history buff. A true, patriotic American. He quizzed me on the possible questions Mrs. Cortez would ask during the interview.

For example, he asked, "Name the first thirteen colonies? What did the Emancipation Proclamation do? Who was President during the Civil War? Name the three branches of government? Name the senators from Florida? Name the president of the United States?"

We arrived at our destination a few minutes early. We walked in. We were directed to the waiting room, a large bland government type room with perhaps one hundred chairs set up in rows. A few people were seated. Dan brought the *Wall Street Journal* and sat as though he was going to spend a few hours in this room. He handed me a section of the paper. We both read silently waiting for someone to call my name. After just a few minutes, the silence was broken by a strong woman's voice calling, "Marie Cécile LeBlanc." I stood up in a flash, walked briskly toward her. She greeted me with a handshake.

"I'm Mrs. Cortez. Please follow me."

Once in her small office filled with piles of folders, she pointed to an empty chair. Without looking at me, she said.

"Please sit down, Miss LeBlanc. Hmm . . . I'm going to do everything today."

"What do you mean everything, Mrs. Cortez?" She looked up, met my eyes and said,

"Everything."

I thought, "Zip it up C.C. Whatever she means by the word 'everything' is good enough for now."

She kept shuffling and looking over the application papers. I watched her nervously in total silence. Then she asked,

"Did you bring pictures?"

"Yes, Mrs. Cortez, here they are."

"Oh! They're a little pale. Hmm . . . don't worry. I'll make them work."

A few minutes later she said,

"Did you study for your test?"

"Yes, I did Mrs. Cortez."

She proceeded to quiz me. I answered each question quickly and correctly. About six or seven questions later, she said,

"That's good enough Miss LeBlanc. You know your stuff. You can go back in the waiting room. Someone will call you in a little bit."

I entered the waiting room. Dan was still reading the Wall Street Journal, his reading glasses on the tip of his nose. As I approached, he looked up over his glasses with questioning eyes. I lifted my shoulders and my arms as if to say, "I don't know." I sat next to him and shared what had taken place in Mrs. Cortez's office.

"C.C., I bet you they will swear you in today."

"Oh Dan, that would be such a dream come true. No, I can't imagine it. I still think they're preparing documents so I can attend the swearing-in ceremony in August."

Just then we heard, "Marie Cécile LeBlanc."

I quickly stood up, walked toward a slender man who greeted me with a handshake and said,

"Miss LeBlanc, I'm Roger Park. Please follow me."

We walked down a long corridor, turned left into another one, and then entered a very small office with a large window, a very large wood table and eight chairs. There was barely enough room to stand. Mr. Park closed the door, looked at my file and asked that I identify myself. I gave him my drivers' license. He looked at it, returned it, and with a smile he said,

"I'm going to swear you in right now Miss LeBlanc."

"Are you? You really are?" With half a smile, I blurted, "Is this for real Mr. Park . . . or are you making a joke?"

Returning the smile, he answered, "No, no, Miss LeBlanc, I'm not joking. I will read you the Oath of Allegiance. At the end of my reading, if you agree, you can say, 'So help me God' or 'I solemnly affirm.' Your choice."

I immediately replied,

"So help me God is good enough for me, Mr. Park."

The United States Oath of Allegiance is an oath that must be taken by all immigrants who wish to become United States citizens. It is usually done in a ceremonial fashion. The oath of citizenship is meant to be a statement of loyalty and patriotism to the United States. Adding an oath to God at the end of the oath is usually optional.

Mr. Park started reading, "I hereby declare, on oath, that I absolutely and entirely renounce and abjure all allegiance and fidelity to any foreign prince, potentate, state, or sovereignty of whom or which I have heretofore been a subject or citizen; that I will support and defend the Constitution and laws of the United States of America against all enemies, foreign and domestic; that I will bear true faith and allegiance to the same; that I will bear arms on behalf of the United States when required by the law; that I will perform noncombatant service in the Armed Forces of the United States when required by the law; that I will perform work of national importance under civilian direction when required by the law; and that I take this obligation freely without any mental reservation or purpose of evasion; so help me God."

With enthusiasm, I firmly and loudly said, "So help me God."

He shook my hand and said, "Congratulations Miss LeBlanc! You are now an American citizen!"

He handed me a small flag and a welcoming envelope.

My heart was beating so fast, I was so happy I wanted to jump and give Mr. Park a hug. I wanted to scream, "I'm an American now! I can now move forward to adopt my children! Thank you God! Thank you Mrs. Louie! Thank you Mrs. Cortez! Thank you Mr. Park! Thank you whomever got me to this point. This battle is won. From now on, I will focus on winning the war. The war will be won when I can tell my children, 'We're Going Home.' *En avant on marche!* Forward we march!"

Mr. Park seemed to enjoy my reaction. With great emotions and moist eyes, I open the envelope and read:

THE WHITE HOUSE

WASHINGTON

Dear Fellow American:

I am pleased to congratulate you on becoming a United States citizen. You are now part of a great and blessed Nation. I know your family and friends are proud of you on this special day.

Americans are united across the generations by grand and enduring ideals. The grandest of these ideals is an unfolding promise that everyone belongs, that everyone deserves a chance, and that no insignificant person was ever born. Our country has never been united by blood or birth or soil. We are bound by principles that move us beyond our backgrounds, lift us above our interests, and teach us what it means to be citizens. Every citizen must uphold these principles. And every new citizen, by embracing these ideals, makes our country more, not less American.

As you begin to participate fully in our democracy, remember that what you do is as important as anything government does. I ask you to serve your new Nation, beginning with your neighbor. I ask you to be citizens building communities of service and a Nation of character. Americans are generous and strong and decent not because we believe in ourselves, but because we hold beliefs beyond ourselves. When this spirit of citizenship is missing, no government program can replace it. When this spirit is present, no wrong can stand against it.

Welcome to the joy, responsibility, and freedom of American citizenship. God bless you and God bless America.

Sincerely,

George W. Bush

I put the letter in my purse. Mr. Park led me out of the room. I thanked him and firmly shook his hand again before entering the waiting room. Holding the American flag with both hands at waist level, I walked toward Dan. His eyes lifted above his reading glasses. He dropped his newspaper to his lap and smiled from ear to ear. As I reached him, he stood up.

"Welcome to America, C.C.! Congratulations!" He gave me big hug. He appeared to be just as happy as I was.

"Thank you, Dan. I am so happy. The door is now open to pursue the adoption. The Certificate of Citizenship will be ready at 1:00 p.m. You were kind enough to drive me here. Would you be my guest for lunch to celebrate this unforgettable moment?"

We walked to the car. The Four Seasons Hotel was just a few blocks away. It was the perfect venue for this special lunch. Walking with the flag between my hands, I blurted to everyone who crossed our path,

"I'm a brand new American! I'm a brand new American!"

When we reached the restaurant, I continued to share this joyful moment with the maître d' and the waiters,

"I'm a brand new American!"

My visible excitement created smiles on everyone's face. Indeed, it was an incredible moment, a memorable piece of my life. After we finished the main course, the maître d' came to our table.

"To celebrate and welcome you as a new citizen of the United States, we offer you a cheesecake for dessert."

We smiled and accepted gracefully.

We left the restaurant, stopped at the immigration office to pick up my brand-new Certificate of Citizenship. We were filled with joy and appreciation. June 10, 2004 was an extraordinarily successful day.

14.

Naples United Church of Christ

*Challenges are gifts that force us to search for a new center
of gravity. Don't fight them. Just find a new way to stand.*
Oprah Winfrey[14]

WHEN I RETURNED HOME, it was almost Happy Hour. I sat
quietly with a glass of red wine. I needed to say thank you, to
count my blessings, to review and to reflect on the events of the
last ten months.

On August 31, 2003, I was introduced to Valerie and Murray
Wise and their newly adopted Russian twins, David and Diana.
That's when the inspiration to adopt and give a chance to two
children came. Unrelentingly, I tap-danced around each challenge until my first goal was reached, United States Citizenship.
Ten months later, I was sworn in. Didn't the *New York Times*
report that it takes an average of twenty-three months for green
card holders to become U.S. citizens? One more time, I convinced
myself that when a cause is good and noble, hard work and determination always pays off in the end. During the process, I must
have touched someone's heart.

Amazingly, I was sworn in alone, as if I were a diplomat.
That could not have been done without the many people who

supported me. Sylvia, in Congressman Goss's office, wrote letters on my behalf to try to accelerate the process. Although I received an acknowledgement from the White House in July 2004, I will never know if the office of First Lady Laura Bush intervened. I believe Mrs. Louie, this wonderful Haitian woman at the INS office in Miami, was a big part of my success. I will never forget her kindness and how meeting with her gave me hope. I will keep her in my precious memories, as well as the wonderful Mrs. Cortez and Mr. Park, who swore me in.

For you, my children, and for everyone reading this book, believe in yourself, never quit. If your cause is noble, fair, reasonable and achievable, work unrelentingly to reach your goals. Pursue your dreams . . . never quit until you hold each dream in the palm of your hand. I learned, one more time, to never take NO for an answer, to be proactive, to make things happen rather than waiting for them to happen.

What else did I learn from this experience? My first thought was that I follow Sir John's advice, "NNNQ" NEVER, NEVER, NEVER QUIT, no matter the challenge. This was Sir John's slogan. He expressed it at the end of every email he sent me. It is from one of Winston Churchill's quotes, "NEVER, NEVER, NEVER GIVE UP." My second thought was a strong conviction that when one works unrelentingly to bring a worthy cause to fruition, God and all the positive energies of the universe will work in synchrony to grant it.

The story of my life is filled with "NNNQ's." I cannot take "No" for an answer when I know my intentions are noble and achievable. I'm repeating myself because I'm so convinced that help will come your way when you work hard, maintain a positive attitude and when your purpose is to achieve something good. Adopting two children was just that and more. To some, I was completely out of my mind, totally insane. Others expressed the words "generous," "brave" and applauded my decision. In my heart, I knew it was what I was asked to do.

In the end, my efforts and my pleas for the benefit of my children must have touched someone's heart, perhaps Mrs. Bush's, for sure Mrs. Louie's or perhaps someone at the INS office. Deep down in my soul, I believed that Mrs. Louie became an Earth angel for us the day we met.

A part of President Bush's welcoming citizenship letter caught my attention. "Our country has never been united by blood or birth or soil. We are bound by principles that move us beyond our backgrounds." This statement so vividly reflects the essence of what took place that day. A woman of French-Canadian blood, birth and soil became a United States Citizen in order to adopt two children, of Russian blood, birth and soil. All three will move beyond their backgrounds to become an integral part of the American fabric. How beautiful!

As soon as I called Sir John to announce that my citizenship had been granted, he was overjoyed. He immediately asked for a copy of my citizenship certificate and a copy of President Bush's welcome letter.

At the next United Church of Christ Sunday service, three days later, June 13, Reverend Paterson made a few announcements, then added,

"One of the participants of this church who has been in this country for many years can now pursue the adoption of her children. After delay upon delay by the INS, she asked her dear friend John if she should address a letter to the First Lady. John, who is sitting next to her this morning, told her to go to the top. C.C. wrote to Mrs. Laura Bush to ask for help."

He continued, "I'm holding a copy of Marie Cécile LeBlanc's citizenship certificate in my hands along with a welcome letter from President Bush."

The congregation applauded. With great emotion, Pastor Patterson read President Bush's letter. He stopped speaking for a few moments then looked at the participants with a very intense gaze.

"I ask the congregation to join me in prayer to thank God for C.C.'s citizenship and to welcome her warmly to the United States of America."

At the end of the service, the tenor sang my favorite Irish blessing. I held Kristina and Anton in my thoughts and in my heart.

May the road rise to meet you,
May the wind always be at your back,
May the sun shine warm upon your face.
And until we meet again,
May the Lord hold you in the palm of His hand.[15]

Silently I added, *May the Lord hold my children in the palm of His hand, until we meet again.*

15.

Reflecting on Motherhood

When you are a mother, you are never really alone
in your thoughts. A mother always has to think twice,
once for herself and once for her child.
Sophia Loren[16]

WITH THE CERTIFICATE OF Citizenship in place, courage was added to my determination, which was stronger than ever. My children had overtaken my heart the moment I made the commitment to adopt them. They were now part and parcel of my being. Moving toward the adoption itself was the new challenge, one that would for sure unfold in a systematic manner. My hopes were high. Before the end of this year, 2004, a new American family would be born.

It seemed ironic that at almost sixty-five years of age, I found myself in the process of adopting two children. My mind drifted to a time when I was between twenty-eight and thirty-two, a time when my maternal instincts were crying to have a baby. The desire was so strong; I could not take the thought of motherhood out of my mind. After long consideration, I concluded that having a child as a single woman would be very selfish on my part. Yes, it would fulfill my maternal needs . . . but what about the child? As I wrote before, a child should have two parents, a mom and a dad. After arguing with my thoughts back and forth,

I finally convinced myself, that without a father for the child, motherhood was out of the question. The thought of adopting never crossed my mind. I was convinced no one would grant me a child without there being a father.

Then my eyes turned to a painting given to me by my special friend, Donald, for Christmas 1969. I was thirty then. The painting is of the face of a most beautiful little girl with big brown eyes. Her face moves in and out of the frame as different lighting illuminates it. A rolling tear dripping on one cheek is always present, no matter how the light moves on the painting. The moment I saw her face, I exclaimed, "This is the little girl I'll never have."

Weeks, months went by and, little by little, the haunting maternal instincts diminished and, life became the way it was to be for me. Although, still, whenever I looked at the painting, I wished I had a little girl just like her.

I continued reflecting. This time, my mind travelled to a time when I was about to reach the iconic age of forty. As the big number approached, I went into a dark hole. A state of depression overpowered me. In a distressed tone I said out loud,

"Half of my life is already lived, gone. In another forty years, the number will climb to eighty. Eighty! Unacceptable! I will never get old, not me, not C.C. LeBlanc. I refuse!"

My spirit was so low; my whole being was in distress. I knew I had to change my attitude, change these negative thoughts, these negative feelings. With no one to turn to, I sat at the kitchen table with a cup of freshly brewed coffee and lit a cigarette. I took a sheet of paper and drew a vertical line down the middle. On the left side, I would write everything that troubled me. On the right side, I would write what I would do to remedy those concerns.

The first concern was "Getting Old." I looked at the cigarette I was smoking and said, "Cigarette, you will never touch my lips again. You are helping the process of aging; in the ashtray you go!"

The second concern was "Married Life." I had never experienced the intimacy of married life. It was my choice not to marry. I had been asked numerous times. At a very young age, I witnessed my cousin, and then, my older sister, being abandoned by their husbands, each with two children and no money. They both had to return to live with their parents. I made a vow to myself then, "No man is born who will take me from the security of a home and drop me on the sidewalk with a couple of children. I will not marry until I become financially comfortable."

There is a price to pay for every decision one makes. Living as a single woman gave me the freedom to move around, to travel, and to have little responsibility other than my work. Many single men and women choose to build a career, not a family. Family may come later.

The third concern was "Motherhood." Yes, Motherhood. The strong desire to be a mother returned. The thought of never experiencing motherhood felt like a dull pain deep in my heart.

I knew that in 1979, pregnancy after the age of forty could have had serious complications. Moreover, *in vitro* fertilization had just begun in 1977. So, at almost forty, with no daddy in sight, I scheduled surgery to have a tubal ligation. My brain understood that tubal ligation was justified, but my heart could not. It was a very emotionally charged decision. With this surgery, I was forever denying myself the joys and the privileges of motherhood. So emotionally charged was I that three days before the scheduled procedure, and for the first time in my life, I experienced an overwhelming anxiety attack. Melinda, a friend and neighbor, suggested I lay down and rest. She took me to my bed and tucked me in.

"Try to sleep, C.C. I'll check with you a little later."

A soon as I heard the door close, the painting of the beautiful brown-eyed little girl with a tear drop on her cheek started flashing in my mind. It picked up speed and accelerated, faster and faster.

"This is the little girl you'll never have! This is the little girl you'll never have!" On and on . . . faster and faster . . . "This is the little girl you'll never have . . . " It would not stop. It was frightening! If you can imagine this beautiful little girl's face was flashing in and out of my brain with lightning speed. The constant flashes were totally uncontrollable and unstoppable. I thought I was going insane.

Melinda came back to check on me. She took one look at my face and immediately called Maureen, a nurse friend in the building. My blood pressure and pulse were both normal, but I was pale and so out of it that they took me to the emergency room. All tests were normal.

I asked the physician, "Should I cancel the tubal ligation procedure?"

"There is no medical or physical reason not to have the procedure. You must discuss your feelings with your surgeon," he responded.

A day or two after the procedure, a very deep sadness again invaded me. The haunting thoughts of never giving birth to a child returned. I was not able to look at a baby, any baby. The pain was so intense that even the sight of a baby carriage passing by created acute pain in my heart. I did my best to isolate myself from contacts with anyone or anyplace where there were babies, or anything related to babies.

Three years later, my significant other and I were invited to dinner at his son's home to celebrate the birth of his first grandson. Just a few minutes after we arrived, the new mom said,

"C.C., would you like to hold the baby?"

"Hmm . . . well . . . maybe . . . lat..."

Before I could mutter the word "later" she put the five-day-old baby in my arms. This was the beginning of the healing process. Little by little, I came to accept that motherhood was not meant for me, and I continued to believe I could not adopt a child as a single woman.

"Motherhood is not going to be part of your life, C.C. Get over it," I told myself.

Now, some twenty plus years later, at an age when my first social security check was in the mail, the process of adopting two children as a single woman had begun. This new venture was so out of the box, so out of sync with the real world, even I could not understand the reasons I was so driven to pursue this cause. But then, who's to judge what qualifies as in the box or out of the box?

I felt an overabundance of love, a love that needed to be shared, to be given away, a love strong enough to fill the heart of someone in need of receiving it.

Then I remembered the song written by Amanda McBroom, recorded in 1980 by Bette Midler for the movie "The Rose." The lyrics, easily found on Google, became a vision for what was happening in my soul. I paraphrase.

The song compares love to a river that takes away abandoned souls. It says that love is a razer that chips away at a hurting heart. Others say love is a craving deep inside our soul, a constant feeling of emptiness. Others say love is like a bud and only we have the power to make it bloom.

We could relate this paragraph to abandoned children who are denied love, whose tender souls have dried up, children who yearn for love, whose hearts have bled to an emptiness we can not fathom, whose hearts are aching and hungry to love and be loved. Wouldn't it be wonderful if we could imagine opening our heart to this wilted flower/child and if we could see ourselves nurturing the kernel, that with our love through adoption, could stop the pain for just one child.

Then the song refers to those afraid of a broken heart, that refuse to fall in love. Their yearnings are pushed aside by the worries of being hurt. It is those who will not bend, who lack the flexibility, those who cannot seem to share, and those who when they die will never know the true meaning of life.

Is it because we're afraid to fail, afraid to be hurt, afraid to take a chance? Is it why we keep our dreams dormant, why we keep them hidden, why we let them pass us by? Or is it because we lack courage that we do not dare to take a chance? If we never take a chance, if we only live in fear, if we never leave our nest, if we never learn to give, will we ever learn to live? Will we ever reach our dreams?

The song goes on: When after so many years of loneliness, and so many years of continued emptiness, do we assume that love, giving and sharing are reserved only for the few? Just know that below the frozen soil a seed is sleeping, waiting for the spring sun to grow into a flower.

When we have spent so many lonely years, and the road of emptiness sees no end, and when we think that motherhood is only for the brave and the strong, should we not remember that far beneath our fears, lies the seed that with our love a child will blossom.

Two young hearts had overtaken mine. How could that be? I was filled with a love I did not understand, but one I would pursue to my last breath.

16.

Preparation of Documents

The key to realizing a dream is to focus not on success but on
significance—and then even the small steps and little victories
along your path will take on greater meaning.
Oprah Winfrey[17]

I REVIEWED THE ADOPTION instruction packet one more time, to assure what was already done was correct and to add the parts that were missing.

Instruction for The Adoption Paperwork Process

Adoption Over-Seas will create an Active File for your family once we have received:

1) Your Application to Adopt, 2) the CampKidHope Service Agreement/Contract, 3) the Child Acceptance Agreement, accompanied by your initial payment of $7,300. All documents must be signed and notarized.

After we create your file, you will start building your Russian dossier to be presented to the Judge in your child's region. Ann will assist you. Concurrently, you also need to work on your Home Study interview and the filing with the Bureau of Citizenship and Immigration Services (BCIS) to gain immigration approval for your adoption.

It may take three months for the United States Citizenship and Immigration Services to complete your request. Once you have submitted your application and paid your fees, an appointment will be scheduled for your fingerprinting. Upon receipt of your Home Study the BCIS [Mrs. Louie's Dept.] will send your immigration clearance or form I-171H, which will be included in your dossier.

I received another form, *Addendum to the Adoption Agreement*, which included additional rules. I signed it immediately. Now that Kristina and Anton had entered my heart, no rules could keep me from pursuing their adoption.

DOSSIER REQUIREMENT

Birth Certificate / Marriage License / Divorce Decrees must be original documents issued from the County Clerk's Office of the County / State where these took place. You will need two originals and certified copies for each child you are adopting.

PASSPORT

A notarized exact front colored copy of photo and signature page of your U.S. passport.

HOME STUDY

You may start preparing your Home Study.

A home study, sometimes called an "adoption study," is a written evaluation done by an authorized social worker to qualify a family who wants to adopt a child. The social worker investigates the home, the financial security, the general health, medical history, criminal record, nearby schools and family background of the potential adoptive parents. If there are other individuals living in the home, they will be interviewed, investigated and included as part of the Home Study. The purpose of the Home Study is to help the courts in both countries determine whether the adoptive parents are qualified to adopt a child, based on each country's legal requirements.

While waiting to become an American citizen, I filled out as much as I could the required forms for the adoption. As suggested by Adoption Over-Seas, I invited Dr. Fleece from the Florida Social Services, to meet at my home on February 4, 2004.

Dr. Fleece was a typical bureaucrat, not particularly impressive, in fact, rather bland. He asked so many questions, some truly personal. I expected him to ask how I came out of my mother's womb . . . . Had he asked, I would have answered, "I don't remember!" His questioning expected me to describe my life in minute details, and that was just a preliminary interview.

Yes, Dr. Fleece, I am heterosexual and, no, Dr. Fleece, I was not forgotten on a windowsill. I received several marriage proposals during the course of my life. No sir, I did not earn my financial comfort through illicit means. I was fortunate enough to work for an outstanding American company. I worked ten to twelve hours a day for years to achieve this comfortable lifestyle. Believe it or not, Dr. Fleece, I earned the financial comfort I am enjoying all by myself. Dr. Fleece, are we to assume a woman cannot accomplish such status without the help of a man?

No, Dr. Fleece, I did not go to college. I was number two in a family of seven children. Growing up, my parents could only afford two dresses a year for my older sister and me. When I was young, boys went to college, girls were supposed to get married and have many children for the church. Did you know it was a mortal sin for a wife to refuse her husband? In fact, Dr. Fleece, when I started working, at sixteen-and-one-half, I did not even have a high school certificate. My last year of school was spent in the United States learning how to speak English. In addition to working full time, I took night classes at McGill, Quincy Junior College and Northeastern University. After I retired at forty-seven, I attended classes at Florida Gulf Coast University. I also spent approximately twenty-four weeks learning the Spanish language at several Spanish Schools of Language, in San Jose, Costa Rica, San Miguel de Allende, Mexico, and in Malaga and Nerja in Spain.

Dr. Fleece looked at me, baffled.

"Dr. Fleece, would you like to include in my home study that I obtained my GED four years ago, at age sixty, and graduated with paroled kids and dropouts in February 2000?"

I became truly annoyed. Did Dr. Fleece have to ask all these questions? Was he overly impressed or was he just curious? Was he puzzled because I had never married? Did he not believe I reached financial security on my own? I rejoiced at the thought I may have shocked all the chauvinistic fibers in his body.

It turned out working with Dr. Fleece was a nightmare. How did he ever become a Ph.D . . . ? Wow! The home study had to be reviewed at least five times. Every time, several parts had to be corrected or rewritten. I offered to type it for him at no cost. He was embarrassed. Then hurricane Charley came. Dr. Fleece's phone and fax lines were out of order for days, which further delayed the process. I reread the home study after it had been sent to Russia. I almost fell out of my chair when I read the words, "She dates a lot."

"What!" I screamed.

It appears Dr. Fleece wanted to explain that even though I had not married, I was heterosexual. Homosexuality was not well accepted in Russia. Wouldn't you think a Ph.D. could have found a more professional way to clarify that point?

ACCEPTANCE AGREEMENTS

I signed these documents to accept each child. The documents were received with faxed pictures of each child in black and white with information as to what happened to their parents. Kristina was described as social, self-confident, adaptable to her surroundings, diligent, even-tempered and not envious. She enjoyed singing and dancing. Anton was described as social, happy, persistent and self-confident. He enjoyed singing and drawing.

No matter what the report may have revealed, Kristina and Anton were already my children. I signed the agreements on June 15, 2004. I attached a personal letter and photos of the children and me to the documents. The letter stated the children and I had bonded during the time we were together, that I had come to love the children as my own and that I wished to adopt them.

FEES, APPLICATION AND REQUIRED DOCUMENTS

The fees to adopt two children are as follows:
#1 Due with the acceptance agreement of two children   *=$ 7,300*
#2 Due prior to Dossier submission to Russia   *= 8,500*
#3 Due upon receipt of Court Date, (prior to travel)   *=$9,500*

Total = 25,300

In addition:

Two children visas:			=	670
Two medical exams in Russia:			=	200
Two Certification Documents:	=	160	to	1,200
Home Study:	=	1,000	to	1,500
Two Immigration filing fees:	=	510	to	560

Additional expenses were for the airline tickets for parents and children, hotel accommodations, meals, transportation, fees for my personal translator, for the translation of the documents, for the driver and, then, there would be the gratuities.

MEDICAL REPORT

My medical report included the following tests: HIV, other STDs, drug addiction, tuberculosis, hepatitis, inhalant use, infectious diseases, disorders of internal organs, disorder of locomotor apparatus, history of substance abuse, mental or neurological disorder, cancer, disabling trauma. All my tests were negative.

Because most of these tests were valid for only one month, by the time the full dossier was forwarded to Russia, I had to return to my doctor for a third visit to redo the tests. On that visit, she said, "C.C., I'm not sending you to the lab again. I know you have not contracted any of these diseases in the last couple of months. I will write a new report with today's date and with the same results. I will not charge you for this visit."

A notarized copy of my doctor's medical license was also required.

POLICE REPORT

The police report was valid for only one month. I went back to the sheriff's department three times. Each time the letter had to be notarized by someone at the police department. On the third time, I said to clerk, "Jose, you will not find any criminal records under my name. I only commit little crimes like speeding, parking in no parking zones, making U-turns where I'm not supposed to. I always pray I won't get caught."

We both laughed.

FINANCIAL REPORT

As a retired person, I did not receive a regular salary. Instead, I lived off annuities, stocks, dividends, interest, etc. It became an issue for the Russian translators to translate these financial terms into the Russia language. Proof of income, of dividends and of assets needed to be validated by my CPA, as well as a copy of my condo's deed with its value. A record or proof that my condo's real estate taxes were paid, and finally a valid notarized copy of the CPA's license were required. The Russian Government wanted more proof. They insisted that I include a letter from a legal firm to confirm that my condo's real estate taxes were paid.

Most of the documents were notarized by the wonderful and beautiful Alicia from Northern Trust. She was a pleasure to work with. Thank you, Alicia.

LETTERS OF RECOMMENDATION

Both the U.S. and the Russian governments requested reference letters. I received glowing recommendations from my mother, Aline LeBlanc, from Sir John, from Claudette my Montreal long-time friend, Dr. Renate and her husband, Naren, and my cousin Louise Sauvé. Reading these positive, revealing accolades brought strong emotions to me. I was not aware my family and friends thought so highly of me. The file was complete. It was mailed to Adoption Over-Seas in Texas, July 1, 2004.

17.

Tidbits

People who lack the clarity, courage,
or determination to follow their own dreams will
often find ways to discourage yours.
Live your truth and don't EVER stop.
Steve Maraboli[18]

NOW THAT THE ADOPTION documents were on their way to Adoption Over-Seas for review, my hopes for a quick process were high. With six months left in 2004, my children could be here for Christmas.

The phone rang.

"This is Gen. I just wanted to share with you that we recommend giving adopted children an American name. It helps them blend better with the American students."

"Gen, I very much like their names, Kristina and Anton. They are already American sounding names. Could I only change their middle name?"

"Yes, that would be fine."

In early June, my dear friend Lidia called.

"C.C., could I come for happy hour today and bring a Russian couple visiting from Washington, DC?"

"Of course you can."

We sat on the lanai sipping a glass of wine. Larisa and Gregory asked a thousand questions. They were fascinated with my decision to adopt two children from Siberia.

When we exhausted my reasons to adopt, we started debating their possible middle names.

Larisa exclaimed, "Kristina Cécile LeBlanc sounds wonderful. Kristina's middle name should be your name C.C."

I was not sure it was a good idea. Lidia argued in favor of Cécile. I gave in. The debate continued to find Anton's middle name. I suggested Anton John. John in honor of my dad, whose actual name was Joseph Maurice, but he always insisted he was Jean Maurice LeBlanc. Then John in honor of my dear friend Sir John and, finally in honor of Jean Philippe, my godchild. Conclusion: Kristina Cécile and Anton John LeBlanc would be their new names.

Convinced the adoption would be successful, I needed to move to a home near the better schools. Several months earlier, a realtor had called asking, "C.C. are you interested in selling your condo? One of my clients is looking to buy a three-bedroom, three-bath condo in your building. She wants a unit facing the Gulf of Mexico. Yours is the perfect one."

At that time, I had no interest in selling, but today was a different story.

I phoned the realtor. Her customer was still interested. We negotiated a price and signed a purchase and sales agreement with a flexible closing date sometime in the fall.

After spending many hours visiting homes in several communities, I found a three-thousand-square-foot estate home, in mint condition, in the gated community of Stonebridge. It had three bedrooms, three baths, a large kitchen, living room, family room, an office, a lanai/pool and a three-car garage.

Stonebridge was located just a few miles from North Naples Middle School where Kristina would attend and only one-half mile from Pelican Marsh Elementary school for Anton. On July 24, 2004, the seller and I signed a purchase and sales agreement with a closing date of October 1. I knew in my heart this was the perfect house for us. As I put my signature on the document, a few emotional tears surfaced. It was such a relief to have found our family home.

You may think I was bored to no end to be immersed in doing and redoing paper work or packing boxes, but on the contrary, just thinking about the final outcome of all these efforts and thinking about the beautiful home in a gated community where my children and I would live, made me happy. To keep my life balanced, I continued to do volunteer work, play tennis with Sir John, Trudy and Dr. Gerard twice a week. I attended some monthly luncheons, and when possible, I met friends for dinner. Everyone knew and respected that my number one priority was to bring Kristina and Anton home as fast as possible.

My Belarus friend, Lidia, was of immeasurable help. She translated all the letters to my children and all communications with the orphanage in Siberia. Each letter was meant to let Kristina and Anton know they were in my heart every day and that I was doing everything possible to bring them to America. Part of the correspondence and the packages I sent included some vitamins, gifts, some crafty fun things to make them laugh or to inspire them as to the possibilities they would have in their new life here in Florida.

Using advertising flyers from various music programs of the Philharmonic of Naples, I replaced the faces of the musicians with my children's faces, making them the violinist, trumpet or bass virtuoso. For Kristina's birthday, April 2004, I made a copy of a painting of a beautiful bouquet of flowers. Using a cutout picture of Kristina's profile extending her hand, I placed it on the painting as though she were reaching for the flowers. At the bottom, a Happy Birthday message with pictures of me, Lidia and Anton were glued on.

For Anton's birthday, I took a page of an ad from a business magazine featuring a large sea turtle with Bill Gates' face. The turtle was loaded with three boxes of products. If you can imagine, to that image, I exchanged Bill Gates' face for an appropriate picture of Anton's face, exchanged the lettering on the boxes for "Happy Birthday to You." Then I found a picture of Kristina speaking on a phone, and carefully glued it on the top box, a smiling Lidia was placed the middle box, and me on the bottom box. Just imagine, Anton was the turtle carrying his sister, Lidia and me on his back. I photocopied each one of these fun pieces of artwork and mailed them on different occasions.

I had been asked to be the Indian bride for an Indian wedding fashion show in Naples. My friend Renate's husband, Naren, an Indian gentleman, still had his authentic Indian wedding clothes. He agreed to be the groom. Wanting to create something fun for Anton, I went to a FedEx office. Using the photocopy machine, I shrunk Naren's wedding picture to child size and I replaced Naren's face with Anton's. Like in the movie "Honey I Shrunk the Kids," Anton, now dressed in Indian wedding clothes, was placed in front of my picture dressed as an Indian Wedding Bride. Photocopy machines created the magic. All this silly work was designed to amuse the children and for sure amused me while I created it.

After the children returned to Russia, at the end of CampKidHope, I wrote to my mother, family and friends announcing my decision to adopt Kristina and Anton. It did not take long before congratulations as well as replies of disbelief came pouring in. The comments were very diversified.

"C.C. you are decidedly a brave woman."

"You're very generous."

"You have lots of courage . . . ."

"Friend Jerry K. said to a mutual friend, 'C.C. is crazy. She is much too old to adopt.' "

One close friend screamed at me begging me not to go forward with this adoption. Her husband had to tell her to stop screaming and not to discuss it anymore. He told her, "C.C. made up her mind. Nothing anyone can say will reverse her decision. Let's just support her choice and wish her well."

A few days later, a younger relative learned of my intent to adopt. She replied with an email. I paraphrase,

Hello Cécile,

I am not surprised by your initiative. I knew before hearing the news you had decided to adopt.

I strongly encourage you to read the rubric "post adoption" text from the following website: http://www.Québecadoption.net. You will find very important information you should read before you finalize your decision. Québec is a province with an enormous number of international adoptions and that for a very long time. As such, there exist valuable records of post-adoption, heart-wrenching difficulties. It would be best for you to be well prepared for all outcomes, and to take the time to "réfléchir," or think of a plan to get out of the commitment before you are caught by surprise.

Russia is a violent country without a moral compass. One can think that these children have suffered enormously. To bring them into your life will be a very demanding commitment, a commitment for at least the next fifteen years. It is doable but you will pay the price.

Happy reading.

I repeated out loud, "A plan to get out of my commitment? Pay the price?"

Her website suggested the following. (I have paraphrased and translated from the French):

There is a euphoric moment of happiness. You have friends and family offering gifts in abundance, but then there is the shock of reality: These children are there to stay. It is no longer the child one tenderly viewed on the pictures and to whom one blew kisses. The arrival of this child turns everyday life upside down. Your dreams, your unrealistic expectations, the delays, the lack of sleep, the shock of the reality and sometimes the deceptions of having a child that does not conform to imaginary expectations, hits you with full force.

All is not as beautiful or as rosy as you expected. Many parents feel guilty when feelings of ambivalence, bitterness, resentment or anger toward their child surface. The popular belief of love, and of instant attachment is imaginary and unrealistic. After the excitement at the onset, there are unexpected difficult adjustments toward the child. According to the parents interviewed during the research period, the veritable attachment to the child takes two to six months.

I have read there are several characteristics of the adopted child. For example: The instinct to survive, difficulty sleeping, the Teflon or Velcro child, a phase of regression, the seductive or indifferent child, an exaggerated fear of rejection or abandonment, a fear of the non-permanence of their new life.

This relative continued to email me the addresses of several more websites that described the many negatives of adopting children from Russia or from other countries. I read some twenty-five thousand words. I found it upsetting. There were no positive comments in any of the websites. It was all negative. I understood there were risks but I also understood there would be profound joys. I knew in my heart and soul no number of negative articles anyone would send me could change the determination I felt deep within. Difficulties along the way would be handled. I was aware that some adoptions were filled with horrible nightmares, but similar nightmares have occurred with biological children. I remember the teenage years of my two sisters and mine. Our poor mother. What she endured!

Truthfully, I could not base my decision to adopt on the fear of a negative experience. On the contrary, my optimism for a positive experience was at the highest level. I could not evaluate if this relative was trying to protect me or warn me against the "horrible teenage years" I would face.

Within my soul, I felt God and the positive energies of the universe were guiding me. Since my retirement, I asked whoever might hear what I needed to do to repay for the incredible privilege of being able to retire at a young age. It took seventeen years to find the answer. The answer was bigger than anything I could have imagined, something so overwhelming I'd never thought I could achieve as a single woman. Accepting this challenge could save the lives of two children, but certainly it would give them opportunities to be successful. Now that I had found my purpose, nothing, I repeat, nothing could change, reverse or alter the course of my decision.

18.

Finalizing the Documents

*In a hierarchy, every employee tends to rise
to his level of incompetence.*
Laurence J. Peter, The Peter Principle[19]

IT WAS NOW PAST mid-July. The documents had been mailed to Adoption Over-Seas July 1, still no news. The turtle speed of this process was teaching me important lessons in patience, a quality I'm short on. I believe in being proactive, not waiting for things to happen.

I called Gen.

"C.C., your file will be hand-carried by a family going to Russia for their own adoption. One family is leaving July 18th, the other one sometime next week. But C.C., your file is not complete. We have not received the corrected Home Study from Dr. Fleece."

Livid, I called Dr. Fleece who said he had been in bed for two days with a cold. I wanted to scream, and scream loudly, but that would make matters worse. I bit my tongue. I took a deep breath and said, "Dr. Fleece, I'd be happy to drive to your office to retype the Home Study."

"Not necessary, C.C. I will mail the packet in a couple of days, on July 19."

This man was the most frustrating person I have ever dealt with. Despite this frustration, a ray of sunshine arrived in the mail.

An envelope containing my children's documents, first to review, then to forward to Mrs. Louie at the Miami Children's Adoption Services. On July 19, I mailed the packet to Mrs. Louie with a note reminding her how we met several months earlier and to thank her again for her help in accelerating my citizenship.

The same day, my Belarus friend Lidia called Ludmilla, the adoption coordinator in Krasnoyarsk, Siberia. The purpose of the call was to inform her that my documents should arrive in her office soon and to ask if it would be possible to process my file quickly since I would be sixty-five on November 22.

Ludmilla promised to place my and the children's dossiers on top of the pile for processing, as soon as they were translated and received.

Time passed. I thought all was moving along when a call from Adoption Over-Seas arrived on Thursday July 29th.

"C.C., Your Home Study with the necessary documents was finally received from Dr. Fleece. The documents look OK, but the financial statement shows the total income in the wrong space. Please fax page five to Dr. Fleece immediately to correct it and initial it. Ask him to return it to us as soon as possible. In the meantime, I will scan some documents to our Moscow office for translation."

My face must have turned Christmas red from anger. In the face of such incompetence, I felt hopeless. What an imbecile! I immediately faxed page five to Dr. Fleece, with a note and left a message of urgency on his answering machine.

By late p.m., the good doctor had not responded. I called his home. His wife answered, "Dr. Fleece will return this evening. He has been out of town for a few days."

The next morning, at 8:30, I left a pleading message on Dr. Fleece's answering machine.

"Dr. Fleece, my dossier is complete except for page five of the financial statement. The dossier cannot move forward until

Adoption Over-Seas receives a corrected copy of page five. Please correct and sign it as soon as possible."

The next day, I corrected and typed page five, faxed it to his home for him to add his initials. A note of urgency to forward the page to Adoption Over-Seas ASAP was added. This incompetent Dr. Fleece received a total of $1,500 to do my home study. Imagine, $1,500 and he kept making mistakes delaying the process. How do people like that get a Ph.D.?

In early August 2004, Valerie and Murray hosted a pool party to reunite the Russian adopted children and their parents. It was a heart-warming experience as I had the chance to speak with many parents and with several children. Gen, from Adoption Over-Seas, attended.

"Gen, I'm getting really nervous. It is imperative that the completed dossier reach Ludmilla in Krasnoyarsk ASAP. The Russian court must grant my petition to adopt Kristina and Anton before I turn sixty-five, on November 22. As requested by the Moscow office, Blue Cross Blue Shield sent a letter confirming my children will be on my medical insurance policy the day of the adoption. Their letter is valid only until I turn sixty-five, at which time the children will need separate policies."

Gen assured me she would do her best. On August 10, I received a phone call from Mrs. Louie of the Children's Adoption Services in Miami.

"Miss LeBlanc, the documents you sent were correct. I will send them to Russia along with form I-71H for the children's advance processing. Your documents will travel to Russia with a family departing in a few days."

This was music to my ears. What a wonderful woman this Mrs. Louie is! A real Earth angel!

The same day, Adoption Over-Seas sent an email.

"C.C., you need to have an attorney prepare a letter stating you are the owner of your condo. You also need to update your Sheriff's Report and your Medical Report as both have expired. Your birth certificate needs to be an original copy in the English language. Remember to notarize all documents and send them to Tallahassee to be apostilled before they come to us. Don't forget, proof of medical coverage for you and for your children must be written on the insurance company's letterhead."

It will never end! As soon as we hung up, I sent an email followed by a telephone call to the Québec Government to ask for an English copy of my birth certificate.

Thick molasses is slow moving, but frozen molasses doesn't move at all. The frustration was unbearable. Every time I felt the process was going forward, something had to be done or redone. But then, deep in my soul, I felt the frozen molasses was starting to thaw, ever so slowly, but thawing . . . Our dossier was moving forward bit by bit. The wait, the delays, the constant redoing of documents were testing my patience every single day . . . . I told myself,

"The rewards will soon come C.C. . . . . You'll see . . . ."

19.

The Baby Shower

Sarah, Abraham's wife, gave him a child at ninety.
Why can't I have two at sixty-five?
C.C. LeBlanc

IN SEPTEMBER, TWO FRIENDS, Fran and Greta, organized a surprise baby shower for me. An 8x10 invitation was sent out featuring a picture of a cuddly teddy bear wearing a large yellow polka dot bow tie. Between his hands, the bear was holding a large heart with the words, "From Russia with Love." Written on the back were these words and a beautiful poem.

"It's a surprise baby shower for C.C. Shhhhhhh. . . . She thinks she's attending a cocktail party.
Invitation for C.C.'s Shower Party
A stork is winging its long, long way
From frigid Russia to sunny Pelican Bay.
But C.C., from the looks of you
It's hard to believe this could be true
That you are an expectant mother,
Especially of two, a sister and a brother.
Kristina and Anton will soon be here.
They will need a lot of American gear,
Jeans, lots of T-shirts and baseball caps,
Not like the Russian style with big ear flaps,

Hot sneakers, coats, shoes and white shorts
For proper wear on the tennis courts.
These children will never long for Russian sables
When they wear chic clothes with Polo labels.
Well, as we all know,
To raise two children takes a lot of dough.
So instead of rain showers
Let's make the day sunny,
And shower C.C. with lots of money.
But more important than any of the above,
Kristina and Anton will receive a lot of love.
Renee S.
When: Sunday, September 26 at 4:00 p.m.
Where: The Barrington Clubhouse
What: Light hors d'oeuvres, wine and tea will be served
Hostess: Fran and Greta
RSVP: By Sept 20.

As often happens with secret celebrations, someone let the cat out of the bag. I surprised everyone when I walked in wearing a medium blue dress with a very protruding tummy. It was obvious the protrusion indicated a near-term pregnancy. Yes, the image was clear: C.C. was pregnant, very pregnant, any day now! This dramatic entrance created bursts of laughter.

The room was filled with approximately twenty-five cheerful women. Many came to feel my tummy or to try to hear the babies' beating hearts. The smiles and the congratulations were abundant. There was high, happy energy coming from everyone. As I looked around, the room was decorated with multicolored balloons, tables with tablecloths, one covered with gifts and the other with food and wine in abundance. In the middle of this joyful celebration, I said a few words, first to offer my heartfelt appreciation to Fran and Greta for organizing this wonderful gathering and to thank those who attended this special celebration. Then I continued, "In the course of my life, I have attended many celebrations for family and friends, such as engagement showers, baby showers, weddings, 25th wedding anniversaries, etc. Today, at almost sixty-five, it is the first time a shower of any kind has been given in my honor. I was never engaged, never married, never had a baby until . . . well . . . soon from the looks of my protrusion. It took many years, almost my whole life, to justify being the recipient a baby shower. Two miracles happened. First, that I am pregnant at almost sixty-five. Was it not Sarah, Abraham's first wife, who became pregnant late in life?"

Carol raised her hand.

"Sarah was ninety, you're only sixty-four-and-a-half C.C.!" Everyone laughed.

As Jack Benny said, "Age is strictly a case of mind over matter. If you don't mind, it doesn't matter."[20] More laughter.

I continued, "The second miracle is not only that I am pregnant, I'm pregnant with fraternal twins already nine and twelve years old."

With each statement I made, I received a roar of laughter.

"Seriously, ladies, the protruding tummy is symbolic of the pregnancy that is occurring in my heart. Yes, since the day I made the decision to adopt my precious children, January 3, 2004, Kristina and Anton have tucked themselves deep in my heart. It is a beautiful and pleasurable feeling to have them constantly with me. Surprisingly, they do not weigh much, if anything. And to my surprise, I have not gained a pound!

"It's been about nine months now, the length of a normal pregnancy. As you can imagine, this pregnancy is totally abnormal."

Laughter.

"As such, my pregnancy may last a little longer than normal. Before long, the birth of my children through adoption will occur. That is when motherhood will begin.

"I am overwhelmed at the thought that not only will I be the instant mother of a teenage girl and of her younger brother, but to complicate matters, for the first time in my life, I will need to join the mom's soccer club . . . ."

Laughter.

"Not only join the club but look the part. I don't even understand soccer .... I come from Québec, you know. Canada is hockey country... you know. When I grew up, every Saturday night was hockey night in Canada. Every family in Québec sat in front of the TV to watch the game, that included my dad and my four brothers."

The laughter continued.

"My old 1993 Fleetwood Caddie will not do. That's for old people. My children would be embarrassed being dropped off to school in an old caddie. A soccer mom must drive a modern SUV. At age sixty-five, I will look pretty cool. By changing my image, I will try to avoid embarrassing my children by being called grandma. Should anyone ask me if I'm the grandma, I will answer, 'No, I'm their mom. I became pregnant through the intervention of the Holy Ghost!'"

An explosion of laughter.

"Seriously, I will do my best to fit in with the young moms of my children's friends.

"Ladies, let me debunk comments such as, 'It's not possible to love an adopted child as much a biological one.' I've not experienced a biological pregnancy, but I can assure you it would not be possible to find more love in my heart and soul than the love I feel for my children, Kristina and Anton. There is no possibility, no room to love them more. The love I feel is overflowing with joy. They have taken my whole being, my thoughts and my dreams."

I explained how it all started with my friends Sir John and Laura introducing me to Valerie and Murray and their twins from Russia. I shared the experience of hosting the children in Tampa with the intent to adopt them if we bonded.

"The epiphany happened on the third day, the day I fell in love. I woke up in the middle of the night, sat on the edge of the bed and asked God, the universe, whomever could hear me, 'What am I to do with these children?'

"The intuition was straight forward and unequivocal, 'These are your children; you are to take care of them.'

"I accepted the challenge. Today, I am proud, ready and happy to announce, with hope in my heart, that in the next few weeks, God willing, a woman from French Canada will adopt two children from Siberia, to form a family in America. This new family with international roots will start their new life right here in Naples, Florida. Isn't it extraordinary?

"Thank you again Fran and Greta, and thank you, all of you, for your contribution but especially for celebrating in my honor. You truly touched my heart."

After all the laughter, I received a rousing applause.

20.

Moving to Stonebridge, Departure for Krasnoyarsk

I can't change the direction of the wind,
but I can adjust my sails
to always reach my destination.
Jimmy Dean[21]

THE BABY SHOWER CELEBRATION was a fun, unforgettable and touching part of "my pregnancy." That night, I lay in bed thinking and realizing how much love and support from so many friends and close acquaintances would be there when we returned home as a family. More friends would have wanted to attend but September is a very quiet and hot month in Naples. The snowbirds will not be arriving from the North until toward the end of the year.

Moving day to our new home in Stonebridge was scheduled for October 1, 2004. I only had four more days to finish packing. That is where my time and energy would now be devoted. Moving is stressful. This one was no exception. My first mistake was to hire a local moving company. Their representative underestimated the size of my belongings. The result was that the truck had to make two trips. The first load was delivered late morning. The second load was to come around 3:00 p.m. The phone rang.

"Miss LeBlanc, don't be upset. Our truck broke down with your second load in it. It'll be fixed this evening. We will deliver your belongings tomorrow at 9:00 a.m."

At this point, it didn't really matter. I had enough to keep me busy.

Monday morning, October 4, the phone rang,

"C.C., this is Gen. I have wonderful news. Your appointment with the judge in Krasnoyarsk is scheduled for October 12th. Because of the twelve-time-zone difference, and the time it takes to travel to Krasnoyarsk, Siberia, you must depart for Russia no later than October 9th. You need to hurry to get your visa. I'm emailing you the name of the visa company in Washington, DC. They are a little more expensive, but they will overnight it right away. Now, C.C., I assume you have purchased all the clothes and other items needed for your children?"

When we hung up the phone, I felt numb for a minute or two. Panic sat in.

"What? Leave for Russia in five days? I just moved! There are boxes everywhere! The bedrooms are not ready! Nothing is ready! The kitchen, OMG, the cabinets are empty! I have to pack for Russia! My clothes are still in boxes . . . ! The children's clothes! I have to buy more! OMG! The measurements . . . ? Where is the children's measurements list? Less than five days to do it all! I'll never make it! *Help! Please, someone help me!* No one's here! No one heard! Where do I begin?" Filled with panic, I called Sir John.

"Don't panic. That's wonderful news, C.C.! I'll call Trudy and a few others. I'll find some help. Email me your info. I'll drive to your home right now to pick up your passport. Don't worry; I'll talk to the visa company."

"But Sir John, I need to book a flight!"

"I'll take care of it. Don't worry. Email me the exact spelling of the city where you will arrive. Laura and I will take you to the airport. One thing at a time, C.C. It will all get done."

God bless Sir John. He calmed me down. He has been and continued to be an unimaginable Earth angel for me and for so many people. Everyone should have a Sir John in his or her life.

Trudy and Liz were called to the task. They took a day each to set up the kitchen. Trudy is German, Liz, Italian. They had only met once at the shower celebration. One would think they were raised by the same mother. Where one left off, after her day of emptying kitchen boxes, washing the contents, and placing the items in the cupboard, the other took over with the same logic. The end result: The kitchen was better organized than if I had done it myself. While they worked, I shopped and packed. Trudy came a second day to help me put the children's bed together. As I write these words, I recall the profound appreciation I felt. It seemed the world was cheering me on for a successful mission. For sure, Trudy and Liz merit the title of "God's Special Earth Angels."

The morning of October 9th, parked at my door was one large suitcase filled with gifts for the children and caregivers at the orphanage. Another suitcase was filled with my children's clothes and toys. A third one was for me. As promised, Sir John and Laura arrived on time for the ride to the airport. They were excited, positive and encouraging.

"All will be well, C.C. We are so looking forward to welcoming you and your children to the United States!"

Even though the day I had been waiting for had arrived, I was filled with swirling emotions, from incredible joy, to incredible anxiety, to a host of "what ifs." But I could not dwell on what ifs. I had to trust that if God and the universe were on my side, then all would go as planned. The timeframe for the process of most adoptions is approximately ten days. Could it be that our new life as a family could start in just ten days?

We arrived at the Airport. John and Laura stayed with me until it was time to go to the gate. We enjoyed a cup of coffee. We held hands. John said a prayer. We hugged. We waved, then I disappeared. The first leg of this journey, Fort Myers to New York City, was short and stress-free. Now at the Kennedy Airport, waiting to board my Delta flight, I felt very alone. I trembled. My mind was racing.

"C.C., are you crazy? You're alone, on your way to Siberia, twelve time zones away, with a language you do not speak, to work with people you've never met, to plead your case in a Russian court to a judge you can't relate to, to adopt two Russian-speaking children, children you barely know, children you fell in love with three days after you met, children you have not seen for ten months. You must really be out of your mind!"

Walking down the aisle to reach my seat, I looked at as many passengers as I could, wondering what the purpose of their visit to Russia was. Were there any passengers on board making the leap to adopt children just like I was? Exhausted from the recent turmoil, and anticipating facing strong emotions once in Russia, I thought it would be best to relax, pray, sleep, and hope that all will be well. I felt surrounded by positive energies. I knew in my heart I was supposed to fulfill the commitment I made in Tampa. I closed my eyes, filled my mind with a vision of my children and fell asleep.

21

Flight to Krasnoyarsk, Seeing my Children Again

We do not need to know the beginning
of a child's story to change the ending.
Fi Newood[22]

I WOKE UP THINKING about this wonderful man John Percy Carey Woodhams—a man I called Sir John. Later promoted to Saint John. When my children arrived, he would become Grandpapa John. Both Laura and John loved children. They were delighted I was adopting two.

Financial success did not change this man. He remained humble and never forgot his meager beginnings. John and Laura helped many people. For example, after they moved to Naples, they continued to pay their cleaning lady in Wichita until she died. He said she was too old to find another job. He continued to support a church in the Bahamas even when he and Laura stopped sailing to that island. He volunteered to teach English to immigrants. He contributed generously to charitable organizations. Most of all, he gave of himself to create happiness around him.

In the fall of 1998, I was sick in bed with a horrible cold. Laura called mid-afternoon to ask how I was feeling.

She said, "John and I are going to the concert at The Phil tonight. We'll stop by your house to bring you dinner."

About 7:15 p.m., their Rolls Royce rolled up in my driveway. John and Laura delivered my dinner on a silver tray, served on their best dishes, their silver utensils, a teapot with a matching cup and saucer and a white linen napkin. They added a small vase with a red rose.

They made me feel so very special. This is one of the many beautiful stories I could share about Sir John and Laura. I miss them, especially Sir John. He was one fine man, a loyal friend. I am so thankful to have been part of their lives for so many years.

The flight landed in Moscow on October 10, at 11:25 a.m. Adoption Over-Seas had arranged for Max, their translator, to meet me at the Moscow airport. He and a driver took me to the Sheremetyevo International Airport for the transfer to the Krasnoyarsk, Siberia flight. The eighty-seven-mile distance between the two airports took nearly two hours.

Max was a pleasant young man. He spoke good English, and he was very informative about the Russian adoption process. As we drove, he became a tourist guide. With pride, he spoke of Russian customs and history. He explained the purpose of various buildings. He also spoke of his personal disappointment and of the despair shared by so many citizens. He thought it unacceptable that his mother's salary as a cardiologist was only the U.S. equivalent of one hundred dollars per month.

The third and final flight of this journey was scheduled to leave around midnight. With a ten-hour layover, Max suggested I rent a nearby hotel room to rest. He arranged for the hotel receptionist to wake me up and shuttle me to the airport by 10:00 p.m.

As soon as I entered the Sheremetyevo Airport that evening, I felt I was in some sort of frantic zoo for two-legged animals. It was packed. I had no idea which direction to take. All the signs and my ticket were in the Cyrillic alphabet and all announcements were in the Russian language. I joined a line hoping to meet someone who spoke English. I turned to the man behind me,

"Sir, do you speak English?"

"I do."

"Would you be so kind to look at my ticket and guide me to the proper gate?"

"With pleasure, follow me."

He walked me to my gate while his wife continued to wait in line. Thank God, numbers are multilingual. The flight to Krasnoyarsk, a city with a population of approximately one million, departed on time at midnight.

The plane was very noisy, disgustingly dirty, and had very uncomfortable seats. The passengers were unfriendly. The stewardesses were stiff but polite. There was no camaraderie.

Do I sense some of you are asking me about the toilets on the plane? You do not want to know. When I needed to, I walked in. I walked out. I held it.

Back in my seat, I chose not to let the discomfort of the next four hours bring my spirits down. Soon, real soon, I will be with my children. The four-hour flight added to the four-hour time zone difference from Moscow, clocked the arrival in Krasnoyarsk, October 11th, at 8:00 a.m. I was warmly greeted by Ludmilla, the coordinator, and Tasha, the translator. They would be my only direct contacts for the duration of my stay.

As soon as the preliminary introductions were over, I asked, "When will I see my children?"

"Boris, the director of their orphanage, is now on his way with Kristina and Anton. They should arrive at the hotel by 5:30 p.m."

Ludmilla was a warm, attractive women of about forty. I immediately felt comfortable with her. Her responsibility was to oversee all details related to the adoption during to my stay in Krasnoyarsk or until my petition to adopt was granted. She was a caring woman with a lucrative position by Russian standards. Tasha was my translator. She would be by my side for the duration of my stay to translate anything related to the adoption. They worked very closely together. Tasha was an attractive, young, stoic and professional woman. She was conservatively dressed and wore very,

very red lipstick. Her face and her body language showed very little emotion. Ludmilla was more of a mother hen while Tasha was more reserved.

Once at the hotel, I unpacked, reviewed the papers needed for the court, and rested. At about 4:30 p.m., I walked outside with my video camera. I began filming what would become the history of my children's adoption. Hotel Kpachorpck was sitting on a large plaza facing the Yenisei River. The art center stood kitty corner to the right of the plaza. The city hall with its impressive clock tower sat at a higher elevation to the left. It was a chilly afternoon, similar to a late November day in Montreal. The sun was piercing its last rays of the day through heavy clouds. There was no snow on the ground. Surprisingly, a few flowers were still hanging on to dear life.

I became fascinated by the people passing by. Most young men wore jeans. A few wore suits. Many walked with pointed shoes, curved upward, reminding me of Pinocchio's slippers. The young women were well dressed. Many wore beautiful A-line winter coats, some wool, some cashmere, big hats and winter boots with skinny high heels. I was mesmerized by their determined way of walking, each one making his or her own sound, with the click clacks of heels. It was almost musical. The older women wore long, cloth coats, low-heel boots, large hats, some in fur. Many older men covered their head with the typical Russian *ushanka*, a fur hat with flaps. There were no friendly gestures, no smiles. No one looked at the other. They walked with a purpose, as if they were in a rush to reach their destinations.

At 5 p.m., I returned and sat at a table on the left side of the lobby, facing the hotel main entrance. I imagined being in the labor room of an obstetric hospital, ready to deliver my two children. They should be here at any moment. My whole being was overwhelmed with excitement, but deep down, fear was looming. There were so many unknowns. Being less than one year away from collecting my first social security check, I feared I was embarking on a mission way over my head.

My eyes were focused on the beautiful large double door entrance of the hotel. It was made with a combination of wood and thick beveled glass. Each time the doors opened my heart vibrated. I was determined these children would have a chance to enjoy a better life and be as successful as they would want to be.

This time, as the doors were opening again, Kristina entered. She immediately recognized me. Anton followed carrying the small brown teddy bear I had sent him for his birthday. Next was the driver, then, Boris, the director of their orphanage, then Ludmilla and Tasha entered with faces filled with smiles.

"Here they are, my precious children!" I exclaimed.

I stopped filming to greet them. They seemed a bit shy, but big, loving hugs were exchanged. We had not seen each other since January 11, nine months earlier, the duration of a normal pregnancy. After some conversation, we set up a time, 6:45 p.m., to join Boris in the lobby for dinner. Ludmilla and Tasha left. The children followed me to my room.

Our hotel suite had a large master bedroom with a king size bed, a long rectangular living room with a sofa, a desk, a TV, a small refrigerator and a shower/bathroom. Kristina scanned the two rooms the moment we entered. She touched the sofa, pointed to herself and said,

"Me C.C., me."

"You want to sleep on the couch Kristina?"

"*Da*"

"That's OK."

I pointed. "This suitcase is for you Kristina, this one is for you Anton."

I gestured while talking. "You can open them, and you can choose the clothes you want to wear for dinner."

I walked to the closet. "See the shelves? These two are for Kristina, the bottom two for you Anton."

Amazing how, for simple exchanges, gestures and pointing become sort of a universal language. How wonderful and touching it was to watch the children unpack their luggage. Today they were unpacking their very own clothes, for their use only.

The first item Kristina took out of her suitcase was a beautiful, pastel blue, winter jacket with a hood. She put it on, looked at herself in the mirror then moved around pretending she was a model. She smiled. I smiled back.

"You like it?"

"*Da.*"

Kristina took out an angora pink sweater. She held it for me to see.

"Pretty color for you Kristina?"

She brought the sweater close to her body and hugged it as if it were her most precious belonging.

She took out a small cosmetic bag, opened the zipper, and then took a little tube out.

"Do you know what that is, Kristina?" She looked up, not understanding what I said.

"It's a lip gloss." I pretended to color my lips. She smiled.

She then took out a large decorative bag and looked inside. It was filled with fancy hairpins, brushes, and ribbons to tie her hair. She looked very happy.

In his suitcase, Anton found a black Adidas jogging suit with red trim, a red winter jacket with a hood, gloves, a black winter woolen hat, two pairs of jeans, khaki and black, sweaters, sneakers, etc. He folded and placed all of his clothes on his two shelves but left the winter jacket on the bed. He unzipped a luggage compartment and found a box filled with two-dozen small trucks. He looked at it for a few minutes, then turned toward me with a smile while bringing the box to his chest.

"Anton, you like your trucks?" He just smiled.

When he was finished unpacking, he put on the jacket and the wool winter hat on his head, then paraded around the room.

Imagine if you were Kristina and Anton and had lived in their orphanage for the last four-and-one-half years. Starting today, they would never again need to go into the bin for their size, to pick up clean underwear or a clean shirt to wear. Those days were over. These new clothes were their very own, not to be worn by anyone else. The beginning of the rest of a better life had begun. Soon they would become citizens of the United States of America. The joy I felt filled every fiber of my body. These were my children, the children God and the universe gave me to care for. I felt honored to have been chosen for this incredible responsibility.

Both children took a quick shower; something they would now be able to do every day, instead of taking a bath once a week and, at times, in someone else's water. They looked exquisite in their new clothes. Proud and confident, they walked back and forth in front of the mirror, making faces, especially eight-year-old Anton.

While the flowers outside were hanging on for dear life, here, in our hotel room, a family was being born. Is this not in some way what the Circle of Life is all about?

As understood, we met Boris in the lobby. He looked at the children with approval. We walked to an elegant restaurant across the plaza and down several steps. It was a bit awkward as we could not converse. Smiles are universal. We exchanged lots of those.

Before the menu arrived, the children talked up a storm with Boris in an excited and happy tone. When they looked at me, I smiled. Boris had no knowledge of the English language, we conversed with our eyes, smiles and gestures.

I opened the menu. "God help me." It was all in the Cyrillic alphabet. Boris talked and gestured to me. I understood he would order the food.

We started with a cup of *solyanka*, a winter soup, often referred to as the King of Russian soups. It is made with a meat broth. It is salty, spicy, and sour with a touch of sweetness. It includes ham, sausage, onions, carrots, garlic, peppers, tomatoes and herbs. It is served with a flat bread. It came to Russia by way of Georgia.

Boris discussed the menu with the children. They decided on Russian kebabs or "*shashlik*." For me, Boris pointed to a dish on the menu. Trusting his choice, I said, "*Da.*"

In addition to ordering half a liter of Vodka, approximately five straight shots, Boris ordered the *olivie*, a Russian salad. It is said, this salad was invented in Russia by a French-Belgian chef.

After we ate our soup, plates of kebabs with rice and vegetables were placed in front of Kristina and Anton. I watched their facial expressions. It was obvious they had not seen such appetizing food in a long time. To my surprise, my dish was a wonderful beef stroganoff. But when Boris's plate was placed in front of him, all eyes were on it. The food was piled up like a miniature Mount Everest with an avalanche of mayonnaise. His dish was appetizingly colorful, filled with diced potatoes, carrots, pickles, peas, eggs and several kinds of meat.

For dessert, Boris chose a *medovik* square, an excellent soft, sticky, crumbly and creamy cake made of ginger, cinnamon-spiced, honeyed pastry built in layers with sweetened sour cream and condensed milk. God knows I have a sweet tooth. It was delicious. I wanted more.

Several times during the dinner, the children, especially twelve-and-one-half year old Kristina, stared at me with questioning eyes, seeming to ask, "Will we be safe with you? Will you care and love us?"

Touching her arm with my eyes fixed on hers, I tried to convey a positive response to reassure her.

During the CampKidHope fourteen-day period when I first met the children in Tampa, with the help of a translator, Boris and I had had long conversations. He understood the love I felt for my children. He understood my desire to adopt Kristina and Anton, and he understood my unflinching determination to do so. I sensed he was on my side from the onset.

With our bellies full, we returned to our hotel. Back in our room, the children played like little puppies, laughing and teasing each other. They truly looked happy and comfortable with me. Perhaps they felt a freedom they had never experienced before. I was excited.

The children changed into their nightclothes. In my rush to pack, I had left their pajamas in Naples. Kristina wore one of my long and pretty t-shirts with a big heart on the front surrounded by the words *"je t'aime"* and "I love you" embroidered in gold thread. Anton wore my red turtleneck shirt, which was long enough to reach his knees and with sleeves twice the length of his arms. Clowning around, flapping the excess fabric lenght of the shirt arms, he reached the TV, rested his elbow on it, crossed his feet and smiled, making different faces. Kristina and I watched him and laughed.

It was time to say good night. We hugged. Anton went under the cover in the master bedroom, holding his brown teddy bear to his chest. His eyes closed. I went back into the living room. Anton sneaked back and hid under Kristina's comforter. He started pulling on it. A pillow fight started. They played to complete exhaustion. We said goodnight one last time in a beautiful bear hug. As I turned off the lights, the beautiful clock hanging on the outside tower of the city hall was ringing 11:00 p m.

22.

Court Day

Trust yourself. You survived a lot,
and you'll survive whatever is coming.
Robert Tew[23]

ON OCTOBER 12, 2004, we would face the judge for the first time. Kristina wore black jeans, a pastel purple sweater, and her blue winter jacket. Anton had his Adidas suit and his black and red winter jacket. I dressed in a navy business suit with a white blouse. Kristina was quiet and pensive. Anton was his usual happy and witty self. As long as his beloved sister was with him, he had no worries.

We followed each other to the breakfast room. Kristina walked slowly around the breakfast buffet table, her eyes wide open, taking in the large variety of food on display. Anton almost ran around it twice, not believing he could have it all. The choices were from pasta-dishes, to various sausages, kielbasa, vegetables of all kinds, eggs cooked in different styles, fish, smoked herring, stews, a variety of bread and sweet rolls. They both filled their plates. What a feast! Their eyes glanced at me as to say, "Will it be like this every morning?"

Ludmilla, the coordinator, Tasha, the translator, and the driver arrived on time, at 9:30 a.m. Boris and the representative from the Ministry of Education met us at the courthouse. Once there, the atmosphere became tense. This was the big moment everyone had been working for. Our fate was in the hands of the judge and of the prosecutor. Shortly after we arrived, I noticed a tall slender woman walking quickly across the lobby, her heels clattering loudly on the granite floor.

I asked Tasha, "Who is that lady?"

She whispered, "She is the judge who will hear your case. I heard she is in a very bad mood. Your case has been delayed."

My heart stopped at hearing those words. I felt a strange, uncomfortable omen hanging over my head. Ludmilla informed Kristina that our case was delayed. I asked, "Tasha, Kristina is very pensive, she seems very stressed. Do you think she has second thoughts about being adopted, or is she reacting to the word that our case is delayed?"

"Kristina is afraid the judge will say no."

It was understood that Ludmilla would stay in the hallway with the children during the hearing. At 12:30 p.m., Boris, the representative from the Ministry of Education, Tasha and I entered the courtroom. In front of where we stood was a balustrade separating us from the court officials. It reminded me of the churches of my youth. On the other side of the balustrade, the space was dominated by an enormous desk, set three steps higher than us. Two steps below the judge's desk were two smaller desks facing each other. One was placed on the very right side of the room, the other on the very left. On our side of the balustrade, there were a few benches and some chairs to sit on. We sat waiting for the court officials. No one spoke. I prayed. I asked for guidance.

A few minutes later, the three officials entered. We stood up. The judge climbed the three steps. The prosecutor sat at the desk on the left, the secretary on the right.

The judge started by identifying the adoption case she was about to hear. She took approximately twenty minutes to question Boris and the Ministry of Education representative. Tasha translated every spoken word.

The judge called my name. I stood up. She stared at me for a few seconds.

"Miss LeBlanc, please identify yourself, and tell us why you are here."

The questioning started, first by the judge and then by the prosecutor.

I answered questions on my life, where I was born, number of siblings, my family life, my upbringing, my parents, my schooling and professional career. It continued with, "Miss LeBlanc, why do you want to adopt two children at your age?

"Why did you not adopt sooner, at a younger age?

"Why did you not get married?

"How were you able to retire at such a young age as a single woman?

"How could you have acquired such a high-valued condominium without marriage?

"Why did you retire so young?

"How can we be sure your medical report is accurate?"

According to available statistics, in 2004, life expectancy in Russia was between sixty-one and sixty-three years of age. In one more month, I would be sixty-five. The court may have thought, "Is this woman crazy to want to adopt two children at her age? She should be dead by now!"

If it was not the judge questioning me, it was the prosecutor. They both took turns asking me the same questions, over and over, using different words. They could not believe I could be healthy at almost sixty-five years of age. They questioned the validity of my doctor's medical license, my financial report, how I acquired financial comfort without marriage and without rich parents. Over and over, they asked, in all sorts of different ways, why I wanted to adopt two children at my age. Why did I not get married, why did I not adopt sooner, what would happen to the children if I died? What sort of education would they have? Would they be allowed to keep their Russian language and more? I answered each question truthfully.

At the end of four-and-one-half hours, they requested reconfirmation of several documents, which were part of the package they had already approved before our court case was scheduled. The judge also requested more documents, such as the value of the assets I received from my former employer, proof my real estate taxes were paid, and proof my condo fees were paid. They asked for a new medical report and for a reconfirmation of my doctor's medical license as well as proof of other documents. It was 5 p.m. I had been standing for four-and-one-half hours without a break and without water. Our case was delayed until the requested documents, notarized and apostilled, were received and reviewed by the court. The court adjourned. It was obvious to me that both the judge and the prosecutor had spent the afternoon trying to catch me lying. They couldn't. The truth never lies. It never changes.

With this twist in our court case, our stay in Siberia would be extended by at least one week, not an appealing thought. Ludmilla informed the children, Tasha translated.

"Kristina and Anton, we will return to court in a few days. The judge asked for additional documents. Don't worry. All will be well."

We were driven back to our hotel. Our spirits had been neutralized. I could not think of a comforting thought. My intuition was predicting challenges ahead. After dinner, the three of us walked to the business center where I emailed Sir John.

"Dear Sir John, the court was very difficult today. The judge is requesting more documents and more proof the documents presented were truthful. The judge and the prosecutor do not seem to believe me." He immediately responded.

"Don't worry C.C. it will all get done. Adoption Over-Seas heard the news from Moscow. They emailed me the list of required documents."

I was amazed the news of the court delay had already reached Naples. Ludmilla had informed the adoption office in Moscow, who informed Adoption Over-Seas in Texas, who informed Sir John in Naples.

No surprise, separated by twelve time zones, that in the middle of the night in Siberia, Hollister Inc. in Chicago and Hollister Ltd. in Toronto both called me to ask permission to divulge my Hollister assets and income to Adoption Over-Seas.

"Yes, you may. I am at the mercy of the Russian court. We must tell it all. We must confirm the documents presented were truthful, and we must be patient."

I'm so thankful my most loyal friend Sir John started the ball rolling the moment he heard the news.

The next day, October 13, we were up at 9:00 a.m. Both my children were coughing. I thought of going to the pharmacy, but every sign was written in the Cyrillic alphabet. I wouldn't be able to tell the difference between a post office, a pharmacy and the public bathroom if there were any on the way.

"Tasha will call soon. I will ask for her suggestions," I thought.

We started the day by repeating the bear hug we shared the previous night at bedtime. Again, my children were playing like little puppies, seemingly enjoying their new lifestyle. They seemed oblivious to the possible consequences the court delay could cause. I was determined to spare them from sensing any stress or anxiety from me. I convinced myself this was just a bump on the road like so many others I've experienced in my life. I reminded myself, "Patience is the mother of all virtue," a virtue I was short on. God or the universe forgot to send some my way.

I repeated to myself several times, "I'm doing something good. I cannot be denied."

The children were coping well with their coughing. After the wonderful buffet breakfast, we studied English for one hour with a small picture dictionary, then Anton entertained himself by popping packing bubbles while Kristina watched TV. Even though yesterday's court put a dark cloud on my hope to bring my children home to America, they were not aware of any possible negative outcomes. As much as I tried to be positive, there were moments I shivered at the thought something dire, something unpredictable was in the making. But as soon as such thoughts came, I prayed God to spare us from such disappointment.

If you were to ask me, "C.C., what was the high note of your day?" I would answer, "The children were happy, wonderful and playful."

As I was asked to do, I called Tasha to inform her that we were leaving the hotel for a long walk. Kristina held on to my arm. Anton, feeling free as a bird, walked on all the curbs and on top of the low stone walls, just like a typical boy. During our walk, we took pictures and made movies, visited some stores and stopped for ice cream. We stopped at the corner deli to purchase our dinner. On the street in front of the deli, vendors came every day to set up their tables filled with fruits and vegetables. We walked to the table of what would become my favorite "fruit lady," an attractive pleasant woman, about forty years of age, who, despite the cold and miserable weather, always had a cheerful smile. Kristina exchanged a few words with the lady who then looked at me and smiled.

Back at the hotel, the children surprised me by putting the groceries away. Then we decided to explore the hotel by walking up and down each floor and hallway. Each floor had a concierge who sat in a beautiful lobby filled with plants and attractive furniture. Each lobby had a large picture window overlooking the plaza and the Yenisei river. We returned to have our first meal in our room. Without a dining table, Kristina placed a clean towel on the coffee table. Both children sat on the couch, I on a chair. The menu consisted of tomato juice, a chicken breast, salad, cheese, bread and chocolate cake.

Anton was his usual self, acting like a clown and making us laugh. Kristina insisted he finish his plate. She tried to spoon-feed him, but he fought her help, spitting the food out of his mouth, laughing hysterically. At several points, he kept his lips tightly sealed while she rested the spoon on his bottom lip ready to shove it in. Anton squirmed and laughed so hard that forcing him to eat was impossible. Both Kristina and I joined in the laughter. After dinner, the children washed the dinner dishes in the bathroom washbasin. They played with the video camera then watched a Russian movie. We said, "I love you" and closed the day with a meaningful family bear hug. In my heart, I said a prayer asking for guidance and protection against the evil forces I sensed were plotting against us.

Thursday, October 14, we repeated the same routine. Every day seemed more and more comfortable for the three of us. At about 11:00 a.m., as I prepared to call Tasha to inform her that we were leaving for our walk, the phone rang.

"C.C., please don't leave the hotel. Ludmilla and I are on our way to speak to you."

They arrived a few minutes later. Tasha started.

"C.C., the judge asked for a new medical report. Ludmilla and I believe the medical report you presented is truthful. Here are the three choices you have to produce this report."

She paused.

"First, you could fly back to the U.S. to obtain a new report. There is no guarantee the judge will accept it. Ludmilla asked the judge if you could have your physical done by a doctor at one of the Krasnoyarsk hospitals. She agreed, but you would be taking the chance of getting an infection or receiving excessive radiation."

She paused again. I remained silent.

"C.C., we do not want you to suffer another blood test nor another chest x-ray. We found a Russian doctor who agreed to prepare a medical record based on the results of the one you presented to the court. You will not have to meet this doctor. If you agree, it will cost you $100."

"But Tasha, that's completely dishonest! All the documents I presented are truthful. This one would be a flagrant lie!"

"Don't worry, we will tell you what to say should the judge ask for specifics. This would be the easiest way for you to obtain a new medical report without taking the risk of catching an infection."

"You're asking me to lie! I hate lies! I hate lies with a passion!" I exclaimed.

Tasha continued, "If the court asks you who was the doctor who did your chest X-ray, you can say it was on the second floor. You do not remember the name of the doctor, but she was of medium height and had dark hair. If the judge asks you about the blood test, you can say it was done on the first floor."

"Tasha you're asking me to lie . . . . What if it backfires? What if it is discovered? I am very uncomfortable with this idea."

They convinced me it was the best way. In the end, very, very reluctantly, I agreed. The salary of a physician in Russia at that time was $100 per month. You read correctly, $100 a month. Based on Russian salaries, this $100 cash, in U.S. dollars, for a fake medical report was indeed very good money.

The truth never lies. By accepting to present a false medical report to the judge, I felt hooked like a fish unable to escape. The falsification of one document to be presented to the court in exchange of $100 haunted me. One fraudulent medical report would now contaminate my otherwise truthful dossier. By doing this, I put myself at the mercy of my two representatives, Ludmilla and Tasha. Should the truth be discovered, should this lie be identified, I could be denied the adoption of my children forever; indeed, a very sobering thought.

23.

Tasha's Visit

The greatest test of courage on earth is
to bear defeat without losing heart
Robert Green Ingersoll[24]

THE FAKE MEDICAL REPORT that would contaminate my dossier haunted me all evening. In my sleep, nightmares punishing me for my action came rolling in and out of my mind. I woke up screaming.

"Please, please, Your Honor, don't throw me out of your courtroom. My medical report was truthful. Please don't send me back to America without my children. Don't punish my children, please, Your Honor."

This was only a nightmare. I couldn't stop thinking of the consequences should the judge discover the one and only false document in my dossier.

What were my choices? 1) Go back home to obtain a second medical report, one-and-one-half travel days each way, without any assurance the judge would accept it, 2) the fear of a possible infection from a contaminated needle, 3) the chance of receiving a radiation overdose? All three possible negatives made Ludmilla and Tasha's offer more acceptable. I suspected this offer was a way for my representatives to make a little extra money. With much reluctance, I tendered the $100.

Each day consisted of similar activities for the three of us. In the morning, the children played with the video camera. Both loved to film and be filmed. Anton was a real clown. They laughed constantly. Kristina had fun trying on some of my jewelry. We took long walks in the cold temperatures. On our way back to the hotel, we stopped to buy needed groceries and visited the fruit lady. We studied English for one hour and communicated using the picture dictionary brought from Naples. While Kristina listened to music on the TV, Anton played with his trucks and small Legos. When finished, he carefully stored his toys under the desk for safekeeping. All was well with our new family, we were happy. We ended each day with several repetitions of "I love you" and lots of group hugs. We were limited in our activities, but we made the best of it while waiting for our next court date.

At the end of each afternoon, we went to the business center to check for email. Most emails were from Sir John, who received from and replied to family and friends asking for the latest news from Russia. A few emails were from Adoption Over-Seas, and fewer were from friends. Sir John would later give me a brown envelope containing printed copies of all the emails he had received from my family and friends during my absence. Reading these emails brought back many emotions. I was touched by the outpouring of love and by so many prayers.

The next day, Friday, October 15, at about 1:00 p.m., I made my usual call to Tasha to inform her we were leaving the hotel to go for our daily walk.

Tasha said, "Please don't leave, C.C. Ludmilla and I will be there in ten minutes."

I felt a sense of urgency in her voice. A distressed feeling invaded my body. A few minutes later, hearing footsteps in the hallway, I opened the door. They came in and greeted all three of us. Their faces were somber. Ill at ease, they both looked down, unsure, hesitant to speak. Their silence seemed an eternity. I glanced at the children. They had their eyes on Ludmilla and

Tasha. I could sense anxiety in both children. Then, softly, Tasha looked at me and said, "C.C., what we are about to say will be very difficult for you and even more so for the children."

I felt my heart sink to the bottom of my feet. I glanced at my children. Kristina seemed to perceive the seriousness of the moment. She became quiet, pensive, almost as if she felt something bad, something very bad was about to happen. Tasha continued.

"The prosecutor, we often refer to her as 'the witch,' is the daughter of the chief justice. She called the children's orphanage and found out the children were with you. She called the Ministry of Education to order that the children be removed from your care and brought back to their orphanage in Dzerzhinsk. The Ministry of Education called Ludmilla to inform her. Boris, the director of the orphanage, is on his way to pick them up."

I froze. I couldn't respond for a few seconds.

"Why?" was the only sound I could muster.

"C.C., the prosecutor wants them back in their orphanage. There is nothing we can do."

Before informing my children, Ludmilla asked Kristina to write a letter dated October 12, which said in part, "After the court delay today, my brother and I asked to stay with C.C. We missed her since we returned to Russia from our visit to America last January."

Kristina signed the letter then gave it to Ludmilla.

After placing the letter in her briefcase, Ludmilla turned to the children. She repeated this horrible news in Russian. Kristina started to sob. She walked the few steps to the couch. Sat. Anton followed. Sat next to his sister. Kristina was sobbing uncontrollably. She bent forward, put both elbows on her knees, and then held her face in her hands. Her beautiful shoulder-length brown hair covered her cheeks. Anton moved closer to his sister. He placed his arm around her back. He managed to put his head under Kristina's hair, then placed his left cheek on his sister's right cheek. Both faces were covered by Kristina's hair, who was crying so hard it was unbearable to witness. I could hear Anton whispering words to comfort her, but to no avail.

It was the most touching sight of brotherly love I had ever seen. Anton, who had been so dependent on his sister since birth was like a little kitten wanting to share the pain of his protector. I felt desperate. How could this be? How could I reassure my children? I can't communicate in their language. Finally, with an emotional and shaky voice, I asked, "Tasha, why is the prosecutor so hard on these children? Haven't they suffered enough? They've received so little since their birth. We were happy, we were bonding as a family."

Firmly, she said, "It's the system, C.C. IT'S THE SYSTEM. . . ."

There was a pause, then she added, "Ludmilla is on the phone trying to have the children stay at a transitional orphanage nearby, rather than sending them back to their orphanage five hours away. If she succeeds, you'll be able to visit them."

What could I say? What could I do? I had no power. I knew no one. How could I reassure my little girl? How could I say all would be OK, when truthfully, I doubted all would be OK?

Ludmilla spent almost a whole hour on the phone. Finally, she announced via the translator, "Permission is granted. The children will stay in a transitional orphanage about forty-five minutes away. Representatives from Social Services are on their way to pick them up."

Slowly, reluctantly, we put on our winter coats. Kristina continued to cry. Anton was numb from witnessing the despair of his sister. I was filled with such anguish. With no other choice, we followed Ludmilla and Tasha to the lobby. With one child on each side of me, my arms around them, we sat on the couch facing the reservation desk. Olea, the only hotel receptionist who spoke English, had become our friend. She looked in our direction. Her eyes seemed to understand what was going on. Kristina continued to cry, now, more softly. Anton remained pale. He looked very sad. Ludmilla and Tasha sat in silence.

First, I heard them, "Click clack, click clack," then I saw them. A tall woman wearing knee high boots with spiky heels. Her beautiful knee-length dark grey cloth coat was left open to display a short black skirt with a matching black top. She was followed by a very tall man with curved-up-tip shoes, Pinocchio style. They were both from Social Services, very official, young, good looking and very well dressed.

They walked directly to the reception desk. Ludmilla recognized them. She stood up and introduced herself. They spoke. The tall woman looked at me. She managed half a smile. I shivered. These people came to take my children away . . . yes, to take my children away. *Can you feel my children's suffocating pain? Can you feel the knife piercing my heart?* They were removing my children from my care, as though some sort of crime had been committed. We were happy. We were bonding. We were in the process of creating a new family. Why such cruelty?

Ludmilla and Tasha introduced us to the "tall people." The three of us stood up holding hands. The tall people gave me a narrow smile. The woman said a few words to my children. I felt unbearably desperate. The tall people talked with Ludmilla for a few more minutes, then Tasha softly touched my shoulder.

"It's time, C.C."

The three of us hugged very tightly for as long as possible. We could feel each other's pain. We could taste each other's salty tears. I spoke softly, with a choking voice, "I will never abandon you, never. You are my children in my heart. I will visit you as often as possible. I love you. I love you forever."

My words were foreign to them, but I hoped the tone and the sincerity in my voice gave them some comfort. Someone separated us. Anton, now a little agitated, walked by Kristina's side. They followed the tall woman. I had a vision they were walking to the gas chamber. They walked outside the main doors of the hotel, then turned right toward the van. I followed with tears still rolling down my cheeks. Alone, I watched their dramatic, heart-wrenching departure. The tall woman guided Kristina and Anton to take a seat in the van. Through the window, I could see Kristina still crying, still blowing her nose. The tall people conversed with Ludmilla and Tasha for a few more minutes. The tall lady sat on the passenger seat. The tall man walked around the van to the driver's seat. The doors closed. The van backed up from its parking space. Kristina, still blowing her nose, managed to wave through the window. She mustered a smile. The van turned the corner. They disappeared. My children were gone.

My heart was broken, the pain unbearable. As I walked toward the hotel entrance, I looked up. The large clock flanking the city hall tower rang 4 p.m.

24.

They Are Gone

*Out of suffering have emerged the strongest souls; the most
massive characters are seared with scars.*
Edwin Hubbell Chapin[25]

BACK IN MY ROOM, I exclaimed out loud, "They're gone! They
took my beautiful children away!"

I threw myself on the bed and sobbed till the tears dried up.
I looked upward and cried out, "God, where are you? How many
more challenges do we need to face? How much more pain will
we have to suffer before the adoption is granted? You too, angels,
have you also abandoned me?"

With a heart overflowing with pain, I walked to the business
center. It was only 4:30 a.m. in Naples, Florida. Sir John, my most
loyal friend, would wake up with very sad news, which he would
share with all my friends, my family and supporters. He kept
everyone informed, including my mother in Québec Province,
and he kept everyone praying.

I believe in Earth angels, those wonderful people who take
over when all breaks loose. Sir John was the Archangel of all Earth
angels. I knew he would find a way to dry my tears, say the right
words to rebuild the confidence I've lost. He would console me.
With his words of wisdom, he would put hope back in my heart

and he would manage to put a smile on my lips, but for certain, he would say, "NNNQ," Never, Never, Never, Quit.

When I finished with the email, I walked to the grocery store. The unimaginable sadness in my heart was unshakeable. I returned to my room with a ready-made chicken dinner and a bottle of wine. After the agonizing emotions of the day, I needed a glass of wine, or two, or . . . who knows how many . . . perhaps the whole bottle. After depositing the groceries on the counter, bottle of wine in hand, I walked down the hallway to the small dining room/bar.

I looked at the young lady behind the bar, showed her the bottle of wine. I smiled, pointed to the wine glasses on the back shelves.

"Could I borrow a wine glass for the evening?"

The young girl, Natasha, took a wine glass in her hand to show me. I said, *"Da."*

She voiced and gestured what I understood to be that she could not give it to me. She put the glass back on the shelf then gestured me to follow her to the door. In Russian, she directed me to the concierge desk by the staircase.

Now, standing in front of the concierge, I pointed at the wine bottle pretending to pour a glass then drink a sip. The concierge lady shook her head left and right while speaking in Russian. I insisted. She led me to see what she had in the closet located behind her desk. Only coffee cups and water glasses were available. I went back to my room. I screamed, "These people don't understand! They just don't understand! My children were taken away from me today. Can't they feel the sadness in my heart? Can't they feel how upset I am? I will not, everyone, hear me, I will not take another rejection today!"

Shaking the bottle I still held in my hand, I shouted, "No one, repeat, no one will prevent me from enjoying this wine in a wine glass. Under no circumstances will I drink this wine in a water glass or worse, in a coffee cup."

Bottle in hand, I walked back to the dining room/bar. Pointing at the bottle, in a controlled voice and using sign language, I said softly, "Natasha, the concierge lady doesn't have wine glasses. Please let me have one, I promise I'll bring it back."

A Russian man who spoke some English heard the commotion. He explained, "Girl no glass out room."

"*Spaciba*," I said.

I walked behind the counter, grabbed a wine glass and walked toward the door. Before exiting, I turned around, looked at Natasha with a smile, "I will bring it back, I promise."

Back in my room, my heart was aching. I felt such emptiness, such sadness. I started to sob, to sob uncontrollably.

"I'm so alone here. There's no one to cry with, no one to hold me, no shoulder to cry on. Even God has abandoned us. Everyone I love is on other side of the planet. Please, someone help us!"

I cried for my children. I cried because I couldn't wipe their tears. I cried because I could not remove their fear. I cried for every parent who has lost a child in some form or another. I cried for anyone who has experienced such excruciating pain. I cried for all the suffering in the world. When, finally, the tears faded, the large city hall clock rang six. Its sad notes penetrated my soul. Its melancholic sounds seemed to express all the pain Russians have suffered for centuries.

I poured one glass of wine, sipped it gazing at the wall. I ate a few bites of chicken, exhausted, completely drained, I prepared for sleep.

When I had made the decision to adopt two children ten months earlier, I had related the process of the adoption to a pregnancy. The difference was that I was pregnant in my heart. After the events of today, I felt as though my children were attacked by a serious illness, which required that they be removed from my care to be admitted into a neonatal intensive care unit. The pain of their departure was aggravated not only by the hourly sad and loud sound of the city hall clock but also by the fear that my petition to adopt them, in the end, would be denied. Completely depleted, I sobbed myself to sleep. Sir John must have felt my desperation. He called me several times during the night and in the following days.

This weekend could have been filled with joy, laughter and hope. Instead, it would be a desperate one for all three of us wondering what our fate would be. The separation was made more painful by the fact there was no visiting at the transitional orphanage on weekends. I told myself, *I must not dwell in negative thoughts. I must switch to positive thinking, pray God to reduce my children's pain, fill my soul with hope, ask for guidance and beg for resolution.*

On Sunday, October 17, I went to an early breakfast where I met a few American families in the process of adopting their children. All were frustrated with the process, but none was as severe as our case. At the end of breakfast, a translator for one of the families heard I was going for a walk. She offered to join me. At one intersection, I noticed several people walking in one direction. I asked where they might be going. She pointed to a Russian Orthodox church. I thanked her for her help, then followed the crowd.

As I entered, magnificent voices filled my ears, voices so soft, so pious, their very sound took me back fifty-plus years, to my boarding school days when the nuns sang in the chapel. If angels could sing, they would sound just like that. I searched for the choir. It was invisible. Their sound came from behind the balustrade, where the priests were performing the service.

There were no pews. Everyone stood. I found a space against the right wall. I let my eyes travel. I first glanced toward the altar. It was filled with intricate artwork of carved wood and pure gold. The windows displayed Russian Orthodox imagery. The parishioners were a combination of young families, middle-aged adults, and many very old-looking people, mostly old *babushkas*. The young families were well dressed. Both men and women wore attractive fabric coats. Most younger women wore high heel boots. The children accompanying their parents were dressed in colorful jackets. They were very well behaved. Looking at the old people, mostly toothless and very wrinkled, I could imagine how tough and desperate life must be for them. If only I could speak their language, I would try to bring them a little sunshine, even if it were only with a smile. No one looked at me. No one looked at anyone else.

The voices stopped. The Bishop raised the Holy Book and read from it. When he was done, several parishioners lined up to kiss his ring. The voices resumed. A little later, the bread and wine were consecrated. It was a very solemn moment. No one spoke. No one moved except when the bell rang, all the heads bowed at the same time. A few priests served communion. Parishioners stood in front of each priest who elevated a chalice as he recited a prayer. A long spoon was dipped in the chalice to collect the wine, the Blood of Christ. The spoon was then emptied in each person's mouth. The priest elevated the chalice again. He recited a prayer after each offering. After receiving the wine, the parishioners walked away with their heads down, holding their arms crossed on their chest. When the available wine was all consumed, the parishioners kissed the priest's large cross hanging on his chest.

Some parishioners walked to a table where an old woman served tea. She filled five or six cups, refilling the cups as parishioners drank from them. Lips belonging to different parishioners drank from the same teacup. To my surprise, the cups were not washed nor wiped during the service. Even the children and the babies were offered a drink of tea out of the communal cups.

While all this was taking place, another priest stood to the left of the balustrade. Mostly older parishioners approached him. For privacy, the priest covered both his and the parishioner's head with a sacred shawl or mantel. I recognized the shawl to be equal to the Roman Catholic confessional booth. It seemed the parishioners who went under the shawl shared their misery or confessed their sins to the priest. I could not imagine what kind of sins these poor desperate people could have committed. Some came out from under the shawl crying, nervous, disorientated.

During my brief time in Siberia, it became obvious that life here was very tough, much tougher than anyone could imagine.

For many, if not most, there was no way out, no light, no rainbow, and no hope of any kind. I felt their sadness, their desperation. I saw the pain in their eyes, confirmed by all the wrinkles on their faces, their missing teeth, their very old coats and hats. I wish I could have done something to alleviate their load . . . even for just one person . . . . I did not know how.

I saw a man who prayed at the *chemin de Croix* (stations of the cross). He prayed so intently at each station, making the sign of the cross four to five time at each one. It sure seemed he was praying, perhaps even begging God to help him, to grant him . . . whatever . . . his needs were. The desperation of so many parishioners was so real, so painful to watch, my heart was crying.

Toward the back of the church, a large narrow, rectangular table was filled with breads of all sorts brought by parishioners to share. Across from this table, on the other side of the church, was a large stand filled with candles, many already lit, others to be lit as a prayer offered to God. In the same area, a priest swung the thurible filled with incense. Parishioners wrote their prayer requests on a piece of paper, which was then placed in a basket. There, I saw an old man leaning on a column, his eyes closed, his head tilted upward. I watched him for a few minutes, his lips were moving in silence, then tears started to wash down his cheeks. He opened his eyes, looked up to the heavens. So intense was his prayer, my heart ached for him. I closed my eyes and asked God to please relieve this poor man of his torments.

The respect and the seriousness of the whole service moved me deeply. I prayed, begged God to take away some of their hardships. As I walked out, the magnificent Angel's voices of the choir continued to fill my ears till I turned the corner. I walked back to the hotel, carrying with me so much of these parishioners' pain. I felt more determined than ever to never abandon, never give up my mission to bring my children to America. I made this promise,

"As long as I'm alive, I will fight with all my might to bring Kristina and Anton to America. As long as I live, they will never experience such hopelessness."

25.

Visit to the
Transitional Orphanage

My children have been punished for sins
they have not committed.
C.C. LeBlanc

IN NAPLES, THE NEWS that the children were removed from my care created quite a stir. In his email, Sir John wrote:

As soon as I received your email reporting your children were taken away, I started stirring things up. Murray could not believe it. Liz M. will call you. I contacted Gen from Adoption Over-Seas. I will call your mom to let her know you will not be back for her nine-tieth birthday, October 29th.

Murray emailed Dawn H., the ultimate sponsor of this program in our area, and wife of a former ambassador to Portugal. She emailed back, that it was the first she had heard of C.C.'s problems. She will follow up.

Murray suggested sending his wife, Valerie, to Krasnoyarsk, if nothing more than to support you, C.C.

This is sick. We have heard of no one who has been treated this way while adopting Russian children. When a friend asked about potential problems in Russia, I told him that once a family secures

138

a date with the court, the judge can ask for a ten-day rule. I WAS VERY WRONG!

Dr. Gerard, a partner in our tennis foursome, emailed Sir John.

Trudy gave me an update. You are a SAINT, John, to help C.C. so much. This is tragic, but things have a way to work out for the best. Perhaps it is not to be for C.C. to adopt these children. A worse scenario would be Kristina could be denied a visa because of TB. That would be a real crisis.

When I read this email, I wanted to scream, "This email is pessimistic. There is no room for pessimism! Everyone! Anyone! Do you hear me? No room for pessimism! I will not accept any negative thoughts. My children will be allowed to come to America if it takes me the rest of my life."

On Sunday, October 17, I wrote, "I'm so grateful for your help Sir John. Your NNNQ is helping me find courage to never, never, never quit. I have to be as strong and as determined as you are."

I was still convinced that the three of us would be able to go home after the next court appointment. I asked Sir John to make flight reservations from Moscow to Fort Myers for October 29. He answered,

"C.C., there are no seats available on that day. I'll let you know the earliest flight I can book."

I wrote back, "Sir John, please call the post office to delay resuming the mail and please call to cancel the cleaning lady. Dear Sir John, you are helping me survive. God bless you and Laura."

Monday, October 18, Tasha arrived mid-morning. She asked me to write a letter to Boris stating that I asked permission for the children to stay with me at the hotel. I was asked to date it October 12, 2004, the day we first met the judge. Later, I realized someone had to cover their behinds in case the prosecutor blamed one of them for letting the children stay with me.

Tasha left with the signed letter to return at 1 p.m. with a driver. It took approximately forty-five minutes to reach the transitional orphanage. Walking toward the main door, I felt ill at ease. We entered the small reception area where my children would meet us. In front of us was an opaque glass wall with a door. It separated the reception area from the rest of the building. On each side of the room, built in, were two curved half-moon bar-height counters. The one on the left hid a receptionist. There were two stuffed chairs and a straight wooden one. Tasha introduced us to the receptionist, who then announced us to the head nurse.

My children entered with a half-smile, looking pale and very sad. Both hugged me at the same time. They hugged me so hard, I sensed they were pleading, "Please do not abandon us here." It melted my heart. I sat on the wooden chair. Kristina sat on my knees. Putting her head on my shoulder, she started to cry, then sob. Anton sat on the stuffed chair, his face white, lifeless. A glance at him would bring tears to anyone's eyes. After a few minutes, I invited Anton to join us. I held him with my right arm. The three of us hugged for several minutes. I held back my tears, but my heart was crying with theirs.

After a while, Kristina and Anton went back to sit on the stuffed chair. Kristina's eyes were red, her face in despair. During the time of my visit, various staff members came into the reception area, one at the time. Each one stopped and stood for a few minutes starring at us while resting one elbow on the high countertop. They were witnessing this heartbreaking scene. I felt we were in a fishbowl with spectators looking in.

I asked Tasha, "Why are these people staring at us. It's very annoying."

"They're curious C.C. They want to see the woman who wants to take these children to America."

Tasha and I tried to entertain the children as best we could. They played with the digital camera, then the video camera. We took pictures of each other. They both had a chance to make a movie. We all looked at it and laughed. After one hour, our visit came to an end. I gave each a bag filled with yogurt, apples, and chocolate.

"We will come back tomorrow."

We hugged. We hugged so tightly it was as though both children would never let go. We had to leave; they had to stay. Their eyes were as sad as little puppies' looking out through a glass window as you walk out of your home.

As we proceeded out of the building, Tasha looked at me with a sad expression in her face, "Anton asked me five times when will C.C. take us out of here."

There was no answer. No one knew if they would ever get out of Russia. Only with God's help will they ever come to America. It was beyond my comprehension how any human beings could be so harsh, so inhuman with children *whose only sin was to have been born.*

26.

Waiting for the Second Court Date

*Having a belief in God, a higher power and the faith
that if we believe in our actions and the actions of others,
all of our prayers can be answered.*
Alexander Neal[26]

THE RIDE BACK TO the hotel was quiet. My heart was numb.
My eyes gazed at the sad, gray, unattractive scenery along the way.
Even Tasha, who was very controlled, seemed filled with sadness.

Back at the hotel, I stopped by the business center. An email
from Sir John informed me he had secured tickets for the three
of us with Delta Air Lines for November 1. He also shared that
Reverend Patterson had placed our names on the church prayer
list until we return to Naples as a family. I wrote to the reverend.

Dear Reverend Patterson,

Thank you for adding our names to the church prayer list.

*The challenging process of this adoption is a test of love, of
strength, of humility, and of faith in a supreme power. I cannot express
in words how brutal this court has been for my children. As an adult,
I can rationalize, but my children are filled with fear and despair that
they will not be able to reach America.*

Your message is giving me hope. Without hope, it would be impossible to stay and live through the hardship this court is imposing on us.

Just as I ended the above message, a second email from Sir John arrived.

Gen from Adoption Over-Seas informed me that your new documents were presented to the court today. Your new court date is scheduled for Wednesday October 20th. She sees that as a good sign, as normally court days are only twice a month, on Tuesday.

Hope returned. Could there be a clearing on the horizon? Maybe this time, we will be able to walk through that big open door, to leave Krasnoyarsk, in the direction of Moscow, then home to God Bless America.

Dinnertime was approaching. Since the concierge lady had loaned me an electric kettle, I could now boil a chicken breast. I walked to the grocery store, which was always an adventure. Most all the products were labeled in the Cyrillic alphabet and priced only in rubles. Since French is my mother tongue, the few French products were easy to recognize. Not to my surprise, there was an abundance of the most internationally known product, vodka, and yes, a bottle of vodka sold at a lower price than a quart of milk.

I could not distinguish between butter, margarine, or cream cheese. All three packages were in the same area and packaged in a similar way. If there was a French product such as *Beurre President* or *Fromage President* (brands of butter and cheese) I would understand. Of course, there was no wonderful "cream cheese 1/3 fat reduced." At the meat counter, I could tell a chicken breast from a filet mignon. A chicken is a chicken and a filet mignon is the same all over the world!

I spotted something that had mushrooms on the package and showed a spread on a piece of bread. I figured it must be cream cheese with mushrooms. It was. Since there was no chicken breast left at the deli, only backs and thighs, I looked for something else for dinner. I saw what appeared to be smoked salmon, nice and pink, ready to eat. With the mushroom cream cheese, that could be dinner! I added the salmon to the basket. I included some Petite Bananas, almonds, milk and water.

Next, I looked for a box of tissue paper, which the hotel did not provide. They only provided rough toilet paper, so rough that one would get a bloody nose using it . . . bad enough one had to use it on one's bottom . . . . I gestured to the young clerk and pretended to blow my nose saying the common name for the brand of tissues. She could not understand for the life of me what I was trying to communicate. I took an old napkin out of my purse and pretended to blow my nose. With a pleasant smile, she gestured me to follow her. The only tissue paper available was in small purse-size packages. My thought was, "Don't they blow their noses here in Siberia? Or do they still use cotton *mouchoirs*?"

The paper tissues were sold in packages of three. I bought a package. The total cost for my purchases came to 797 rubles. I offered my credit card. The credit card company rejected it. I discretely reached under my blouse, took some cash out of my money belt and paid the bill.

Back at the hotel, I placed all the food in the refrigerator, and for dinner, I decided to have some of the leftover breakfast food. Alone, twelve time zones away from home, on the other side of the planet, I made it a point to appreciate the small blessings sent my way. I was very fortunate to have a safe hotel room, food, incredible support from family and friends and Russian representatives who wanted this adoption to succeed.

This period of my life was by far the most challenging and the most painful I had ever experienced. At the end of it all, it may very well be the most rewarding. I knew I couldn't give up. I rarely or never give up.

My intuition tells me that you want to know how I occupied my time, all alone in a country with both a foreign language and a foreign alphabet. Pretend you are walking beside me for a moment. First, I have not been able to find anything written in English, French or Spanish. I even asked the reception ladies if any American families had left any books behind. *"Nyet"* was their answer. Every weekday, the round trip to my children's orphanage took about three hours. Every day I went to the deli and I walked to explore the neighborhood. In addition, whenever I could, I watched the two-hour news channel offered in the English language. I wrote notes to myself with the intent of writing this book. I went to the business center to read and answer emails. I prayed and meditated. I tried to connect psychically with my children hoping to take away some of their fears. I cried.

At times, I sat in the lobby of the hotel and watched people go by. There, I met a young American woman waiting to adopt her child. We sat together a few times. Sadly, she had to return home childless one more time. The court said she was missing documents. She didn't have a Sir John to help her.

One day, while on my walk, I found a small museum near the river. To my surprise, the lower floor had a display of aboriginal people who looked just like our aboriginal people, "First Nation People," at home. The same canoes, the same teepees, the same clothing and jewelry I had seen in the Indian reserve neighboring where I lived in the Province of Québec. How could they be the same on the other side of the planet?

The days went by. Night came. It was time to sleep. I would fall asleep, visualizing Kristina, Mama C.C. and Anton holding hands walking under a large double-arched door toward a magnificent rainbow leading us to America.

On Tuesday, October 19, I was informed that our court date was delayed until the new documents arrived. Didn't Sir John send an email earlier informing me the court had been presented with the new documents that day? Was someone playing games with me? Early afternoon, Vera, a driver, Tasha and I drove to the transitional orphanage. The children walked into the reception area dressed in the same orphanage clothes they had worn the day before. Their faces were so sad it would make the hardest criminal cry. This time, two caregivers came to watch us. We amused ourselves the same way we did the day before. The hour went by quickly. Our visit was over. I left them more yogurt, chocolate and fruit. We hugged. Filled with sadness, Tasha and I watched them leave the reception area with their caregiver.

27

More Heartbreak

When everything seems to be going against you.
Remember that the airplane takes off
against the wind, not with it.
Henry Ford[27]

IN ORDER TO HAVE breakfast, a $5 voucher had to be obtained at the front desk. A young girl stood at each entrance of the two hotel dining rooms. With gaze down, the young girls collected the voucher from each customer entering. Strange, I thought, eyes never met. There was no emotion, no smile, no welcome, no fraternizing. Today however, no one was at the entrance. I walked in, went directly to the buffet counter, poured a cup of coffee, filled my plate and looked for an available table. There was none. I looked for an empty chair. I noticed three people were sitting at a table for six.

"May I join you?" I asked.

Only one person looked at me. He slightly nodded his head yes. I sat. No one acknowledged my presence. I might as well have been a ghost sitting at the end of their table. I had breakfast in total silence. I looked around to find someone with a friendly gesture. There was none. I finished eating, brought the tray to the conveyer, walked out without tendering the meal ticket. *I'll use it another day*, I thought. I felt a little guilty, but I was so upset that my children had been taken away, I dismissed the guilt.

On Wednesday, October 20, Tasha and I arrived at the transitional orphanage.

"We have good news for you today, my children. Tomorrow, we have a court date."

For the first time in several days, our spirits were up. I brought several little gifts. Some they could leave with the children of this orphanage. Kristina received a lip balm, a watch and a little purse. Anton received a watch and a magic "electric" ball. Every time he squeezed it, it would light up like a Christmas tree. If he threw it on the floor, again, it would light up in several flashes of various colors. Both Kristina and Anton were fascinated with this little ball. We played catch. Several times, Anton threw it on the floor and watched the shimmering lights in total amazement. We took pictures. Both children filmed with the video camera. Some caregivers came to the reception area to watch us. Today was a happy visit, one filled with hope that the beautiful rainbow was on its way. Our hugs were filled with smiles and excitement. Tomorrow would be the birth of our family, the beginning of the rest of our lives together. We waved goodbye.

Late that afternoon, there was a knock on my hotel room door. Unannounced, Tasha and Ludmilla walked in. We talked for several minutes. They left. I sat quietly, thinking, trying to make sense of it all. I turned the video camera on and pointed it toward me. I wanted to remember my words, to remember the emotions I felt at this very moment. I wanted that someday, my children would be able to know how I felt, how I suffered along with them through all these delays. I started talking.

Today my children, we had a wonderful visit. Tasha and I brought you good news. We announced that tomorrow, Thursday, we would be at the court. I brought you the clothes you would wear for the judge. I brought you yogurt, fruit, kiwis, a few gifts you can leave at the transitional orphanage. Tomorrow was to be the start of our life together. It would be the start of our life together if the judge agrees to let me

adopt you. We shared wonderful hugs. We said, "I love you." We had
hope in our hearts. I came back to the hotel room happy. Life was good.

However, at about 5:45 p.m., there was a knock at the door. I opened
it. Ludmilla and Tasha were there. Surprised I said, "Oh! Hello! Come
in. I'm repacking the gifts for Boris to take to his orphanage tomorrow."
Tasha said,
"No gift C.C. Tomorrow . . . tomorrow there will be no gifts."
I looked at them with questioning eyes.
"Why?"
With an emotional voice she said,
"Because tomorrow, we do not have court. . . . There will be no court
tomorrow. The judge will not accept your photocopied documents."
"But Tasha! The judge agreed to process our case with photocopies
of the newly requested documents. Has she gone back on her word?"
Tasha spoke a few more words, but I could not hear anymore. I
was numb. Frozen. Stunned. They left. I sat on the couch lifeless.
Except for the sadness that invaded my whole being, I felt no other
emotion. It appears that the public prosecutor will not hold a court
session unless all newly requested documents are received, nota-
rized and apostilled even though the judge had agreed to process
our case with photocopies.

With an emotional voice, and crying through much of what
I said, these exact words were registered in the video camera.

Needless to say, my children, my heart is broken. I can barely feel
my heart beat. I cannot bear the pain you will have tomorrow when
we have to tell you that . . . that . . . what we promised you earlier
today is not going to happen. As your future mama, I don't know
how to break your heart in that way. I don't know how to tell you
tomorrow . . . that we have to wait. . . . We have to wait. . . . I don't
know how long . . . but we have to wait. . . . That's the system you see. . . .
That's the system! Some people relish making the system happen.

Now, I was crying. With a shaky voice, I continued.

Some people don't care about hurting other people, hurting inno-
cent children like you, and hurting a mama like me who wants noth-
ing more than to love you, give you security, a home, an education

and help develop whatever talents you have. But that is not important, the system is important!

My children, I cannot express these thoughts to you in your language, but someday, when you speak English, you will understand the excruciating pain in my heart. Right now, I want to share with you, that it is very painful for me . . . [crying] and I know tomorrow it will be very painful for you . . . but there is nothing I can do . . . . There is absolutely nothing I know that can be done. I could ask people to help but who? And help how? [now choking] Perhaps I could write a letter to Putin . . . touch a tender cord in his heart . . . if he even has a heart, but it would take so long . . . .

Everyone in Naples is waiting for us. They are waiting for you, Kristina. They are waiting for you, Anton John, and they are waiting for me. They already love us. They will celebrate us. But right now, in your country . . . in your country . . . my children [crying] we have to wait. We have to wait. I don't know how to tell you tomorrow. I don't want to break your heart again.

Tasha and Ludmilla said this is one of God's tests. God's tests . . . ? Test? You, my children, have been tested from the day you were born. You've had such a difficult life as it is, you don't need to be tested anymore, not now, not ever. I had such joy preparing for your adoption. Like a mama who prepares the crib for the baby she carries in her tummy, I prepared a home for the young girl Kristina and the young boy Anton I carried in my heart. But now, the delivery part, the labor part, is unbearable . . . Unbearable . . . . I'm alone here in this hotel. I do not understand the language. With a few exceptions, the people are rude, distant, and cold. There is no friendliness. The people have no joy, no spirit. It's gone. It's dead.

I'm completely at the mercy of whomever. Your fate will be decided not by me. I already know I love you. I already know I want to take care of you. I already know I want to adopt you and take you home with me. But I have no power here. I must wait . . . wait . . . and wait . . . until the system grants my petition to adopt you.

Someday, my children, when you read or listen to this message, you will understand how heavy my heart is. My heart is feeling the pain you will have tomorrow when you hear of yet another delay. It's beyond my comprehension such people are imposing such pain on young children like you. I want nothing more than to take you from an orphanage and give you a chance for a better life. Somehow this judge and this prosecutor do not want that to happen. We are at their mercy. [crying] *I think I've said it all for now my children. Just know I love and miss you and . . .* [crying . . . losing my voice] *I'm praying everything will be OK.*

The large city hall clock rang 7:00 p.m. The sad, choking sound of its notes penetrated my soul, adding to the despair.

Upon hearing the news of yet another delay, Murray sent an email to Sir John.

"John, Valerie and I are thinking of flying to Russia to bring the documents. We found an agency who could expedite a Russian Visa."

At the same time, Valerie, his wife, emailed Adoption Over-Seas, to ask Gen how the new apostilled documents could most quickly reach Krasnoyarsk and,

"Gen would you please tell us how we can help C.C. We are ready to fly to Russia if we need to."

The next day Gen informed Sir John, Murray and Valerie that the documents would be hand-carried to Moscow on Saturday and couriered to Krasnoyarsk.

Later in the evening, I wrote to Sir John to inform him that the Thursday court scheduled for 2 p.m. was cancelled by the prosecutor, even though the judge had accepted to proceed with only the notarized copies. My email continued,

I cannot express in words the heaviness in my heart. I cannot tell you how, as I write this memo, I am holding on to my tears so I can see the screen. I cannot tell you how much pain I feel for my children. I said to Tasha, "We as Americans come here with our heart in our hands, ready to take your children, give them love, a home and a future." This system is so disdainful, once we leave here as a family, I will never want to set foot in Russia again, and my children may never want to do so either.

These prosecutors and judges know that we, adopting parents, will not abandon the children we have come to love as our own. They use that knowledge to lay the frustrations they feel from their own system on us.

God be my witness, once I leave this forsaken country with my children, I will never return!

28.

How to Explain

*We must accept finite disappointment,
but never lose infinite hope*
Martin Luther King, Jr.[28]

THURSDAY OCTOBER 21, AS the city hall clock rang 6 a.m.,
I was already sitting at the desk writing this memo.

*Yesterday, my children, once again, there was a small clearing in
the sky, a chance to see a beautiful rainbow. But, alas, another hidden storm was on its way. It totally covered that little slice of hope
we had. One more time, it took away our dream, the dream to be
united as a family and the dream to reach America.*

*My dearest children, how sad I feel for your young hearts when,
later today, you hear the news of yet another delay. How can you
understand the confusing bureaucratic process of this court, which
for days now has lifted our hearts with hope only to take that hope
away in the next breath?*

*In this adversity we have to be strong, my children. We have to have
faith. We have to forgive and not hold feelings of hatred in our heart.
We must remember and promise we will never be the cause of such
emotional torture toward another human being. This is a sad day for
us, a sad day for Krasnoyarsk and a sad day for its powerless people.*

My stomach was rumbling. Numb and beaten, I walked to the
dining room. Similar to previous days, I filled two bowls with

the granola cereal, garnished a large plate from the food selection of the breakfast island and filled two large cups of coffee. Many mornings, as I walked towards the exit with the breakfast tray, a server voiced in her Russian language what I understood to be, "You cannot take food out of the dining room."

Each morning, smiling and pretending that I didn't understand, I kept walking. Each morning, the server watched me leave without uttering another word. The next day, when I returned the dishes and the tray, I smiled and said, "*Spaciba.*" Again today no one collected the voucher. I had breakfast compliments of the hotel, sweet revenge for all the pain and suffering.

As I entered my room, the phone rang.

"This is Tasha. Can we meet this morning, C.C.? I need to better understand your financial statement before the next court appointment."

Tasha arrived a few minutes later. We sat facing each other.

I explained, "My income is based on shares I purchased from Hollister Inc., the medical supply company I worked for. When I retired in 1987, these shares were converted into a promissory note based on the book value of the company the day I retired. This promissory note will collect an interest of nine percent per year until it is fully paid. The principal will be refunded to me in equal monthly payments for a period of twenty-two years. The interest will decrease monthly as the principal is reduced. I also have an income for the duration of my life from a large annuity."

Her eyes were blank. I stopped talking.

"Tasha, you don't understand, do you?"

"No, I'm sorry C.C., I don't."

"Do you understand if I say that my bank is paying six percent interest on my savings account?"

"No."

"Tasha, do you have a bank account?"

She shook her head no. Surprised, I blurted,

"You don't have a bank account? What do you do with your money?"

"I hide it."

"You hide it? What do you mean you hide it? Why?"

"Because I don't trust the government."

"C.C., most people who adopt children are young professionals who receive a salary from their employer. The vocabulary of your financial statement is totally foreign to me."

"I've been retired since 1987, Tasha. I have no salary. I live off my investments. Can you find a financial adviser or an accountant who could review my financial statement and help you understand it and explain it to the court in the Russian language? Tasha, my income is legitimate and is more than sufficient to care for two children."

She left promising to get help.

I dreaded the day's visit with my children. How can Tasha and I announce yet another court delay. How could we take away the happy news of yesterday's visit? On our way, I rehearsed different words, different approaches that could lighten the impact of this new delay, knowing full well that whatever I say would be meaningless.

Upon hearing the news, Kristina's face turned white. Her eyes moistened more and more then slowly the tears started. My mind went blank. I could not find the scenarios I rehearsed on the way to the orphanage. I quickly prayed for inspiration to express the correct words and with the correct tone.

"Please God, how can I renew their hope one more time? How can I convince them that, with time and patience, we will prevail? Please God, help me find the right words."

I started speaking slowly to give Tasha a chance to translate correctly.

"Kristina, everyone's life includes many challenges. All of us must be able to ride over every bump we encounter along our life's journey. We must have faith and be able to climb above all obstacles that come our way so we can reach our dreams. What we are experiencing, my dearest love, feels like we are climbing a very steep and tortuous mountain. We are being tested to the maximum of our capacity, but we must not give up, we must not give in to adversity, we must overcome each difficulty along the way, with hope in our heart, until we reach the top of our mountain."

I stopped talking for a few seconds, I asked Tasha for a sheet of paper.

"How about if the three of us draw a tall and steep mountain. We'll call it 'The KACC Mountain,' K for Kristina, A for Anton then CC for me."

I drew our mountain.

"Now, I'll write Krasnoyarsk on the bottom left side of our mountain. Kristina, can you write Moscow at the top? Then Anton will write America at the bottom on the right side."

With eyes filled with tears, she smiled then looked at me with questioning eyes while Anton, still sitting on the stuffed chair, listened to every word, looking at our mountain.

I continued, "Let's draw little arrows starting in Krasnoyarsk pointing upward in the direction of Moscow. Once in Moscow, we won't need to draw arrows pointing down. We'll draw an airplane pointing straight to America."

She smiled.

"Kristina, you're looking at me wondering if I'm telling the truth, if I really believe we'll make it to America. My dearest Kristina, this is the only truth I know. My only wish is for all three of us to leave Russia and go home to America. When I go back to my room alone, I cry. I cry for you my love, I cry for Anton, for all the other children left at the orphanage. But we can't give up Kristina, we need to hope, we need to hope God or our angels from heaven and our special Earth angels will help us."

I waited a few minutes to let the silence be our friend. I continued to hold Kristina on my knees then invited Anton to come closer.

"Anton, will you help Kristina be strong? Will you both be strong and wait with me? We are a team now. We must wait together with hope that God will prevail."

How can children comprehend all this turmoil? Yet we had no choice. I continued to hold them in silence. Little by little, the tears subsided.

In the meantime, Tasha obtained permission to take the children outside to play in the snow. The laughter returned once we started throwing snowballs at each other. I purposely kept missing them to give them a chance to hit me. When they did, they laughed and laughed as I pretended to be hurt. Both children pulled on me, trying to drag me in the snow. I pretended I was afraid of being pulled and tried to make it difficult for them to succeed by pulling back and letting my boots slide in the snow. When they succeeded, they laughed and laughed again, as children should. While outside, Kristina pointed to her bedroom window which was secured with a metal grid. I thought, *Should there be a fire, how would they ever be able to escape?*

We returned inside refreshed and happy. Anton started filming with my camera while Kristina sat on my lap. After a few minutes, it was Kristina's turn to film while Anton came to sit on me, such beautiful moments. He was laughing and cuddling. I tickled him. Both had such happy faces. We talked about making a real movie. Kristina wanted to be in charge and be the camera operator. Anton wanted to be the main actor. The mood was upbeat and happy, finally, the way it should be for children.

Toward the end of our visit, I turned around only to notice a total of seven caregivers, including the physician and the assistant director of the orphanage, standing in the reception area. I asked Tasha why so many people today.

"They're just all so curious about you C.C. They want to know who is the woman that will take Kristina and Anton to America."

"Tasha, could you translate?"

I stood up and shook hands with each person present. Then I said, "My name is C.C. LeBlanc. I'm Canadian-born from a French family of seven children. In 1976, the American medical supply company I worked for offered me a transfer to the United States, which I accepted. After retiring in 1987, I moved to Naples, Florida.

Recently, I met a couple who had adopted two Russian children. I was so inspired by their action that it led me to follow their example. I will be sixty-five years old next month. That is why my choice was to adopt older children. I fell in love with Kristina and Anton. I hope to give them love, a family, security, and an education that will help them achieve whatever their talents lead them to."

The assistant director of the orphanage made a step forward. Tasha translated her words as follows,

"We are very happy to meet you. We appreciate the Canadians, the Americans and the Europeans who come to this country to adopt the children our government cannot take care of."

I thanked her for her kind words. We looked at each other. I was wishing we could spend more time together, but without involving Tasha, it was impossible. She stood there, looking at me with wondering eyes. She came closer and gave me a hug. I responded in kind. Tasha translated as I looked straight in her eyes and said, "Oh, how I wish we could communicate. There is so much we could share."

Her eyes filled with tears as she continued to look at me. She held my hands while Tasha translated her words.

"These children are very fortunate. Thank you."

Everyone appeared a little emotional. Little by little, they left the reception area except for the physician who tended both her hands to me. I took them. With sincerity in her eyes, she softly said, *Spaciba.* She gave me a hug and left.

No more words were spoken. I was astonished by what just took place. I had been flabbergasted to hear the assistant director's words, "to adopt the children our government cannot take care of."

I sensed the orphanage representatives were genuinely appreciative that other nations were willing to adopt their children in order to give them a chance for better life. Tasha shared with me later that there were over one million children in Russian orphanages.

Our visit ended. Again, I gave my children yogurt, fruit and chocolate. When we parted there was a sense of relief. One more time, there was a clearing in the sky. There was hope that next week will bring a positive outcome. Could it be that next week, our dream will be granted?

Back at the hotel, a group of barbershop singers from Ireland were entertaining the guests in the lobby. I watched them for a few minutes, then went to the business center.

I wrote Sir John an email to relate today's story at the transitional orphanage then added, "All your messages are keeping me alive. Thank you so very much for your love and your support. The next batch of documents will arrive this weekend. Please keep praying, Sir John, so we can soon reach our God Bless America."

Since the concierge lady on the floor had loaned me an electric tea kettle, I walked to the grocery store, bought a chicken breast with the intention to boil it in the tea kettle. I filled the tea kettle with water, placed it on top of the very old-fashion big CRT (cathode ray tube) TV set. I plugged the kettle into the electric outlet. I put the breast of chicken in the kettle. While the chicken was cooking, I sat on the couch to listen to the English Channel news hour.

All of a sudden, the TV screen went crazy. Pink, blue, yellow colors flashed quickly a couple of times then POOF! It died. OMG! I ran to the TV to unplug the kettle. The chicken bouillon in the kettle had overflowed and leaked into the back of this old-fashioned TV. OMG! Imagine! This Russian TV drank a shot of chicken bouillon and died! It might have survived a couple shots of vodka, but chicken bouillon? No can do.

I quickly fetched a towel from the bathroom to wipe up what I could. I decided to let the TV dry out for a couple of days. After two days, I called the reception to report my TV stopped working. A middle-aged maintenance man who only spoke Russian came in ready with his toolbox. He took the back panel cover off, appeared to look at everything, plugged the TV back into the electric outlet, tried to turn it on several times, to no avail. I watched in silence, smiling to myself.

Looking frustrated, he explained what I understood to be that he would bring this TV to the shop to fix it and bring me another one. How many times during his career was he called to fix a TV that drank a shot of chicken bouillon? He left. I laughed . . . and I laughed. Only in the heart of Siberia . . . .

I fell asleep hoping for better days, but my intuition was stirring up my thoughts. It was telling me more nuages noirs, black clouds, were on their way. I fought with these dark thoughts with all my might. How could there be more? What else could this court come up with?

So many people were praying for us. Mom was inquiète, worried. When I left for Russia, the adoption process was to take a total of ten days. It had been two weeks now and still no decision.

"Mom do not worry, I'm still alive; sad but determined. The children and I will survive this ordeal. We will be stronger for it."

Pictures from the Family Album

Segment 1, Wise family, CampKidHope, Tampa, Florida, Pictures 1 to 9.

Segment 2. Waiting for US citizenship and court date. Pictures 10 to 12.

Segment 3. First trip to Krasnoyarsk, Russia. Pictures 13 to 25.

Segment 4. April 2005, return to Russia. Pictures 26 to 37.

Segment 5. America we are here! Pictures 38 to 46.

Segment 1, Wise family, CampKidHope, Tampa, Florida.

1. The Wise family, who were my inspiration to adopt, Valerie, Murray and their two Russian adopted children, Diana and David.

2. CampKidHope, Kristina and Anton at bed time on our second night. Family Album.

3. CampKidHope, Kristina, C.C., Anton bonding in our hotel suite in Tampa, December 31, 2003. Family Album.

4. Anton entered my heart when he ran into my arms and gave me this very intense hug, December 31, 2003. Family Album.

5. Evening at the hotel, dinner, doing crafts, bedtime. Family Album.

6. Bush Garden, January 1, 2004. Kristina learning to use the video camera. Family Album.

7. CampKidHope. Learning to play ping pong and pool. Family Album.

8. CampKidHope.
Kristina and Anton,
Santa's Visit. Family
Album.

9. CampKidHope is over. The children are returning to Russia. A very sad and emotional day. Family Album.

Segment 2. Waiting for US citizenship and court date.

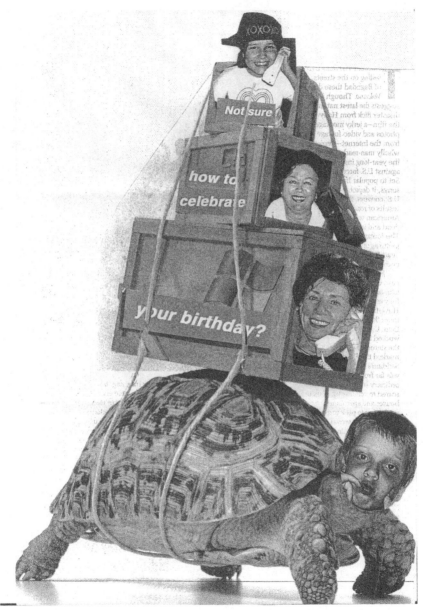

11. A collage created by C.C. for Anton's 9th birthday. Family Album.

10. June 10, 2004. Celebrating C.C.'s citizenship with Sir John, his wife Laura and Trudy at the tennis courts. Family Album.

BABY SHOWER
SEPT 26, 2004

12. Baby Shower, September 26, 2004, before departing for Siberia for the court hearing. Family Album.

Segment 3. First trip to Krasnoyarsk, Russia.

13. Krasnoyarsk, October 11, 2004. The children arrive at the hotel after a separation of ten months. Family Album.

14. Dinner with Boris the day before our first court day. Family Album.

15. Bonding with my future daughter, Krasnoyarsk, Siberia, October 2004. Family Album.

16. Bonding with my future son, Krasnoyarsk, Siberia, October 2004.
Family Album.

17. October 15, 2004. The children are removed from my care and moved to a transition orphanage. Family Album.

18. Kristina and Anton leaving the hotel for the transition orphanage with the tall lady from social services. Family Album.

19. Kristina is still crying in the van taking her and her brother to the transition orphanage. Family Album.

20. Transition orphanage, notice the sadness, especially the fear, in Anton's eyes. Family Album.

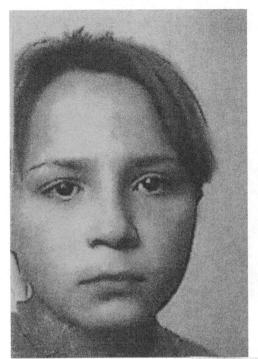

21. Picture taken from a computer at the transition orphanage. Notice the sadness and lack of life as seen in her face. Family Album.

22. Picture taken from a computer at the transition orphanage. Again, notice the sadness and desperation in his face. Family album.

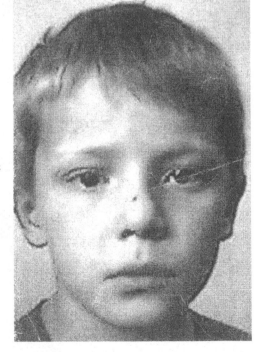

23. Transition orphanage, tears sadness and fear as my children learn of more delays. Family Album.

24. October 27, 2004. The adoption is denied, a devastating moment. My children have to go back to their orphanage. Picture is of poor quality. It was taken by my video camera which I had placed on top of the TV to record the event. Family Album.

25. October 27-2004. A heartbreaking good bye. We lost this battle. They must return to their orphanage. My eyes are saying, "You're not done with me, I'm coming back." Family Album.

Segment 4. April 2005, return to Russia.

26. Siberia, April 2005, at my children's orphanage. Look into their eyes, "Why Can't you take me too?" Family Album.

27. April 26, 2005, announcing more delays. Kristina loses hope one more time, they must return to their orphanage (a 5-hour drive) until the next court day. This picture still brings tears to my eyes. Family Album.

28 This police woman is shooing these two babushkas away. Their only sin was wanting to enjoy the marathon taking place on the street below. Chapter 42, Family Album.

29. April 29, 2005. We won! The adoption is granted, "We're Going Home."
Family Album.

30. April 29. Our first official happy family picture, celebrating our successful adoption. Kristina is thirteen today. Family Album

31. Happy Birthday Kristina. After many tries, she gives up on extinguishing the magic candles. Family Album.

32. Anton and Victor come to the rescue. Victor used his saliva to finally extinguish the magic candles. Family Album.

33. Kristina is holding this beautiful baby girl just adopted by a young couple from North Carolina. Family Album.

34. Happiness is knowing we are on our way to America. Family Album.

35. Anton using his energy... just like a typical boy. Family Album.

36. At the Krasnoyarsk's museum, playing with computers. Family Album.

37. Saying goodbye to our wonderful fruit lady. Family Album.

38. Red Square in festive mode, no cars allowed. It is the 60th anniversary of the end of WWII. Putin is hosting dignitaries from around the world. Family Album.

Segment 5. America we are here!

39. Naples, Fl. Grandpa John and Laura going to the Beach with Kristina and
Anton, June 2005. Family Album.

40. My mom at 91 years with Kristina and Anton, summer 2005. In the background is the site of the Manoir Richelieu on the St-Laurence River, Quebec Province, Canada. Family Album.

41. Summer 2005. Kristina and Anton painting Anton's desk green. Family Album.

42. Playful Anton tries to make mama C.C. fly. Family Album.

43. First day of school in America, August 2005. Family Album.

44. Spring 2006, Crested Butte ski trip. Family Album.

45. April 29, 2006. Kristina is fourteen, Anton could not wait to wake her up with his good wishes. Family album.

46. Our dear Lidia from Belarus with Kristina and Anton December 2007.
To know Lidia is to love Lidia. Family Album.

47. The C.C. LeBlanc family. Christmas 2007. Family Album.

29.

Theater, Shopping, Visit

F-E-A-R has two meanings:
"Forget Everything and Run,"
or
"Face Everything and Rise."
The choice is yours.
Zig Ziglar[29]

FRIDAY, OCTOBER 22

The thought of returning to the transitional orphanage this day was very painful. I could only imagine the children's state of mind. I had to maintain a positive spirit, even when my expectations of having a successful adoption were switching from, "Yes we will succeed," to, "Not so sure anymore." It was hard to imagine a positive ending. I could not share my true fears with my children. I had to give them hope.

When they first walked into the reception area, the sadness in their face created a feeling of total desperation in my soul, desperation I had to overcome one more time. During the visit, there were a few tears but, in the end, we left exchanging hugs and smiles. We had another chance to succeed next week. We could not give up.

When I returned to the hotel, as usual, I went to the business center to check for emails. Finding nothing urgent and feeling mentally exhausted, I went back to my room, lay flat on my bed and meditated. Around 8 p.m., I looked in the refrigerator, found a good piece of bread and made a sandwich out of the leftover boiled chicken from the day before. I sat on the couch, turned on the TV to a Russian concert that seemed to have an affinity to a wild American rock concert. I took a bite of my sandwich. Oh! Something crunched. Better take a look! I put the sandwich aside and I spit the contents of my mouth into my hand. I walked to the bathroom, looked in the mirror. I grinned.

"OMG, I lost a crown! My eyetooth is gone. All there is left is an ugly post protruding from my gum! Oh my God! I'm whistling! It's Friday night! It's past 8:30! What am I to do? OMG, my court appointment is next week!"

I returned to the couch, still holding the contents of my mouth in my hand. I looked at it hoping to find the crown, in whatever condition.

"There it is," I whistled. "I must quickly find a dentist who can fix this ugly gap, even temporarily."

I called the reception desk. What a blessing, Olea was on duty. I explained my urgent situation.

"Olea, what do you suggest?"

"C.C., did you know there is a dentist's office on your floor? It's open till 10 p.m. As you walk toward the restaurant/bar, her office is in room 400. I will call her to let her know you're on your way."

"You're an angel, Olea, thank you."

After washing the crown, I left my room holding it in my hand as if it was a most precious gem.

Knock, knock, knock. A beautiful ten-year-old girl opened the door.

"Is your mama here?"

"*Da*, come." She led me to her beautiful and young mother sitting at her desk.

I smiled. She saw the gap. I opened my hand. I showed her the crown. I placed it on the post left in my gum and asked her if she could use some dental glue and put it back.

Her beautiful little girl translated the best she could. The mother looked at me gesturing and talking. I understood it was not possible to glue it back. She guided me to her dentist's chair. Not able to understand her explanations, we called Olea. She immediately came up. She translated.

I said, "I trust you doctor. Please start the procedure."

At the end one hour and ten minutes, past her closing time, my tooth was back. The dentist rebuilt it using resin-based composites and a dental curing light.

I asked, "How much do I owe you?"

She wrote $70 on a piece of paper. I gave her $100. She deserved every bit of it. Now ladies and gentlemen, do you think I really needed this extra adventure, all alone in the heart of Siberia?

Sunday, October 24

Sundays were a leisure day. I took the morning to rest and reorganize the clothes and the gifts I had brought for the orphanage. After enjoying a late breakfast, I decided to go for a walk. I noticed well-groomed children accompanied by well-dressed adults lining up in front of the Art Center. Hmm! Attending a Russian program would be an interesting way to spend a Sunday afternoon.

After most of the crowd had entered the theater, I presented myself at the ticket window. Speaking slowly, I asked the young lady, "Do you have any tickets available?"

She answered in Russian while gesturing what I understood to be, "Wait a minute." She came around outside her cubicle and gestured for me to follow her. She introduced me to a young woman behind a small souvenir counter. This young lady could not understand me either. She gestured for me to wait. A lovely professionally dressed mid-thirties woman arrived. Gently I asked, "What is the program today and could I attend it?"

In a very thick accent, she explained, "Is children program. Yes, you attend. Please come ticket widow."

"*Spaciba.*"

"Where you from?"

"I'm Canadian born, but I now live in the state of Florida."

197

"Why come Krasnoyarsk?" she asked.

"I'm in the process of adopting a young girl and her brother."

She stopped walking, turned toward me and stared into my eyes for a few seconds.

"Children lucky, thank you."

At the ticket window she addressed the young lady, informed me the price was 20 rubles. When the transaction was completed, she walked me to my seat. I thanked her. She smiled and left.

My seat was one of the best in the house. It was about eight rows from the stage and it extended into the center isle by one seat. With no one in front, I had a clear view of the stage. The theater was about seventy-five percent full. Of course, I could not understand any of the words, but I felt that the children on stage and those in the audience thoroughly enjoyed the performance. They laughed and applauded throughout.

During the intermission, I stood in the lobby to observe. Over half of the attendees were children. They were very well behaved. The adults accompanying the children appeared to be mothers or grandmothers. There were very few men. Everyone was elegantly dressed. There were small clusters of two to four people, every cluster keeping to themselves. I smiled toward some of them, but no one returned my gesture. The voices were low. Not once did I hear a loud laugh nor a loud voice.

At the end of the performance, the attendees exited the hall in a very orderly manner. They directed themselves toward the cloak room, then quietly left the theater. As I watched them walk out, I admired the beautiful ankle-length, A-line fabric coats that most younger women wore. Many of the coats had an additional hood bordered with fur. These beautiful coats added sheer elegance and beauty to the plaza of this Russian, picture-perfect winter scene, complete with large snowflakes falling softly to the ground. Children dressed in colorful clothing of red, pink and purple, were holding their parents' hands as they walked across the plaza in various directions. Older women wore more conventional coats and big fur hats while the few men wore the typical Russian *ushanka* hat with ear flaps. That night, I fell asleep dreaming I would return home with a cloth coat with a hood bordered with fur.

Monday, October 25

Since the visit with my children was scheduled for mid-afternoon, a little shopping spree would lift my spirits. My only wish was to find a beautiful fabric coat with a hood bordered in fur like so many women wore at the theater the day before. After an early breakfast, I stopped at the reception desk to ask for direction to a store where such coats were sold. My receptionist friend, Olea, was off. The receptionist on duty could barely speak English. I showed her a picture of the coat and I asked her if she could direct me to a store where I could buy one. She repeated Mira Street several times.

"Where on Mira Street, Tanya? Can you give me a street number? Do you have a telephone directory to check the address?"

She wrote a name in Cyrillic on a piece of paper, handed it to me. "*Spaciba.*"

I thought I could ask someone on the street for directions. For sure, someone would know where this store is.

Determined to find a coat, I walked to Mira Street. A middle-aged woman was walking toward me. In a very soft voice, showing her the piece of paper, I asked, "Excuse me, could you direct me to this store?"

The lady gave me a dirty look, jaywalked across the street without ever turning back.

Perhaps she's in a bad mood. Maybe she had a fight with her husband. Who knows?

I continued to walk. Two mature ladies were walking toward me. Again, I asked in my sweetest voice, "Excuse me, do you speak English?"

The ladies spoke quickly to each other, gave me a dirty look, pretended I did not exist and continued to walk.

What is going on with these people? Are they afraid of me?

Two more ladies in the distance were walking in my direction. With the piece of paper in my hand, I pretended to look for an address. As they approached, I asked, "Excuse me, could you help me?"

Before I had a chance to complete the question, their disgusted looks hit me like bullets. They kept walking. At that point, I became very emotional. I wanted to cry. I felt totally rejected.

Why do they behave this way? Do I scare them? Do they resent me for speaking English?

Still I would not give up. Two young girls were approaching.

"Excuse me, would you be able to help me find this store?"

"You buy . . . um . . . um . . . what?"

Very slowly, pronouncing one word at a time, using my hands to describe the coat, I answered, "A . . . beautiful . . . winter . . . coat . . . with . . . a hood. Can . . . you . . . direct . . . me . . . to a store?"

"Yes, yes. Come."

What a difference between the older ladies and these two beautiful young girls. They were both sixteen-year-old students who spoke very little English.

"Where you from?"

"I am Canadian-born, but I live in Florida in the United States."

"Why you come here?"

"To adopt two children."

"Good. OK talk Canada, talk United States."

They asked several questions. We kept walking. They kept asking. We turned a corner. They continued their questioning. They even asked about Madonna. All this time, I thought we were walking toward the store where I could buy the coat. After thirty minutes, they reached their school. Both gave me a hug, said goodbye, and left smiling. I was left standing, dumbfounded, and totally ignorant as to where I could find a store to buy my dream coat . . . . I returned to the hotel empty handed, but with an experience I'll never forget.

The next day, Tasha explained that in the time of Stalin and Khrushchev, Russian people were forbidden to speak with strangers. If they did, the punishment was severe, such as beatings, prison, or worse. This fear was still present in the older generation, but totally gone with the younger one. *Perestroika* took away the fear. The young people took every occasion to speak to foreigners to learn more about the West.

On our way to visit the children, Tasha announced the Moscow office did not have time to have the new documents apostilled in Moscow. She would spend the better part of the day reviewing each document to be sure the translation was correct, then she would notarize them as a true translation. She would then have them apostilled in Krasnoyarsk, at a cost of 150 rubbles for each document.

I emailed the following thoughts to Sir John.

I feel I'm being milked to death. I'm completely at the mercy of anyone involved with this adoption process, the coordinator, the translator, the judges, not to forget the system. I have to accept whatever they tell me, smile, in order not to jeopardize the eventual success of my mission. For example, the original price of this adoption included the Russian translations, notarization and the apostille fees, yet I am still asked to pay for these. Another example of their abuse is one of the drivers is Ludmilla's son. The fee is $15 per hour. It took twenty minutes each way to take me to court and back to the hotel. The total fee should have been, at most, for one hour each way, $30. Instead, I paid for six hours, a total of $90 US. That is very good pay for smoking and napping in his van while waiting for the court to end. As a reference, physicians and university professors make $100 per month. I had suggested taking a cab to the court. "Cabs are not reliable." There was no room to discuss further.

At the transitional orphanage, the news that the latest documents had arrived generated a happy mood. One more time, all indications were toward a positive outcome. Even with this good news, my heart was very heavy going to and returning from the visit with my children. An alarm was sounding in my being, an intuition that another devastating "something" was about to drop.

"C.C., dismiss these negative thoughts," I told myself.

An email from Murray and Valerie, who successfully adopted two Russian children in 2003, simply said, "Dear C.C., It is all just unbelievable. We are praying."

On October 26, the visit with my children was happy and positive. Hope was high for the next day's court decision.

At the end of the day, I visited the business center. There was a copy of a message from Adoption Over-Seas.

Hello C.C.'s fans,

It appears definite the court time for C.C. is scheduled for 10 a.m. tomorrow 10-27. I will let you know as soon as I hear. Another family successfully completed a Krasnoyarsk adoption today. Hopefully, C.C. will be able to depart for Moscow, with her children, on Saturday, at long last.

I emailed:

Dearest Sir John,

You will be asleep when the court makes its decision tomorrow a.m. I will let you know the result as soon as I can get to a computer. I have no contingency plan. I cannot fathom anything but a YES answer.

My dearest friend, please tell everyone to keep everything crossed, and pray hard. While my heart is trembling and a lump remains constantly in my throat, I will do my best to convince the court my documents are truthful and that I'm emotionally, physically and financially able to take care of two children aged twelve and nine.

Please thank my brother Roger for keeping Maman and the family informed about the day-by-day changes in Siberia.

At bedtime, wanting to be well rested in the morning, I took a sleeping pill.

30.

The Prayer

My eyes have grown dim with grief;
my whole frame is but a shadow.
Job 17: 7

OCTOBER 27

I rose early and well rested. Yes, I felt anxious about the court appointment scheduled for 10 a.m. but I chose to maintain positive thoughts. I dressed professionally, wearing a dark suit with a light beige top. I applied very little make up. I took a quick look in the mirror and was satisfied with the result.

My imagination soared. In a few hours, my children and I would become a family. Our next stop would be Moscow, and then home to America.

At 9:30 a.m., the phone rang. Tasha was hesitant then with a somber voice she announced "C.C., your court time was delayed to twelve noon."

I felt a jab straight toward my heart. She continued,

"The judge ordered the children not be brought to court." This time, the knife penetrated my heart.

"They will be brought only if the documents are approved. We will pick you up at 11:30."

I was speechless. The moment Tasha said the judge ordered the children not be brought to court, a sense of despair invaded me.

My body was trembling. Tears were gathering in the corners of my eyes. My intuition told me this was bad. It told me the judge had already made her decision. The decision was not to grant me the children. I so wanted to be wrong. So desperate, feeling so alone, I needed a friend. I needed to speak to someone, but to whom? Through tears and a choking voice, I called my loyal friend Sir John to share the latest news. He sent an email to Gen from Adoption Over-Seas.

Her answer was, "I am not sure why the judge did not want Kristina to be present. Anton is too young. It's not unusual for a court to be postponed a few hours if they need more time to prepare documents. I'm sure any changes give C.C. cause to worry. I will call you as soon as I hear more."

From the moment I made the decision to adopt, God, my angels, the forces of the universe, were all present to guide me through this process. I felt so many joyful moments then. Since my arrival in Krasnoyarsk, this mystical presence has disappeared. I sat on the couch thinking, meditating, and trying to understand what I would have to face in the courtroom today. I took my video camera, pressed the record button and through tears recorded the following prayer.

God, my angels, where are you? You did not land with me in Krasnoyarsk. I can no longer feel your presence. Why have you abandoned me? From the time I committed to give a better future to two children, I felt you were always by my side, guiding me, guiding this noble process. I've done everything possible to prepare for the arrival of my children. I did it with love and with hope in my heart. Every day, I woke up with a purpose. I worked hard to accelerate my American citizenship. And I worked hard to finalize all the necessary documents for the United States government and for the Russian court. Every day I felt your presence. There was such joy, such hope in my heart then.

I'm here God. I'm here to fulfill my mission. I'm all alone on the other side of the globe, twelve time zones away from home. I'm here able, ready and willing to take responsibility for Kristina and Anton.

You are my only friend here, the only one I can share my deepest thoughts with, but you have deserted me. I can't find you. I cannot feel your presence anymore. Where are you? Instead, there is a big dark cloud hovering over my head. Is this evil cloud so thick, even YOU cannot penetrate it? I've done everything possible to prepare a nest for my children. We will share a new house. I registered them in their schools. I already made medical appointments. From the day I agreed to give a future to two children, I felt You so close to me.

When I said, "I'll do it, but I will need Your help, I can't do this alone." I felt you would be with me the whole time. I'm here now God, I'm here for the delivery of my children. It's been nine plus months. Why have you abandoned me? Why have you deserted me?

I had so many dreams for my children. My love for them grew more and more each day. When I left for Siberia, I worried about my ability to be a good mother. Nevertheless, I boarded the plane happy. I was ready to fulfill this noble cause to the best of my abilities. I left feeling sure the mission would succeed. Now I'm doubtful. I sense that this very thick, black, evil cloud surrounding me will prevail. Evil could win, God! Is this cloud so dark and too thick and so filled with destruction that even YOU cannot push it away?

I don't know what to do GOD. I am at Your mercy, and at the mercy of the court. I will do my part, answer the questions truthfully, to the best of my ability, and with Your inspiration, say the right words. I will try to convince the court that I will do everything in my power to be a good mama.

You've taken us to this point, God. You've given us hope, but right now, I don't feel your presence. I don't understand your silence. Are you testing my limits again? Are you testing how strong I am? It's very hard right now, God. It's especially very hard for my children. I feel very flat now, I have a body but not a soul. I breathe, but I feel numb. I'm here, but I'm afraid.

I can't imagine going back home alone. I can't imagine leaving my children behind. Their pain would be insufferable. Their beautiful dreams would vanish. Please God, stay with us today. We need your help.

31.

Court Day, October 27th

Success is not final, failure is not fatal:
It is the courage to continue that counts.
Adapted from a quote by George F. Tilton[30]

AT 11:30 A.M., TASHA, Ludmilla, a driver and I departed for the courthouse. Conversation was minimal. Tasha said, "Try to stay positive, C.C."

"Tasha, no matter how I feel inside, I have no other choice but to stay positive. I will answer all questions truthfully as I have done during the first court appointment."

Boris, the orphanage director, and Tamara from the Ministry of Education greeted us in the courthouse lobby. The mood was tense. A few minutes later, we entered the courtroom. We sat waiting for the officials to enter. We stood up as soon as the door opened. The judge, Lappo Alevtina S., the Public Prosecutor, Karsnopeeva Oksana V., and the secretary entered. Their body language felt as if they were ill-at-ease. My heart was beating fast. I felt jittery, weak.

All five of us remained standing until the judge gave us permission to sit. She shuffled a few papers and looked at me for a moment. Tasha translated.

"The judge asks you to identify yourself."

I stood up immediately. Once the court confirmed my identity, the questioning started:

"Tell the court about your childhood. What kind of family did you grow up in?'

"Tell us about your career."

"Miss LeBlanc, what motivates you to adopt two children?"

"Why did you not adopt earlier in your life?"

"Why did you not get married?"

"What makes you think you have the capability to raise two older children?"

"Why did you wait so late in your life before you decided to adopt?"

"What makes you think you will live long enough to raise these children?"

"Why did you not get married?"

"What makes you think you will be a good mother?"

"How did you earn your money?"

"How do we know you have enough money to educate the children?"

"What makes you think you will be able to financially take care of two children?"

"Please explain your financial report."

"Don't you think you are a little old to take care of two children?"

"Have you informed your family of your intentions? What do they think?"

"How do you receive your income?"

The same questions with different wording were asked and repeated over and over, if not by the judge, by the prosecutor. I felt they were both trying to catch me lying. I couldn't lie. I did not have to lie. All my documents were truthful. The only lie in my documents was the fake medical report signed by a Krasnoyarsk physician at a cost of $100.

I wondered if the judge had really rejected my original medical report. Was the judge presented with the fake report? Or did someone trick me out of an extra $100? I remember signing a paper in the Cyrillic alphabet. But I was never given a copy of it. There was no translation of it. How would I ever know?

After explaining and re-explaining my financial report, the prosecutor stood up, read a litany of what she did not understand in it. They questioned everything I owned, everything I worked so hard for. I sensed they could not imagine a single woman succeeding to that level.

Except for when the judge took twenty minutes to question Boris, the orphanage director, and Tamara, the representative from the Ministry of Education, I stood for five hours. Not a glass of water nor a bathroom break was offered. No one left the room. At about 5 p.m., the questioning ended.

The judge said, "I will return shortly with my decision."

She came down from her perch. The prosecutor and the secretary followed her out. The five of us remained in the room. No one spoke. I thought of my children, who had been waiting all day in the transitional orphanage to hear their fate. We could only imagine how they felt. I sensed a bad aura around me. The evil, black cloud hovering above my head was still there. I sat, closed my eyes.

"God, let me be wrong. Tell me the black cloud is gone. Tell me You dissipated it."

Whisperings between Ludmilla and Tasha were the only sounds in the courtroom. At 5:25 p.m., we heard the click clack of someone's high heels. The judge entered the courtroom alone, climbed the few steps to her perch. Looking like a lioness at a zoo, she read the verdict. Tasha translated. "Miss LeBlanc provided the appropriate documents . . . " On and on . . . It all sounded positive. My hopes began to rise. *Yes, yes, it's all good. The adoption will be granted.* The hope and the joy I felt at that moment was indescribable.

The judge kept talking. Tasha stopped translating. Then the words, "The petition of Marie Cécile LeBlanc to adopt Kristina Bajenova Sergeevna and Anton Bajenov Sergeevich is DENIED."

The judge gave me an intensely arrogant look. The right corner of her mouth went up half an inch as if to say, "Got you." She quickly left the courtroom clacking her heels.

Hearing the word "denied" felt like a thousand wasps landing on my body. I felt each of their stings. I could not move. There were no tears, no emotion. I felt nothing. At the word "DENIED," my soul died. Whatever energy I had left drained out of my body as if through the open gash of a horrible stab wound. I stood in disbelief. My mind was screaming the words, "DENIED! DENIED! DENIED!"

Tasha touched my shoulder. I looked around. Ludmilla was sobbing uncontrollably. Boris, looking at the floor, stood teary eyed. Tamara of the Ministry of Education kept her head down. After a few minutes, Ludmilla spoke to Boris and Tamara to decide what the next step should be. This was a new crisis. I had to be strong, control myself and deal with it. I turned to Tasha. In a choking voice, I asked, "Tasha, could you ask Boris if I could go to the transitional orphanage to say goodbye to my children?"

She returned.

"C.C., someone will drive you to your hotel. Boris will bring the children to your room."

Those of you reading, be with me in thoughts and feelings. Experience the heart-wrenching emotions of this moment with me. There were no words to describe the pain in my heart, no words to describe the feelings of desperation invading my body, no words to describe what my children's unbearable, devastating distress would be when they heard this dreadful news. This was an indescribable moment of unbearable emotional suffering that no one present could understand.

Back at the hotel, waiting for my children, I wanted to record what was about to happen because I felt no one would otherwise believe it. I placed the video camera on the TV, pointing it to the couch. When I heard footsteps in the hallway, I pressed the recording button.

The children entered first. They immediately came toward me, their faces in distress. Kristina looked very anxious. They both put their arms around my body. We hugged. I helped them take their coats off. Ludmilla, Tasha, Boris and Tamara entered with red eyes. No one talked. Everyone was tense. Kristina's eyes were already filling up with tears. She must have sensed she was about to hear something very bad, something devastating.

I asked, "Tasha, do the children know?"

"No C.C., they don't."

"I have to be the one to give them the bad news?"

She nodded.

Ludmilla stood behind the couch. Boris and Tamara stood in silence by the bedroom wall, with their heads down. We sat on the couch, Kristina in the middle, me on the left, Anton on the right next to his sister. Feeling the sadness and the tension in the room, Kristina's tears started to fall, and fall they did. I took her in my arms, held her tight for a few minutes while Anton looked on. My eyes were filling up.

How can I announce this heartbreaking, devastating news? What words do I use? How can I soften their pain? How can I reduce their fear of being abandoned again? Please my angels, guide my thoughts, guide my words . . . .

Tasha translated.

"Kristina my dearest love, we were in court for five hours today. The judge said I could not take you and your brother to America just yet. There are documents the judge and the prosecutor do not understand. I will continue to fight. I'm a very good fighter. I had really, really hoped to take you both home with me today, but I can't right now. The judge won't give me permission. My heart is very, very sad."

I invited Anton to come closer. I held them both in my arms. The silence in the room was broken only by the sound of Ludmilla sobbing and the three of us crying in each other's arms. Tasha continued to translate, "Kristina and Anton, you must not be discouraged. When we really, really want something, and that something is worthy, we must be willing to wait for it and to fight for it until we succeed."

I stopped talking. Except for stoic Tasha, everyone was crying. Kristina continued wiping her face with her sleeves. Anton looked like his blood was drained out of his body. Speechless, he observed his sister. I continued.

"Kristina and Anton, I want you to know, both Boris and Tamara gave their consent. Everything was going well, but the prosecutor did not understand certain parts of my financial report. I want you to believe I love you both with all my heart. I will continue to fight until we go home together as a family. Please, do not give up hope. Do not give up my dearest children. You must believe and trust I will return for you. Do you understand?"

I stopped talking for a few minutes, put my arm around Kristina and brought her head on my shoulder. I held Anton's hand, who sat there numb. I continued with tears rolling down my cheeks.

"Your hearts are broken I know. I am powerless here. My heart is crying with yours my dearest children. You and Anton must go back to school, study hard. I will return as soon as I can. You must believe me. I will go to Putin if I have to. I promise, I will communicate with you from America. You must believe me, my children. You must believe me."

I looked at Tasha. "There must be someone in Krasnoyarsk who can understand my income. We need to know exactly what the court does not understand in my financial report. Every time the request for more documents is fulfilled, the judge asked for something else. Could we have another court hearing tomorrow? Could I have an interview with the chief justice? If I could meet with him, I could explain my financial report. I'm sure he would understand it. If that does not work, I want to try to meet with Putin. I'll stand at the door of the Kremlin till someone takes me to him. I must do this before my visa expires."

"C.C., it's not possible to reopen your dossier. Once a dossier is closed, it cannot be reopened. There is no court tomorrow, and we do not have a copy of the judgment yet. We must wait till Monday. You have ten days to bring a complaint against the judgment."

"Tasha, the chief justice can get a copy of the judgment right now if he wants to, he is the chief justice! I have ten days before my visa expires. I want to lodge a complaint with the chief justice before I go over his head. The judge had no reason to refuse me. The fact that the prosecutor doesn't understand my financial statement is not a reason to deny me."

While the Russians were speaking to each other, I continued to hold my children and rub their backs. Kristina kept crying. Anton's face was disconsolate. He kept looking at his sister, then looked at me, trying to understand. With such a language barrier, I was at a loss to find a way to console them.

"C.C., when Ludmilla finishes her conversation, we'll ask her to make an appointment with the chief justice on Monday. If he refuses, we will give him a copy of your complaint. Even if you leave, we will give him a copy of your complaint on Monday. By then, he will have the file with your judgment."

"These are my children Tasha. Over my dead body will they stay in Russia. I will pursue their adoption if it takes me the rest of my life. When I return to the states, I will contact every magazine and newspaper. Krasnoyarsk will be on the map because of this ignorant prosecutor. She should have studied finance in addition to law. My children should not suffer this hell just because these justices are stupid and ignorant."

"C.C., the Moscow and St. Petersburg offices will inform Adoption Over-Seas. They will hire a lawyer who will take responsibility for everything. They will appeal for you in Moscow."

"Ludmilla, who will pay for this?" I asked.

"I don't know."

Boris, Tamara and the children had a five-hour drive back to their orphanage. It was getting late and the roads were slippery. We all put our coats on. Kristina was sobbing so hard I held her for a few more minutes. When we separated, I gave her two motion sickness bracelets for Anton, one for each wrist, and I gave Anton half of a motion sickness pill. I gave Boris the gifts to bring to the children and to the caregivers of his orphanage. I handed a bag of food to Kristina.

I followed the group out of the hotel. The children sat in the back of the car. Kristina was still crying. It was an excruciating moment, a moment of unbearable sadness. It could not be! This could not be happening! I came to Russia filled with love, to adopt and give two children a chance for a better life, and I'm returning home alone, empty handed. Unthinkable! The black cloud hovering over our heads persisted throughout the day. God did not come to our rescue. "Why?"

32.

Reflection

A river cuts through a rock not because
of its power, but its persistence
James N. Watkins[31]

I sat in silence in my room, numb, shattered, terrified our dream was lost. Little by little, reality slowly returned. One more time, my children were gone. This time not just a few miles away . . . . This time back in their orphanage for an undetermined period of time. A new challenge had begun.

I prayed to whomever could hear me although I felt nobody was listening.

"Someone, anyone, if you can hear me, be with us right now, surround us with your love, protect us, give each of us the strength we need to continue to fight. Replace my children's fear with hope, their despair with faith."

If you, my readers, only understood the depth of my love for my children. If you only knew how I have loved and continue to love my little girl, Kristina, and her younger brother, Anton, how I have carried both in my heart for the past ten months. At one-month shy of sixty-five years old and for the first time in my life, I felt pregnant. The love inside me was so powerful, as powerful as if my children grew in my tummy. A biological pregnancy could not have been more powerful. I came to Krasnoyarsk, Siberia, with one purpose, one purpose only, to give birth to two children via their adoption. The judge denied it, refused . . . .

Sitting alone in my room, I remembered so vividly the phone call, October 4th, that I had a court appointment and that I could expect to return home with my children approximately ten days later.

The devastating truth was that, after twenty-one days in Russia, I would be returning home childless. The project, the vision, the plans, the dreams I had for my children, all vanished. With this brutal news, the beautiful image of our life together was punctured, shred to pieces. The desire and the joy to give back, to share some of what I've received in my life, disappeared with the denial of the court. The hope for a better life I so happily offered two children was gone. My dearest Kristina and Anton were now back in their orphanage. It made me feel like a mother whose newborn baby is transferred to a neonatal intensive care unit, and the horrible fear the baby may not survive.

For my children, to survive would mean being granted their adoption and becoming Americans. To die would be the harsh, final denial of the adoption. I will fight. At this moment, the decision is in the hands of God, but where is He today? For sure, I will fight heaven and earth to deserve and to be granted the care of my children.

I had no more use here. I felt empty, tired, depleted. I needed to go home, to hug Sir John, Laura and all my friends, speak with my family. I needed to rest, regroup and figure out how to over-come this court's incomprehensible decision. My friends and family had kept me alive during this horrible journey. A part of my soul would remain in Siberia with my children. I would continue to carry them in my heart. I would continue to fight until a solution is found. For now, I had to leave Krasnoyarsk and prepare a plan of action to overcome this new challenge.

Just then, the sad, penetrating sounds of the city hall clock rang 7 p.m.

Murray called to comfort me. Our conversation ended, "All will be resolved C.C., have faith. Get some rest, we'll talk tomorrow."

I walked to the business center. Several emails had been forwarded to me.

Gen from Adoption Over-Seas wrote, *I just talked to C.C. who said she spent the worst five hours of her life in a failed attempt to adopt Kristina and Anton. She is angry and devastated. Once the children are returned to their orphanage, the reality will be overwhelmingly difficult. At the moment, we are gathering as much information as possible to determine the next option.*

C.C. said the prosecutor convinced the judge that she does not understand how C.C. could have an independent income and own property without the benefit of marriage.

Greta's husband wrote, "What an evil system and with such narrow-minded people! C.C. needs a court-signed document which explains the reason for not allowing the adoption."

Lidia from Belarus wrote, "We try to keep smiling, we are very, very sad."

Liz wrote this email to Adoption Over-Seas, *I'm writing with a heavy heart for my dear friend C.C. It's just unfathomable. Is there someone from Adoption Over-Seas with her? Is someone by her side to confide in? Is anyone helping her?*

All of us who have been through this ordeal in Russia are very sympathetic. We are all wondering how C.C. can face this alone. We can all remember the somber and the vacant stares of the officials in the courtroom and how frightening and intimidating they try to make us feel. Some action has to be taken so she doesn't give up the fight and come home alone. The lives of two innocent children are at stake here.

It's no longer a business matter but a matter of the heart. This judge has to be stopped before she destroys these children.

I'm begging you to take affirmative action and hire someone to go to her aid immediately.

Clara wrote, *I'm dumbfounded! Don't they know the streets are paved with gold here? Was the prosecutor making a personal affront?*

Can someone help? C.C. certainly has determination. Her intelligence and vibrancy should have been so apparent in the proceeding. What are the Russians thinking? She would be such a great mother for the children.

Murray wrote, *I visited with C.C. by phone this morning. I encouraged her to return home. I'm going to hire a Russian lawyer to see if he can give us some insight. Gen suggested we redo our home study, declare ourselves the children's guardian and have C.C., Valerie and I go into court together.*

Murray communicated with a lawyer named Igor. He provided a list of international agencies. He added, "These agencies are accredited by the Russian Federation Ministry of Justice to work in Russia. These agencies will follow code 126.1 of the Russian Family Code."

Back in my room, my eyes locked on a small bottle of wine sitting on top of the refrigerator. I sipped the wine slowly, thinking and reliving the agonizing five hours in the courtroom followed by the heartbreaking departure of my children. The court did not believe anything I said, nor the documents I produced. My health, what I owned, what I'd worked for, what I invested in was not accepted by the court. For this judge and this prosecutor, it was inconceivable that a single woman could accomplish so much. I shouted, "Here in America, Madame Prosecutor, anyone, man or women, determined and hardworking can achieve the American Dream."

I wiped away my tears, blew my nose, had another sip of wine, and then shouted, "Your ignorance of financial statements and your ignorance of the American way of life should not punish innocent children!"

I wanted to send them straight to hell, but what was the point? I was not even sure where hell was . . . . No one could hear me . . . unless THE SYSTEM had planted a camera or microphone in my room to spy on me.

I remembered so vividly the profound words spoken just a few days before, by the assistant director at my children's transitional orphanage.

"We appreciate the Canadians, the Americans and the Europeans who adopt the children our government cannot take care of."

My children had received very little since birth. They were older, twelve-and-one-half and nine. Why deny them because of my age. I'd be sixty-five the next month. I was a healthy and fit sixty-five-year-old woman. I looked like a Russian woman of forty. My mom would be ninety this week. She still tilled the soil in her garden. I brought pictures of my family, pictures of mom sitting in the pool in Naples at eighty-nine. I gave the court a copy of the U.S. statistics for woman's life expectancy starting at sixty-five-years old and, starting at seventy. My life expectancy was in the nineties!

Spiritually, this denial was creating conflicts in my mind. Had God abandoned me? Had there ever been a God overlooking the adoption. I had been so convinced that Kristina and Anton would be part of my life's journey.

When I traveled to Krasnoyarsk, it seemed that the universe, God, and my angels did not travel with me. Instead of all the positive intuitions I had previously felt, there was silence. A thick, dark and evil cloud hovered over my head. Why was I, so positively guided up to this point and, once in Krasnoyarsk, ready to fulfill my mission, abandoned? Why? What am I to think? What am I supposed to do? Were my children and I chosen to be the catalysts that would cause changes in the Russian adoption process? One thing for sure, my children would reach America, if my life depended on it.

Thursday, I met with Tasha and Ludmilla. We wrote a letter to the chief justice. We asked for his help, and we informed him I planned to go to the Supreme Court of the Russia Federation in Moscow to plead for a reversal of this denial. The letter added I would also lodge a complaint with the European Children's Rights Organization, although I was not quite sure what this organization did or if they even did anything.

Tasha and Ludmilla presented me with an invoice. I always thought, "When one pays for something, one gets something in return." Thirty-five thousand dollars later, I had nothing to show for it. I was going home alone. Think about that for a moment.

33.

Flight to Moscow

Be fearless in the pursuit of what sets your soul on fire.
Jennifer Lee[32]

I woke up thinking about my mom. It was her ninetieth birthday. When she found out the news, she would feel the sadness in my heart. I boarded the van for the ride to the airport. The sky had its dull color with many gray clouds floating above us. Ludmilla sat next to the driver. Tasha sat next to me in the back seat. Tasha and Ludmilla were silent. They looked defeated. *We definitely lost that battle but, God willing, we will win the war. These children will live in America if my name is C.C. LeBlanc.* Looking out the window, I remembered so vividly, the joy I felt landing in Krasnoyarsk eighteen days earlier. The mission failed. I was going home alone.

I thanked Tasha and Ludmilla. We hugged, holding back tears. Choking I was able to say, "I'm not letting go. I'll be back."

"C.C., have faith, it will happen," Tasha answered.

In the terminal, I sat lifeless waiting for departure. A few happy parents were seated nearby, entertaining their newly adopted children. I ached with envy.

"God, why were my children denied? What have *they* done?"

I took my assigned aisle seat in the emergency exit row. A very tall man walked down with his head bowed to avoid touching the ceiling. He sat behind me. His legs were so long they were cramped in a right angle with his knees pushing on the back of my seat. When he extended his right leg in the aisle to get relief, his colossal foot reached two-feet in front of my seat . . . sort of comical. I felt miserable and hated all Russians this morning . . . but seeing his foot, sensing his discomfort, my heart softened. This man did not need to pay the price for my suffering. I offered this giant my seat. Looking pleasantly surprised, he twisted himself out of his seat, smiled as he said, "*Spaciba*."

After a four-hour flight and a four-hour time zone difference, we landed at the Sheremetyevo International Airport. Max, the translator for Adoption Over-Seas gave me a hug.

"I'm sorry, C.C."

"So am I."

We kept silent until we reached the main highway. For the following two hours, Max entertained me with the history, the culture and the political atmosphere of the moment. He pointed to the various buildings and parks along the way. When I asked what changes he would like to see in Russia in the next several years, he answered with frustration in his voice, "My mother works as a cardiologist in a military clinic. I would like her monthly $100 U.S. salary to be increased to meet the standard of other professions."

We arrived at the Marriott Tverskaya. I checked in. An hour later, Pyotr, from Adoption Over-Seas Moscow office, came to my room. We worked on a letter directed to the chief justice in Krasnoyarsk, asking for a reversal of the court's decision.

As we finalized the appeal letter, Pyotr explained, "C.C., the judge will issue a report on Monday, November 1st, to disclose the reasons for the denial. Only then can we begin to respond. When Ludmilla receives the court documents, she will fax them to Adoption Over-Seas in Texas. You will have ten days to respond."

He added, "According to Russian laws, a denied case such as yours, cannot be reopened, unless it is in the best interest of all.

If the judge refuses to reopen it, the appeal process will begin."
Pyotr left.

After a short rest, I went down to the lobby to explore the hotel and find a restaurant. While in Siberia, the only English conversations I had had were with Olea, the receptionist, and Tasha, my translator. I was starving to speak English with anyone who would speak with me. Waiting in line for the concierge, I asked a slender, tall, blond, blue-eyed, Scandinavian-looking man standing behind me, "I'm curious Sir, what brings you to Moscow?" He smiled.

"I'm from Sweden. My company has business interests in the pulp and paper industry."

I told him that my dad and two brothers had made their living in that industry in Québec. I was also reminded of a few friends in Naples who became involved with a pulp and paper company in Russia and lost their investment.

I spoke to a few couples from Canada and the United States who had just arrived in Moscow for the adoption of their children. I wished them well without revealing my own heartbreaking denial by the judge.

Looking around, I saw a small coffee/bar restaurant with a large opening to the lobby. I walked in. Only two small tables were available. Being alone, I chose to be the only woman to sit at the bar. At almost age sixty-five, I didn't think anyone would eye me for a quick roll in the hay. The three men sitting to my left were laughing, drinking, joking and yes, they spoke English. I asked the man sitting next to me, "What brings you to Russia?"

"Oh! The three of us work on a pipeline way up in the Arctic. I'm from Canada, the guy next to me is from Scotland, the other guy lives in Atlanta."

"How interesting! I've never met anyone in your type of work. Can you tell me more about it?"

"Well . . . the job is very tough. We work in constant glacial temperatures. Our schedule is one month on and one month off. The company flies us home and back every month. The three of us are on our way home now.

"They must pay you a good penny to work in this frigid climate?"

"Yep! They sure do."

I smiled, "If you continue to work there for some time and save your money, in just a few years, you'll be able to buy yourself a castle anywhere in the world."

"It doesn't work quite like that ma'am. I'm not saving much money."

"How so? Where could you possibly be spending money there? Are there any big stores, casinos . . . or . . . ?"

"You see, ma'am, when we arrive in town, we have to pay the mayor for protection. Then . . . well . . . I don't know how to say this . . . (he hesitated) but there's the girls . . . ."

"The girls? What do you mean the girls?"

"Well . . . how to say . . . well, ma'am . . . it's a little embarrassing . . . uh . . . I can't tell you how many virgins I've had since I've worked there. I don't have enough fingers to count them."

I felt sick.

"Virgins? How do they get there?"

"Well, ma'am . . . the mafia . . . these girls . . . well . . . they're brought here for the guys you know . . . but you gotta pay . . . ."

I couldn't listen anymore. I stopped eating. I asked for the check, signed it and left. Now, I understood why some politicians on the English Krasnoyarsk TV channel asked to take those billboards down. The billboards invited young girls to interview for a well-paying job abroad. Naive young woman, or orphan girls fresh out of an orphanage, with no family to go to, could end up in the claws of this mafia. These young girls, flown to the frigid Arctic, were used as sex slaves to . . . dare I say . . . to . . . to never be seen again. Yes, once taken, they would never be seen again. All the more my determination to bring my beautiful Kristina home to America.

Once I was tucked in for the night, sleep was interrupted with tossing and turning and with one nightmare after another. Scenes of my children being mistreated invaded my mind. I got up, searched for my video camera, turned it on and registered my thoughts.

My dearest children, it's now 2:30 a.m. I'm awake. There's a big lump in my heart. While in Krasnoyarsk, I felt the forces of evil. I felt the despair, the lifelessness, the fear of so many people. I felt their souls were in limbo. I felt death was their only hope to escape the misery of their life. So many people just exist there. There is so much poverty, so much uncertainty and so little hope. Few people, with good professions can prosper . . . by toeing the line of the hard-core government rules. But the masses, God help them!

My children, the judge and the prosecutor knew the status of your parents. They knew of your aunts and uncles who were still alive but did not have the means to care for you. They knew that some children visited their families or went to summer camps. They knew Anton only left the orphanage a few times to play with the son of one of his teachers, and you Kristina, you left the orphanage only once to attend your dad's funeral in 2002. Why this court denied both of you the chance to have a better life in the United States is incomprehensible. There must be a lesson to be learned from this denial. Something of value must come from all this pain. Perhaps the challenges you are facing will fine-tune your characters and make you stronger. Perhaps these struggles will encourage both of you to be better American citizens. Just know my children, I miss you and I love you. I will continue to fight. I will be back.

Recording this conversation for my children calmed me. It allowed me to have a peaceful sleep for a few hours.

Saturday mid-morning, video camera in hand, I walked the approximately two miles to Red Square. I appreciated the mid-rise buildings in lieu of skyscrapers. The wide-open streets, the clear view of the sky gave one a refreshing sense of openness rarely encountered in big cities.

I walked slowly. I stopped to film and to observe people walking by. I became fascinated with the policemen on the street. They were planted approximately twenty yards apart, stopping car after car. As each car stopped, the driver's window came down. Words were exchanged. Papers were presented to the policemen. The policemen looked at them. The papers were either returned or the papers were exchanged for cash. Then, the driver was waved to go ahead. This scenario was non-stop all the way to Red Square.

Even though it was a cold gray day, Red Square was a pleasure for the eyes. The architecture was breath taking. There were many groups of different cultures and languages accompanied by tour guides. As often as I could, I stood near English or French speaking groups to absorb the information given. I learned and later read that Red Square is perhaps one of the most known landmarks in Russia. In the late 15th century, Prince Ivan III, known as Ivan the Great, wanted to expand the Kremlin fortress to accommodate Moscow's growing power. The State Historical Museum, the mausoleum with Vladimir Lenin's remains, the enormous and famous GUM Department store were all on Red Square. Saint Basil's church with its many domes, towers, cupolas, spires and arches, is one of the most recognizable buildings in Russia. All are part of Red Square where, during the 20th century, large-scale military parades and other demonstrations took place to showcase Soviet strength.

I also found out that UNESCO designated Red Square as one of its World Heritage sites. The enormous GUM Department Store, a symbol of the Soviet era, covers the square's entire eastern end. It is now known as a high-end shopping destination. At the northern end, the red brick State Historical Museum (built in 1873-75) is filled with art and displays of Russian history. And while fewer people visit Lenin's tomb than in the Soviet era, crowds continue to amass to Red Square for rock concerts, festivals and other events.

The sun was going down, it was getting colder. I took a bus back to the hotel. I tendered a bunch of rubbles to the driver. He took what was needed, dropped it in the fare box. To make sure I got off at the right stop, I repeated the words Marriott Hotel to people around me. A woman kindly pointed it out when we arrived at its bus stop.

34.

Unusual Encounter

Honesty is a very expensive gift.
Don't expect it from cheap people.
Warren Buffett[33]

IN THE SUMMER OF 2004, I attended a pool party at Valerie and Murray Wise's home reuniting the adopted Russian children of Southwest Florida. There, I met Derick, the Eurasia CEO for Hope for World's Children. Derick explained that part of his nonprofit organization's mission is to help with difficult adoptions. He gave me his card and offered that I call him if needed. Today, while in Moscow and faced with the adoption denial, I sent him an email. He replied that he was in Moscow visiting with Vladimir, the responsible person for their Moscow office. They would both be happy to meet with me.

I invited Derick and Vladimir to join me for brunch on Sunday morning at the Marriott Hotel.

After sharing my experience with the Krasnoyarsk court, they were teary-eyed.

"This story is horrible, C.C.," Derick said.

"Perhaps if Ludmilla could ask the judge to have coffee or lunch outside the courtroom, she could ask what went wrong with your case, what killed it," added Vladimir.

Derick continued, "Everything in Russia works with bribes. Try to find out if the court would accept you giving a contribution to a charitable organization, or if you could offer to bring them to Florida to see where you live . . . Ludmilla may find a round-about way to get them to say yes."

Derick gave me the name of a children's rights agency in Atlanta run by Russians.

I asked, "Derick, you are an adviser to the United Nations, could you ask for their help on our behalf?"

He responded quickly, "The United Nations is good for nothing. Can't expect anything from an organization which does nothing. The UN is corrupt."

We ended our visit with their promise to look for an international lawyer.

My intuition told me to expect nothing from these two men. I believe some non-profit organizations are created for self-enrichment using other people's money. In this case, Derick and his wife spent much of their time traveling between Jamaica, the US, Europe and Russia. It would be interesting to know how many children were helped as a result of their interventions. I did not expect to hear from them again.

My mind continued to do some creative thinking.

There was more than one way to skin a cat. I needed to find the right one. If for some reason I did not succeed, Murray and Valerie suggested they could adopt my children and once in America, the adoption could be reassigned to me. That, of course, would be as a last resort.

I'll have to keep fighting. I've been a fighter all my life, either fighting for someone or for a cause. If one wants to accomplish something, one has to work hard and replace the negative or defeatist thoughts with positive ones until success is reached . . . NNNQ.

I emailed my Belarus friend in Naples.

"Lidia could you email and ask Ludmilla in Krasnoyarsk to ask if offering a donation to a charitable organization or to an orphanage would help?"

Lidia replied to my email immediately.

"C.C., I think the judge and the prosecutor wanted to milk a rich America lady."

The next day, Lidia emailed me Ludmilla's opinion.

"It's a very slippery slope. I do not advise C.C. to go forward with an offer. If the judge decided not to grant her the children, a bribe could or would forever deny her the adoption."

October 31, 2004, I went to bed about 9 p.m. It was now 4:30 a.m., Moscow time. I had been awake for some time. There was a lump in my throat, a lump that wouldn't go away. I was thinking about Krasnoyarsk. In that city and for the first time, as unimaginable as it was, I repeat again, *I felt the forces of evil.* As I tried to sleep, I visualized my children and cried. I wondered what they were thinking, what were their hopes. Did they have any hopes? What would happen to them from now until I would be able to bring them home? *I know there are many more children in the same condition. I wish I could help them all. I'm only able to care for two, perhaps three.*

The judge and the prosecutor drilled me on why I would want to be a mother at my age. First, because of my age, I was adopting older children who were at the age limit to be adoptable. I gave the court statistics on life expectancy in the United States to back up my case. If I live another eighteen to twenty years, Kristina would be between thirty-one and thirty-three and Anton would be between twenty-seven and twenty-nine. I explained to the court that I had the financial means to support my children and to lead them to a successful life. I failed to impress them. These judges just did not have a clue about what life is like in Canada or in the U.S.

I spent the afternoon writing a letter to the chief justice. Early Monday morning, on my way to the airport, I would have the letter notarized. It would then be sent to Ludmilla who had my power of attorney and was, therefore, able to represent me. With the help of Pyotr, the letter was written in such a way that we hoped the chief justice would consider reopening our case.

Otherwise we would present our case to the Supreme Court of the Russian Federation.

The silence as we drove to the airport reflected the disappointment we both felt. Everyone involved with this adoption, outside of the court, felt a complete letdown. There was nothing to say nor add. The confirmed fact was that the adoption was denied. I was going home alone. Will my children and I ever be together again? What a terrible thought!

My assigned seat was on the right aisle bulkhead seat of the middle part of a Boing 747. My traveling companions were a young Russian couple.

I asked, "What is the purpose of your trip to America." With a big smile and a heavy accent, he replied, "We very lucky. Russian friend got electrical job me in Colorado."

The young woman asked, "You come Russia adopt children?"

I shared my story.

She said, "We from Krasnoyarsk. What name judge and name prosecutor?"

When she heard the name of the prosecutor, Krasnopeeva Oksana V., she raised her eyebrows.

"She high society. She witch!"

"Why would you say that?"

"I go school Oksana. Father important lawyer. Now chief justice. Power of dad go Oksana head. Oksana think she better than us. She tell us, 'I do what I want. Dad protect me.' "

She continued, "We all scared she report bad thing we say. When finish high school, Oksana go law school. Now, she prosecutor. Dad protect her. Many lawyer nervous when work with Oksana."

She gave me the name of the dean of the university and the name of a lawyer. She said I should not bribe directly but I could go on an around about way by offering a trip to Florida to the chief justice and his daughter or to the judge. She suggested that I could try to work through the Rotary Club or the Kiwanis Club in Krasnoyarsk, or with organizations that help children's causes.

These organizations could lodge a complaint or appeal to the Supreme Court of the Russian Federation."

I added, "Or can I appeal to Putin directly?" She smiled.

After our conversation, I decided to walk in the aisles to speak with some happy parents and some hopeful ones who were on the plane. One couple shared, "After several attempts to adopt, we were denied our child for no comprehensible reason. We pursued, only to find out the child was taken off the adoptable list because his eighty-two-year-old grandfather had visited him in the orphanage six months before."

A man by the name of Mark gave me the telephone number of a man in New Jersey named Herb. This is what Herb shared when I later called him.

"I hired a lawyer, Irina, from St Petersburg. She said our case was denied on suspicion of seven points. It appears the Regional Court had anti-American sentiments. Nothing negative was found in our home study. The judge assigned to our case reported terrible contortions of the facts. She questioned our medical reports. That judge even questioned the validity of our apostilled documents."

He continued, "The U.S. Embassy wrote to the Supreme Court of the Russian Federation to report that the Regional Court was in violation of the Hague Agreement, whereby apostille documents were to be mutually recognized. Lawyer Irena's appeal was successful in the granting of our adoption. Friends, who were also denied, hired lawyers who were able to reverse the judgment of denial. Your chances are good. Have faith."

I returned to my seat reassured. I thought, "Does it make any sense to think that something good will come from all this pain, all these tears? There must be something to learn from all of this turmoil, but what? Perhaps something of value that we do not know now. What I'm left with is hope, hope that someday my children will be granted the privilege of living in a free country, the United States of America."

I wrapped myself in the airline blanket and fell asleep. A mixture of emotions pursued me as we landed at Kennedy Airport.

There was no time to be emotional or pensive. I collected my bags, went through customs, then on to catch a flight to Atlanta. After a long wait, I boarded my connecting flight to South West Florida International Airport. The flight landed in Fort Myers at 1:00 a.m. When, finally, the passengers were allowed to disembark, I felt very tired and depleted. My heart was aching. My children were missing. I felt like a drunk person without direction.

35.

Going Home Alone

There are times when the adoption process
is exhausting and painful and makes you want to scream.
But I am told, so does childbirth.
Scott Simon[34]

As I exited the airport security zone, Lidia from Belarus, Fran and Greta were there to greet me. Overwhelmed by their presence, I totally broke down and started sobbing. All three rushed toward me. We exchanged a bear hug. Greta took my carry-on bag. Lidia and Fran supported me on each side, guiding me to the escalator, then to baggage claim.

Greta said, "I'll quickly get the car. I'll pick you up at the curb."

On the way home, I couldn't talk. I sobbed all the tears left in my body. My friends cried with me. Forty minutes later, we arrived at my new home in Stonebridge. Earlier, my wonderful friend Sir John had filled the refrigerator. Lidia made coffee for us. We sat in the living room. I shared my stories. They listened. I kept crying, blowing my nose. Lidia, Fran and Greta could not help but cry with me like people do at a sad movie. Through tears, we laughed when I retold the story of how the TV received a shot of chicken bouillon and died, and when I told them how, on a Friday night, I lost the crown of my eyetooth, only to find it in my sandwich. All that, alone, in the middle of

Siberia. They could now feel all the emotions and the desperate moments they had read about in my emails during the last twenty-plus days. Around 4:00 a.m., all our tears spent, Lidia and Fran left. They were working in the morning. Greta stayed with me the rest of the night. She slept in what would have been Kristina's bedroom.

Returning home and being greeted by dear friends was the best gift I could have received. In the sad state of mind that I was in, it was a most touching gesture. I did not expect anyone as it was so late. But there they were. It melted my heart. Thank you.

It was wonderful to wake up in my own bed, with my own pillows, and in my own home. I opened the sliding doors to walk onto the lanai (pool deck). Inhaling the smells of Florida, hearing the birds chirp was wonderful. But I felt a mixture of joy and sadness. I pretended my children were with me, still sleeping in their bedrooms. Pretending is not truthful. I knew the truth. They were far, far away, perhaps sad, without hope, crying in their orphanage.

Sir John and Laura arrived with muffins and coffee. We talked. We cried. John repeated his slogan.

"NNNQ. Never, never, never quit, C.C. With perseverance and determination, you will succeed. I know you."

In the next several days, through many phone calls, visits, lunches and dinners, no one allowed me to lose hope. My friends did much to keep my spirits high. Their support was immeasurably heartwarming, with one exception. A distant acquaintance had asked, "Why do you keep chasing these children, C.C.? Why do you continue to hurt yourself? The judge said no. The answer is no. Leave them in Russia; you don't even know these children."

"Obviously, Clara, you don't understand the love I feel for my children. If you had a biological child born with a critical health problem, would you abandoned him in the hospital and move on with your life, or would you do everything in your power to save your baby's life? My children, Clara, went back to their orphanage. Figuratively speaking, my dear, their orphanage represents a neonatal intensive care unit. I will continue to chase them until I'm no longer part of this planet."

Clara was speechless.

"Clara, for anyone who questions if adoptive parents are able to love their adopted children as much as their biological ones, here's what I have to offer: An adopted child is not an accident that happened from copulating with a husband or a boyfriend, nor is an adopted child an accident that happened while enjoying unprotected sex at a drinking party. An adopted child is one you choose to have. Repeat, an adopted child is one you *choose* to have and take care of. Clara, as soon as I made the decision to adopt Kristina and Anton, they entered my heart, where an overabundance of love was waiting. Clara, do you have any conception how powerful that love is? For me, the love I feel for my children is indestructible, even more so after we experienced the despair of the judge's decision just a few weeks ago. End of conversation!

"To this day, I still remember what I lived through in Krasnoyarsk. There were many sweet, loving people there, but many were very rude, especially the men. My sense or my impression is that a large percentage of Russian adults live their lives in extreme frustration, despair, and fear of the unknown. They have no power, no hope, no reason to believe that someday their lives will be improved. If a Russian citizen is not part of the elite, the mafia, the police, or has a successful business, there is no reason to believe there will be a rainbow at the end of the dark tunnel they live in. Perhaps it is more so in Siberia. I have seen the desperation in their faces. In my observation, I find Russian society to be a very obedient society. There seems to be a sense of uneasiness when they have to venture out to make a decision. I did catch a glimpse of hope for Russian society when I spoke with a few young students who displayed a more positive outlook for their future."

When I was again in Russia, in 2005, the Krasnoyarsk TV news showed the following comments by a Russian politician: "We are losing our youth by allowing so many adoptions abroad.

We must encourage Russian families to adopt our children and stop their adoption by foreign lands."

2005 statistics stated that if nothing changed by the year 2050, the population of Russia would be reduced by half. Russians are having few babies, one, two, or none at all. Abortions are free, but I was told one must pay for condoms. Many babies and young children were adopted by foreigners. Russian families are now encouraged to adopt the children of their orphanages. As of this writing, Italy is the only country in the Western world allowed to adopt Russian children. We can remember the feud between President Obama and President Putin. Putin vowed not to allow any more Russian children to be adopted in the United States. On January 1, 2013, the law, No 272-FZ, was put in place banning Americans from adopting Russian children.

According to https://travel.state.gov/content/adoptionsabroad/en/about-us/statistics.html, the number of Russian children adopted by U.S. citizens have dropped:

2004: 5,862

2005: 4,631

2006: 2,303

2007: 1,857

2008: 1586

2009: 1079

2010: 962.

2011: 749

2012: 250

2013: 2

2014: 0

2015: 0

36

Moscow Lawyer, NUCC

Patience, persistence and perspiration
make an unbeatable combination for success.
Napoleon Hill[35]

AN EMAIL FROM PYOTR in Moscow stated that he had found an attorney, Irina B., who agreed to take on our case. Her fee to prepare the appeal was between $200 and $300. To present our case to the Supreme Court of the Russian Federation would add an additional $500 to $700. However, if she won the case, her fee would rise from $500 to $1,000.

A few hours later, a second, contradictory, email from Pyotr arrived. Note the difference in fees.

I found a lawyer with work experience with the Supreme Court of the Russian Federation, and with adoption cases. Her name is Irina B. We do not have much time. Monday is a holiday. Irina can start preparing the appeal as soon as confirmation is received that Miss LeBlanc agrees to her fees of $200 to $300 to prepare the appeal and $3,000 to present the case to the court. I will assist her to be sure all points are covered.

A request was made to the Krasnoyarsk Court to submit their October 27th denial decision. When received, Irina will file an appeal to the Supreme Court of the Russian Federation in Moscow on C.C.'s behalf. If the Krasnoyarsk court refuses our request, Irina will file an appeal to order them to release their documents.

Miss LeBlanc must obtain an additional letter from her CPA describing her financial qualifications. She must ask her real estate agent to confirm her condo can be sold for the amount she quoted in her financial report. These two letters will help prove her financial stability.

As requested, I gathered the necessary documents. Yes, the *Purchase and Sales Agreement* for the Pelican Bay condo would be acceptable. I obtained a copy of the deed of our new home in Stonebridge and a copy of my portfolio statement. I hated sharing this private information with so many people. My financial assets were being divulged to whomever wanted to intrude.

I signed a power of attorney, addressed to the Judicial Division of Civil Cases of the Supreme Court of the Russian Federation, allowing Irina to plead on my behalf. It took some time, but in the end the Krasnoyarsk documents were transferred to the lawyer.

Irina would plead that every document was properly filed, that nothing illegal was found, and that Miss LeBlanc had followed all the rules. Irina hoped that the Supreme Court of the Russian Federation would agree to hear my case. They could decide 1) to rule to reverse the lower court's decision and grant me the adoption, or 2) to transfer the case back to the Krasnoyarsk Court for a rehearing.

The anxiety of not knowing was mounting. Adoption Over-Seas became difficult to work with. Gen often did not take my calls. She and/or her staff would not call back when promised. It was most frustrating. Their interest in my adoption had taken a third or fourth priority. They had received the full payment. The incentive to work hard on our behalf no longer had money value, yet my children were still in Russia, waiting in their orphanage.

Some days, no one was in the office except Ted who only took care of finances. I was told excuses like, "Gen was closing on a mortgage," or "Gen was driving the children to school." "Louisa was at the doctor." "Neta just moved to her new home." "Suzie took her dog to the vet."

I would scream, "Ted, my children are waiting in a Siberian orphanage, I need answers."

As frustrating as it was, optimistic thoughts greeted me every morning. The adoption had to be granted. To adopt two children was a good thing. I was still convinced it couldn't fail. Someday soon we would overcome all these difficulties.

On November 10, 2004, the Naples United Church of Christ hosted a dinner in honor of veterans here and gone. Sir John and his wife Laura, strong supporters of this church, suggested I be invited to speak on becoming a U.S. citizen. The LeBlanc name was known in this church since Sir John had asked that Kristina, Anton and I be placed on the prayer list shortly after I arrived in Krasnoyarsk.

I dressed in a dark suit wrapped in a patriotic large blue shawl adorned with butterflies in the colors of the American flag. After recognizing Reverend Patterson and the other officials, I shared the beautiful story of how, on June 10, 2004, I was sworn in as a United States citizen in a private ceremony in Miami. I related how it only took me ten months to become an American Citizen as oppose to the New York Time's advertised twenty-three months for green card holders. This was the first miracle in my quest to adopt two children. Becoming a citizen opened the door to reach the second miracle which will be when my children and I come home as a family.

"As many of you know, after I spent a total of twenty-one days of incredible mental and emotional torture, the petition to adopt my children was denied in the Krasnoyarsk Courts in Siberia. Even with your many prayers, the forces of evil won this battle. But we, all of us as a team, will win the war. Once we defeat evil, the second miracle will occur. I will fight this cause if it takes me a lifetime. Please continue to pray for us until we reach the soil of freedom in these beautiful United States of America."

I continued, "In this room, there is a gentleman I refer to as Sir John. During the agonizing days of the month of October, this man's love, friendship, loyalty and unrelenting support was the lifeline that kept me sane when despair came, that gave me hope when hope was gone, that kept me strong when strength was depleted. Sir John, please stand. I want to share with you a conversation I had with God yesterday."

Laughter!

"First, I thanked God for granting me such a wonderful friend and I shared so many flowery comments about you, Sir John.

"In reply, God shouted, 'C.C. Stop! That's enough! I know this man better than you do. I watch what he does every single day!'

"God's screaming got my attention. I stopped talking. God asked, 'Why are you telling me all this?'

"I replied, 'Because I want your permission to promote my exceptional friend to sainthood.'

"God answered, 'The goodness and the qualities of John Percy Carey Woodhams from Naples, Florida cannot be denied. You have my permission.'

"Sir John, as decreed by God Almighty, I have been given the power to promote you to sainthood. From this day on, you will be known as, *Saint John of Naples.*"

Everyone laughed and clapped.

In late November, Sir, now Saint, John and Laura extended an invitation for me to join them for dinner at their Bay Colony Club to celebrate my sixty-fifth birthday. Not knowing what to wear, I wore an old leopard dress that had made a former boyfriend's heart flutter. For sure, a male leopard could have thought I was for the taking. The sole purpose of wearing this dress was to ask Laura if I should give it to charity . . . .

Laura and John greeted me warmly at the entrance to the club. We chit-chatted as we walked toward the private room at the end of the spacious clubhouse. Two waiters in tuxedos opened the double doors to the private dining room. I was overwhelmed at the sight of approximately twenty-five friends singing "Happy Birthday Dear C.C...." I wanted to find myself six feet under ground or to run home to change out of the embarrassing leopard dress into something more elegant. Red as a beet,

I accepted the good wishes, the hugs and a glass of champagne offered by the waiter. When it became quiet, I was informed that John and Laura and Dr. Renate and Naren Chevli had join forces to secretly prepare this wonderful *fête*. I thanked them profusely and thanked everyone for their presence. I explained my shock at seeing their beautiful faces and I explained the reason why I looked like an African leopardess. Everyone laughed. It was a stunning surprise. The joke was on me . . . . Before dessert was served, "the roasting" started with Sir John, then Naren. I was lovingly teased and made fun of, with, I must admit, some embarrassing stories I had forgotten. More than a few times, my face turned red like a boiled lobster. As for the leopard dress, I did not wait for Laura's comment. I gave it to a charity the very next day. I promised myself I will never look like a leopardess in heat ever again.

Life continued without my children who were nonetheless always present, always in my heart.

37.

The Year End, 2004

Il faut rire tout haut pour ne pas s'entendre pleurer tout bas.
We must laugh out loud not to hear ourselves cry inside.
My mom, Aline Laurin LeBlanc

CHRISTMAS SPIRIT WAS IN the air. Days went by spent with friends in various festivities. On November 27, Stonebridge Golf and Country Club, where we will live as a family, hosted the lighting of their Christmas tree. It would have been Kristina and Anton's first American Christmas experience. I missed them. I invited Sir John and Laura, and several other friends to join me. Then there was the Galiana's phenomenal Christmas party. A few days later, a ride on the Christmas Trolley with my friends, the Hopkins, took us all over town. Christmas Eve was at Greta's. Christmas day dinner was at Margie's. Then, cocktails and dinner were with the Gaudreaults. The Year 2005 would start with a New Year's open house I hosted at our new Stonebridge home.

The sadness I felt had to be balanced with moments of joy shared with friends. I joined in as many activities as I could. These distractions were helpful until the sadness returned when I found myself home alone in a big house purchased specifically to create a safe home for my children.

A most welcome Christmas gift arrived on December 23 from Adoption Over-Seas. The Supreme Court of the Russian Federation in Moscow agreed to hear our case on January 18, 2005. I immediately asked if I could attend. Irina, the Moscow lawyer, wrote the following response to Adoption Over-Seas.

If C.C. is part of the hearings, the judges may ask her questions. Her answers may vary from what has been presented in the documents, or the translation of her statements may be flawed. If there are any discrepancies, I would not be able to help her. It took two weeks for the Krasnoyarsk court to forward her file to Moscow. It will take at least another two weeks for the Supreme Court to return it to Krasnoyarsk. C.C. could end up spending three to five weeks in Russia. It would be best if she would send me a power of attorney to represent her.

I immediately wrote a power of attorney for Irina and a letter to thank her for agreeing to represent us. I suggested she communicate with my friend Polina M. with whom she already had several conversations.

Polina is from Moscow, now living in Naples. I met her, her husband and their little boy at the Naples United Church of Christ. She is a trustworthy intermediary.

Irina, if my age is a concern, my family enjoys longevity. I'm number two of seven children, all living and healthy. My dad died at eighty-two. My mom is a strong ninety and she still takes the bus alone to visit her sister in Montreal, 350 miles away.

In Naples, the children will be surrounded by surrogate aunts and uncles. Several families with adopted Russian children maintain contact with each other. Polina from Moscow, and Lidia from Belarus, are on standby to help the children with translation.

The Krasnoyarsk court questioned the value of my home. I'm including the most recent data of real estate sales in the last several months. In my community, ninety-two sales closed at an average sale price $897,000.

If clarification is needed regarding my sexual preference, I did not marry by choice. I am heterosexual. I was devoted to my family and to my demanding career. I said no to marriage several times. Kristina and Anton will have my complete attention once we form a family.

Irina, I've already contacted a pediatrician, a dentist and a tutor. I've purchased children's books and videos. Our neighbors are ready to embrace Kristina and Anton.

My children have a younger brother named Sasha. They haven't seen him since mid-2000. They don't know where he is. If that becomes an issue, I will adopt him too.

I'm confident you will succeed in convincing the court that I have provided the correct information and that I am fully qualified under the Russian Laws to adopt and give Kristina and Anton a chance for a better life.

I couldn't wait to share the good news with my children. I wrote a letter to inform them a lawyer would present our case at the Supreme Court of the Russian Federation in Moscow. "You are in my heart every day, every hour, every minute. I will never abandon you." I told them their bedrooms were ready, their teachers were looking forward to introducing them to their classmates. "Do not give up hope my dearest children. I will write again as soon as there is more news to share. I love you, Mama C.C."

On December 30th, the thoughts of my children were intense and constant. The sheer distance . . . on the other side of the planet . . . close to Mongolia . . . seemed so unreachable. Our new home was silent except for the murmur of the refrigerator, the tweeting of a bird or the sound of a golf ball hitting the center of a Big Bertha. I relied on prayers and on God for strength. That very day, at that very moment, I felt an overwhelmingly strong presence of Kristina and Anton. I sat at my desk, took up a pen and I started writing these words as they flowed out of my heart.

They say we must pray
But . . . what are prayers?
Pray? Pray to whom?
To a God we've never seen?
To angels with wings?
To loved ones now gone?

Someone please tell me,
Do they hear our words?
Can they share our joys?
Do they feel our pain?
Can they heal our soul?
Is there anyone out there?

Are prayers desperate words we write?
Are they words we speak to ourselves?
Words that reach deep into our heart
To mesh with the despair of our soul?
Are they the final cries we release out there,
Somewhere in the Infinite? But where?

Do prayers truly bounce here and there
In this silent and cold universe?
Do they stop anywhere?
Where God is?
Where angels live?
Where loved ones' eternal rest is?

Today, I pray only for my children.
I'm reaching out to you, you and you.
Can you hear me? Can anyone hear me?
Someone give me a sign. Hear this prayer.
Can you feel my children's fears?
Can you comfort them, dry their tears?

I ask you . . . anyone one of you . . .
Fill my children with your magical love.
Surround them with your miraculous power.
Erase the damage done to their soul.
I beg of you, help me bring them home
To the Land of the Free, yes, the Land of the Free.
Amen.

—C.C. LeBlanc. 12-30-2004

38.

The Appeal

*It's always something to know you've done
the most you could. But don't leave off hoping, or it's of
no use doing anything. Hope, hope to the last.*
Charles Dickens[36]

ON JANUARY 18, 2005, my attorney, Irina, filed the follow-ing appeal with the Supreme Court of the Russian Federation in Moscow. Because all my documents had been filed under the address of my previous condominium, the lawyer recom-mended proceeding with the appeal using that address.

LeBlanc Marie Cécile
6001 Pelican Bay Blvd, # 1602
Naples, FL 34108
APPEAL
Against the Krasnoyarsk Regional Court Decision dated October 27, 2004.
I have been denied the petition to finalize the adoption of minors Bajenova, Kristina S. and Bajevov, Anton S. by decision of the Krasnoyarsk Regional Court issued October 27, 2004.
I ask that the Decision be recalled due to the incorrect Court under-standing of my documents.

The court has found that the minors Kristina Bajenova, born in 1992, and Anton Bajenov, born in 1995, are left without parental care for various reasons, one of which is the passing of their father in 2002. As such, the children qualify as legally available for adoption in accordance with Article 124 of the Russian Federated Family Code.

Refusing to satisfy my petition to finalize the adoption, the Court has stated in its Decision that my home evaluation report, income statement and confirmation of ownership do not meet the requirements specified in Article 271 of the RF (Russian Federation) Code of Civil Procedure.

The finding of the Court does not correspond to the materials presented for the case. All documents specified in Article 271 of the RF Code of Civil Procedure have been presented by me.

—Medical statements (pages 80, 170 in the file);

—Financial statements (pages 59, 63, 69, 76);

—Documents confirming the ownership of my condominium (pages 34, 41, 45);

—Conclusion of the competent USA authority on my living conditions and capability to become an adoptive mother (page 20 in the file).

The above-mentioned documents have been made and executed in accordance with the requirements stipulated in Article 271, Part IV of the RF Code of Civil Procedure: The documents have been legalized, translated into the Russian language. The translation was confirmed by a notary and the documents are considered to be appropriately written evidence under Article 271 of the RF Code of Civil Procedure.

The Court has established that I own my 2,583 square feet (240 square meter) condominium on the 16th floor of the Grosvenor high rise building in Naples, Florida, USA. In addition to the living areas, the condominium includes three bedrooms and three bathrooms, as confirmed in the confidential Home Study prepared by the South Florida Adoption Services (page 20 in the file, Part: Community, Finances); letter from the Grosvenor condominium management (page 36 in the file); estimated assets value (page 45 in the file); attorney's statement (page 41 in the file).

Having properly defined the factual situation, the Court has made an inadequate conclusion, finding the ownership of my condo unconfirmed.

In this regard, the Court stated that it does not view the attorney's statement and Warranty Deed to be appropriate evidence of my ownership. However, my ownership of the condo has been confirmed by other documents investigated in the case hearing and entered into the case file, namely: Confidential home study report prepared by the South Florida Adoption Services (page 20 in file, Part: Community, Finances); Letter from the Condominium Grosvenor management (page 36); estimated assets value (page 45). The above said papers have been documented in full compliance with the requirements specified in the Article 271, part IV of the RF Code of Civil Procedure and, therefore, are the appropriate evidence as required by Article 59, 60,71, of the RF Code of Civil Procedure.

Additionally, I consider the Court's dismissal of the Warranty Deed, dated September 1999, in evidence of my title for the above described condominium to be unfounded.

As stated in the Deed issued on September 29, 1999, I bought the above described condominium from Herbert H., joined by his wife Mathilde.

Under U.S. federal law, the said Deed is a document that acknowledges the acquisition of the right for the property which comes into force from the moment of state registration made in the official records of Collier county, Florida, USA on October 7, 1999, which is confirmed by the stamp on the Deed.

The estimation of the condominium value owned by the petitioner is not the subject of probation in the adoption case (Article 271 of the RF Code of Civil Procedure). Consequently, the Court's impossibility to satisfy my petition for adoption due to non-correspondence of the market value of the condominium declared by me to its purchased price value is not confirmed by law.

The Court's conclusion on my unproved financial stability does not correspond to the factual situation of the case.

The court has established that I am retired and receive benefits. However, the Court's finding of the amount of the pension benefit and payment terms does not correspond to the factual situation.

As stated in the letter received from "The Firm of John Dickinson Schneider, Inc." dated October 12, 2004 (pages 69, 76), I receive quarterly benefits from the said company in the amount of $xx U.S. dollars, plus yearly interest to be paid until April 2009. The statement received from "Hollister Limited," Canada, dated October 12, 2004, states the quarterly benefits are in the amount of $xx U.S. until October 2009, plus interest (page 59).

The letter from Metropolitan Life Insurance, dated October 15, 2004 (page 63), states that under their contract with Hollister Inc., I am eligible for a pension benefit, in the amount of $xx a year, for the rest of my life, starting in October 2006.

The above-mentioned documents are executed in full compliance with the requirements specified in Article 271 part IV of the RF Code of Civil Procedure. They are considered to be proper evidence under Articles 59, 60, 71.

The estimation of the total value of the petitioner's assets is not the subject of probation in the adoption case. Consequently, the Court's impossibility to satisfy my petition for adoption due to its rejection of my declaration of the total value of my assets of more than $xx is not confirmed by law.

The Plenum of the RF Supreme Court in its resolution dated July 4, 1997, "On administration of Legislation by Courts in Hearing Cases on Finalizing the Adoption," clarified that in case the petition is filed by a foreign citizen, a petitioner is obliged to present in court the conclusion on his/her living conditions and his/her capability to become adoptive parent issued by the competent state authority located in his/her country of citizenship (clause 5).

I have met this requirement having presented the confidential home study report prepared by South Florida Adoption Services made July 17, 2004.

As defined in the above said Resolution, the child's interests, which under Article 124, S-4 of the RF Family Code, must determine the adoptive parents are able to provide the child's good physical, mental and intellectual development.

In the process of the lawsuit, it has been established that the children will live in a 5-room condominium and each child will have their own room/bathroom, there is an entertainment center in the unit; the residence is located near and with a view of the Gulf of Mexico. I have an active life: I attend lectures, read, travel, swim, play tennis, go on ski trips in winter. I enjoy classical music. I speak fluently in French, English and Spanish. Therefore, my living conditions, my skills and interests demonstrate my ability to provide the adoptees with the conditions conducive to their positive physical, mental and intellectual development.

The court has all the documents required by law to finalize my petition to adopt.

The court has not established any reasons against my capability to become an adoptive mother (Article 127, 128 of the RF Family Code); the headmaster of the Social Orphanage for teenagers where Kristina and Anton are staying has given his consent for the adoption; according to the conclusion made by the Authorities of Custody and Guardianship, the adoption is deemed to be eligible as it is fully in the children's best interests; the minor Bajenova Kristina, born in 1992, has given her consent for adoption under Article 132 of the RF Family Code.

Having established the factual situation of the case fully and properly, the Court has made the improper conclusion that the adoption does not comply with the minor Bajenova Kristina and Bajenov Anton's interests. That is why the Decision is to be recalled under Article 362 of the RF Code of Civil Procedure.

Taking into consideration all the above mentioned and under Articles 361, 362, of the RSFSR Code of Civil Procedure,

I REQUEST

The reversal of the Krasnoyarsk Regional Court Decision, dated October 27, 2004, and

a decision to finalize the adoption of the minors Bajenova Kristina S. and Bajenov Anton S.

Marie Cécile LeBlanc

39.

Hope Renewed

We may encounter many defeats,
but we must not be defeated.
Maya Angelou[37]

As you recall, the October 2004 trip to Russia to adopt my children was filled with beautiful expectations, which turned into devastating nightmares. The news the Supreme Court of the Russian Federation would hear our case January 18, 2005 reenergized my optimism. I now could visualize, one more time, the moment when the judge would proclaim, "The petition of Marie Cécile LeBlanc is granted."

Without the children, our brand-new home was just an empty house. The thought that this empty house would be filled with laughter and busyness and become a home was so invigorating. The "what to do list" to prepare for their arrival was reactivated. I met again with the school principal and some teachers in both schools. Kristina would take the bus to North Naples Middle School with other students from our community, a distance of four miles. Anton would be car-pooled to Pelican Marsh Elementary School, only half a mile away.

Learning English would require a change from the Cyrillic alphabet to our Latin one. I reserved an English tutor and purchased children's books. At the onset, my friends Lidia from

Belarus and Paulina from Moscow would help us with translation as well as help the children maintain their Russian language. Friends and neighbors loaned us Disney movies. I collected several videos from the National Geographic on birds, fish and land animals. I subscribed to the educational editions of magazines for children such as *National Geographic* and *Discovery*. I've inquired at the library about various children's programs.

To help them integrate with American children, I met with five families in my community who had children of Kristina and Anton's ages. They offered their help. I asked their children to help Kristina and Anton with English, sports and to help them fit into the American way of life. Friends offered to read to the children, take them fishing, teach them to ride a bike. A neighbor John Z. offered to teach Anton how to fix things. Later he became a true mentor for Anton. I met the manager at the YMCA to familiarize myself with their programs. I saved old telephones and old electronic equipment so the children could open them up to find how they're made inside. I prepared little projects such as painting an old desk for Anton's room and painting four old dining room chairs for the lanai. I purchased a bird feeder and a bird bath. I inquired about summer camps for swimming, tennis, golf, all available in our community. The Naples United Church of Christ had a children's summer camp available, as well.

Members of my family in Québec looked forward to meeting my children in the summer. My mother said she would welcome adding two grandchildren to her list, for a total of thirteen. Reverend Patterson and the parishioners of The Naples United Church of Christ would continue to pray until we return safely as a family. Most special, Laura and Sir/Saint John honored us by offering to be surrogate grandparents to Kristina and Anton, an invaluable gift for my children.

It never crossed my mind an adoption could be granted without a "daddy." That all changed when I met Valerie and Murray, August 31, 2003. They informed me they were aware of a single man, about my age, who successfully adopted two

Russian children. Added to the beautiful image of successfully adopting two children, my wild imagination further envisioned, "Someday I may hold a baby grandchild against my heart and fill it with love."

It was now late February and I still had no news from the Russian Supreme Court nor from my lawyer. I became impatient. I asked Polina to call Irina. Irina responded,

"Polina, I no hear Court decision. I not pressure Court for answer. C.C. must wait."

Polina wasted no time to tell me in her strong accent, "C.C., you patient. Hmm, people no hope when take long time. All friends clapping hands for you. You trust in God. All be OK. When Sasha [her six-year-old son] hear C.C. in church, he say, 'Mama, pray for C.C.' Patience is virtue, C.C. It will happen."

"Thank you, Polina. My patience is always in short supply, but this time I have no choice."

On March 4th, an email from Adoption Over-Seas announced, "C.C., the Supreme Court of the Russian Federation has ruled in your favor. An English translation of their decision will follow in a few days."

This was cause for prayers of gratitude and for celebration. The news spread like wildfire. The next day, I wrote to my children to share the good news and to tell them that, this time, I was confident we would succeed.

Finally, on March 7, the translated decision of the Supreme Court of the Russian Federation arrived. A panel of three civil judges considered the facts presented by lawyer Irina. Here is a brief summary:

After examining the case materials, discussing the pleading of the appeal by attorney Irina B., the Panel of Civil Judges considers the Krasnoyarsk Court decision to be subject to annulment on the following grounds:

Deciding not to grant the petition to adopt, the Court proceeded from the fact that no due evidence was presented by the Petitioner, LeBlanc, Marie Cécile, of her ability to provide the children with

proper conditions necessary for their full physical, emotional and spiritual development. However, coming to such conclusion, the Court has wrongly determined the material facts.

During the Court hearing of October 12, 2004, it was found necessary for the Petitioner to present additional documents confirming, including but not limited to, her financial position and living conditions. The hearing was adjourned. But the date of a new hearing was not determined by the Court, contrary to the code of law of the Russian Federation.

The decision not to grant the adoption was decreed on October 27, 2004, only two weeks from the date of the original hearing. In such cases, a date for a new hearing shall be appointed taking into account the period of time necessary for collecting evidence. In this case the requirements of the Law were not satisfied.

Further, in the hearing of the case, the Court has committed gross contravention of the Law of Practice, entailing the reversal of judgment according to the Civil Code of Practice. The Court Decision was decreed on October 27, 2005, however, the minutes of the hearing as of that date are not available in the case materials.

Under the circumstances, the Court Decision, as decreed with violation of common-law practice, is declared invalid and it is subject to reversal, with transmission of the case for a new hearing to the court of original jurisdiction. To declare a new decision in this case is not considered to be possible as violations committed by the court of original jurisdiction cannot be removed by the court of appeal.

According to Articles 362, 364 of the Civil Code, the Panel of Civil Judges of the Supreme Court of the Russian Federation decides to reverse the Decision by Krasnoyarsk Regional court of October 27, 2004, and to submit the case for a new hearing to the court of original jurisdiction.

Wow! Reading the above words from the Supreme Court meant *my dream* was still alive.

On March 23rd, Adoption Over-Seas announced a new hearing was scheduled for April 19, 2005, at the Krasnoyarsk court.

40.

Panic

Panic causes tunnel vision. Calm acceptance
of danger allows us to more easily
assess the situation and see the options.
Simon Sinek[38]

BECAUSE MANY DOCUMENTS ARE valid for only thirty days, several needed to be renewed. For example, the Collier County property appraiser's office needed to reconfirm that the property was mine. For the fourth time, the Collier County sheriff's office had to confirm that I had not been a criminal in the past ten years. Also, for the fourth time, my physician had to repeat all the approximately fifteen tests she had done before, to reassure the court I was healthy and drug free.

On March 30, I emailed Gen of Adoption-Over-Seas that the above documents will be delivered to Corporate Access, in Tallahassee, to be apostilled, on March 31. I faxed copies of those documents to Gen's office that evening. The documents would be carried by a family leaving for Moscow on Saturday. The Moscow office would start the translation right away.

A business visa was requested through an agency in Washington, D.C. The visa would arrive at the latest on April 16. My flights were confirmed—from Fort Myers to Kennedy, then to Moscow, arriving at 11:15 a.m. on April 17, Moscow time.

Three return flight tickets were secured to depart Moscow, direction Kennedy Airport, on April 28.

On March 24, the wonderful Mrs. Louie of the Department of Homeland Security in Miami informed me she had forwarded the children's advance processing application to the American Consulate in Moscow. In addition, I asked Gen to be sure the children's orphanage director was aware of these new developments. I also asked her to forward the name of the judge and of the public prosecutor who would hear our case.

April 6, 2005, the phone rang. "This is Gen, C.C. You must contact Mrs. Louie of the Immigration Office in Miami immediately. Your FBI fingerprints will expire April 8th, and you must leave for Russia on April 16th."

Mrs. Louie's responsibility is to coordinate immigration documents for the American Consulate for foreign children being adopted by American parents. If you remember, I was referred to this wonderful Haitian woman mistakenly when I was trying to accelerate my citizenship. I immediately emailed Mrs. Louie to explain the urgency of the situation and to say,

"I'm in a panic, Mrs. Louie. The flight for Russia departs the 16th. Can the fingerprint expiration date be extended? What do you suggest?"

The next day, via email, Mrs. Louie requested I write her a letter asking for the FBI to re-fingerprint me ASAP. The letter, with a check, left via FedEx to be delivered on April 8, by 10:30 a.m.

Four days later, I wrote to Mrs. Louie, "Dear Mrs. Louie, I'm now in a severe panic mode. It's now April 12th, the FBI has yet to confirm my fingerprint appointment. I'm leaving for Russia in four days."

In the meantime, late in the day April 13, 2005, Gen from Adoption Over-Seas sent an email with Attorney Irina's invoice for the work done at the Supreme Court of the Russian Federation and the cost for accompanying me to the hearing in Krasnoyarsk April 19th. She ended her email this way, "C.C., prior to your departure, please sign Irina's agreement and FedEx it along with the full payment. We will wire the attorney's fees to Russia. Please note, Irina will not accompany you to Krasnoyarsk unless you pay the full amount prior to your departure."

"This doesn't make sense," I thought. There is something fishy here. The total invoice Gen sent was $5,496. It included $1,700 to prepare and present at the Moscow court, $3,000 to accompany me to Krasnoyarsk and $796 for Irina's flight, hotel and meals, but the contract did not have the attorney's signature! As per the original agreement, I owed Irina $1,500 for her work at the Supreme Court in Moscow. To trust sending an extra $3,996 to Adoption Over-Seas for the attorney to represent me in Krasnoyarsk, but without the attorney's signature, was very suspicious. One must remember that, generally, Russian professional people, such as physicians or university professors, only earn about $100 U.S. a month.

On April 14th, I wrote, "Gen, my flight to Moscow leaves April 16th, the day after tomorrow. There is an eight-hour delay to connect with the Krasnoyarsk flight. I plan to meet with Irina in Moscow, to pay the $1,500 I owe her and discuss the arrangements to represent me in Krasnoyarsk."

In addition, Gen had been insisting I pay her $500 to register my children with the Consular Division of the Russian Federation in Washington, DC.

I added to the above email, "Gen, regarding the registration of my children, I spoke to a representative in the Washington DC office who assured me I do not have to register them through an adoption agency nor to register them in Russia. She, in fact, recommended they be registered here in the U.S. within thirty days of their arrival. Gen, there must be some misunderstanding."

Somehow, I wanted to get to her. I added, "Gen, have you forgotten to send me the list of documents needed for the American Consulate in Moscow? Hopefully, I will have all that is needed." I also informed her, "I drove to the FBI office in Miami on April 13 to have my fingerprints taken. The fingerprint report will be forwarded to Mrs. Louie by April 15."

Finally, I told her, "Gen, you do not need to send me my children's shoe sizes and foot measurements as I had previously asked you to do. We called Boris directly to obtain that information."

Immediately after writing this email, I called Polina, my friend from Moscow, to ask her to call the attorney, Irina, to review the accuracy of the contract received from Adoption Over-Seas.

Polina called me back as soon as she hung up with Irina.

"Oh C.C.! Irina very angry. She very upset. Much bad, very bad."

Polina started speaking at the speed of a cheetah chasing a gazelle. With her thick accent, I couldn't understand a word she was saying.

"Polina, Polina! Stop! Take a deep breath. How about if you and Sasha [her son] come for dinner. I'll invite Lidia. Together, we'll discuss your conversation with Irina."

We sat around the table with a glass of wine and some appetizers.

In her thick accent, Polina started, "C.C., told Irina adoption agency say, C.C. need pay $5,496, but contract no have Irina signature. Contract say work in Moscow $1,500, work Krasnoyarsk $3,000, Irina flight Krasnoyarsk $796. Adoption agency want C.C send money before fly Russia or Irina not represent C.C. in Krasnoyarsk court."

Lidia asked Polina, "What did Irina say?"

"Irina furious. Say agency tell her C.C. no want pay her, C.C. no need her, no want her Krasnoyarsk.

"I say, 'Irina, C.C. want pay you, need you Krasnoyarsk. C.C. want know what cost Krasnoyarsk.'

"Irina say, 'Court Moscow and court Krasnoyarsk $3,000, plus pay flight, pay hotel cost.'

"Irina, you say $3,000 both courts?

"*Da*, both courts."

"If Krasnoyarsk court more three days, what cost?

" 'Each plus day, $100.' "

She then told Irina I would arrive in Moscow at noon on the 17th, that I would ask Max to drive me to her office to discuss and sign the Krasnoyarsk contract, and pay her what I owed her."

You can just imagine the conversation that followed between Polina, Lidia and myself. Adoption Over-Seas was asking me to pay $1,500 over what I owed. My suspicions were correct. Gen's demand did not add up.

On a more pleasant note, the day before departure, Polina arranged for a gathering of well-wishers to cheer me on. I included Kristina and Anton in the festive evening by bringing a framed picture of each one. We sipped delicious wines and enjoyed delectable appetizers brought by everyone. A delicious, decorated cake with the words "GOOD LUCK C.C.," was served. Good wishes and hugs from the twenty-five or so people attending were very touching. Only success would be acceptable. Polina said a prayer. Everyone stood holding hands to sing "God Bless America." It was truly an emotional evening filled with love and good wishes for me and for the children they had yet to meet.

On departure day, I sensed God and my angels were back at their posts . . . . I felt hopeful. *All will be well . . . but will it?* Deep inside, fear of another failure was still lurking. As much as I wanted to stay positive, I felt little stabs of doubt. Will the big, black, evil cloud return once I'm in Krasnoyarsk?

On the 16th, the suitcases were at the door early. A beige money bag filled with $7,000 in cash was wrapped around my waist. With my dearest friends, Sir John and Laura, we drove to the airport. With a mixture of moist eyes and smiles we hugged.

Sir John said, "God be with you C.C. I'm confident Kristina and Anton will be on the flight when you return home this time. Laura and I are so looking forward to embracing them."

41.

Moscow, Krasnoyarsk, Visit to the Orphanage

Every adversity, every failure, every heartbreak,
carries with it the seed of an equal or greater benefit.
Napoleon Hill[39]

AFTER A TWO-HOUR WAIT at Kennedy Airport, I boarded the Delta flight, direction Moscow. More palpitations, so many unknowns. Wanting to save energy, I slept, prayed and re-read my documents. The eight-hour flight landed on time. Max and Alina, both translators, greeted me.

We drove to Irina's office where a big discussion took place. Max insisted I pay $200 to refund Pyotr who advanced the money to register the appeal. I also paid $3,000 plus another $1,000 in various fees, all in cash, using clean $100 bills from the little beige cotton body pouch secured around my waist.

We decided it would be best if Irina represented me in the Krasnoyarsk court proceedings. Max suggested that I prepay for Irina's flight, hotel and meals in Krasnoyarsk. I insisted I would pay those expenses with my credit card as they arose.

At about 10:30 p.m., Irina and I were chauffeured to the Sheremetyevo International Airport, twenty-nine kilometers northwest of central Moscow. After a four-hour flight and a four-hour time zone difference, we arrived in Krasnoyarsk at 7:30 a.m. We were met by Tasha, the translator, and Vera, the driver. I was so tired, so very tired, I walked and talked as if I were drunk. I had not laid flat since 6:30 a.m., Naples time, the day before. I only slept by bits and pieces on the plane. As soon as we arrived at the hotel, Tasha informed us, "You may freshen up and have breakfast. Ludmilla is planning a meeting with both of you at 10:00 a.m. We will meet in your room, C.C., to discuss the court's procedures and what to expect."

The meeting was cordial and short. There was nothing new. The children would arrive with Boris in the morning. When the judge was ready, she'd bring Kristina in. Ludmilla would give us the court time as soon as she found out.

Tasha and Ludmilla left. Irina went back to her room. I laid down to rest. At 3 p.m., the phone rang.

"C.C., Tasha here. Ludmilla, Irina and I are on our way to your room."

Ludmilla started speaking in Russian. Tasha translated.

"C.C., Ludmilla was just informed by the court that the hearing will be delayed by one week."

My jaw dropped. She continued, "The judge is on a medical leave. While on vacation, she hurt both her knees. She will not be able to hold court until next week."

I exclaimed, "This cannot be! You mean Irina flew all night for nothing? Wasn't this information known three days ago before I left the U.S., or even last night before we left Moscow?"

"C.C., there is nothing we can do. It is the way it is."

That meant, end of conversation. It was decided Irina would fly back to Moscow on the first available flight the next day. Ludmilla and Tasha left my room. Alone with Irina I asked, "What about your fee Irina, what do I owe you? In her broken English she replied, "C.C., don't know. I . . . um . . . do nothing. Pay $200. $200 OK?"

I felt she was very reasonable. I chose to pay her $300. Irina would fly a total of eight hours for nothing. She wasted a whole day away from her office. With all the stress and exhaustion, I had forgotten that I had already paid her in Moscow the agreed sum of $3,000 for both court hearings. This felt like *déjà vu*. The milking continued. The thought of yet another delay made me nauseated. One more time, my patience was tested. One more time, I was at their mercy.

Now, alone in my room, I felt furious. I started to talk, almost scream, to myself, "Didn't somebody know the judge could not hold court three days ago? Or did somebody want me in Krasnoyarsk to increase their paycheck?"

I found out that Ludmilla did not have any other families to work with this week. Simple conclusion, no customers, no revenue. Tasha suggested I visit the orphanage twice during the week to demonstrate and prove to the judge my strong interest in the adoption of my children. I wanted to tell her, "After all I endured, how much stronger can my interest be? I'm here, am I not?"

This last curveball was so suspicious, I felt so hopeless. If I refused to visit the orphanage, they could sabotage the whole adoption process. I remembered Lidia's comment in Naples, "C.C., they want to milk a rich lady." I said, "They want to milk a rich lady dry."

A visit to the orphanage would take approximately twelve hours. The drive would be four-and-one-half to five hours each way, plus two hours to spend with my children. The cost would be $25 per hour, $15 for the driver and $10 for the translator, for a total cost of $300 plus gratuities. Considering that physicians and university teachers make $100 a month . . . this is very rich. Think about it. For whose benefit was it that I came a week early? Let that simmer in your mind.

"Of course, now that I'm here, I want to see my children. But twice in one week, when a few days later, if my petition is granted, we will be together for a lifetime? Isn't this more for their financial benefit than for ours?"

The next morning, we left at 8 a.m. I was filled with joy anticipating seeing my children after six months of separation. Within twenty minutes, we were driving on a two-lane narrow road lined with several small villages and summer cottages. We passed beautiful birch forests, which brought back memories of my youth in Québec Province. En route, to relieve oneself, gas stations provided an outhouse, but no toilet paper, no water and no soap. Bring your own or do without . . . . Remember, "Never leave home without soap and toilet paper." You may leave your credit cards home but never, ever, leave without your soap and your toilet paper, at least not in Russia.

We arrived in the small village of Dzerzhinsk District at 1 p.m. As we approached the wide, one-story gray building, my heart was pounding. It was early spring. The yard was muddy. Wood planks were laid down to create a dry walking surface to reach the main door. One young teenager was standing on the porch, shivering while smoking a cigarette. Another young girl went inside to announce we had arrived. Kristina came out followed by several young girls. We embraced for a long time. In that embrace I was hoping Kristina would feel my love deep in her heart. Once we let go, Anton jumped into my arms. He hugged me as though he would never let go. The other children were watching, smiling, giggling with each other, curious to see who Kristina and Anton's new mama would be.

All the children kept their eyes on me. I was a curiosity. It was only the second time in a long time an adoptive parent had visited their orphanage. Kristina was dressed in black. She seemed timid. Her big black eyes were focused on me. Boris arrived with a big smile. He shook my hand and led us to his office. The children first stood near him, seemingly waiting for guidance from their director. Then they joined me. We took pictures. Then Kristina led me on a tour of what had been their home for almost five years.

First, we walked through a large happy room filled with sunlight and large green plants. It was very clean, had a beautiful wood floor, and an open credenza with electronic entertainment equipment, a few sofa chairs and a coffee table. We moved on to a long corridor. To the left, we entered a large room with a TV and with toys for boys. A caregiver was sitting at her desk. Anton ran to her, sat on her lap. He made gestures and funny faces to attract my attention, attention that I gave him with my eyes and my smiles. Twelve to fifteen young boys surrounded the teacher. They were all agitated, smiling, joking with each other. The room was filled with high energy. Through Tasha, I thanked the teacher for caring for my children. We moved back to the hallway. The next stop was a visit to the boy's bedroom a rectangular room with a large window and ten beds. Anton ran ahead of the group. When we entered, he was pretending to sleep in his bed located against the wall near the entrance.

I asked, "Is this your bed Anton?"

Shyly he answered, *"Da."*

We walked to the sleeping quarters for teenage girls, a room similar to the boys' but without a window. Kristina pointed to her bed, which was against the wall in the left corner. She had to walk on top of several beds to reach hers. The shower room was strange. I saw a large room with three or four very wide barrels filled with water . . . a brownish colored water. I still do not understand their purpose.

Nature called. On my way to the outhouse, I walked on wobbly planks laid down on the muddy spring ground. As I walked by, I looked into the TV room. Approximately ten older children were sitting around. I frowned at the sight of a young girl and a young boy holding each other in a romantic, compromising way.

When I returned, the children joyfully introduced me to some of their caregivers. Each one greeted me warmly. We could only smile. I spoke to all the children in English. In a shy way, they reacted by looking at each other giggling. I showed them how to use the video camera and the still camera. Several children took pictures of each other. As it was with my children, we were separated by language. Through the camera, especially the video camera, we found a way to communicate with each other.

I asked for the video camera back. I gestured to five or six young boys to sit on the couch then I filmed them one at a time.

The real fun started when I reversed the camera screen to let them see their own faces. As they saw themselves on a video screen for the first time, making funny faces, sticking their tongues out, they looked surprised as if to say, "Is this really me?" As they recognized themselves, their laughter filled the room. When a five-year-old boy saw his face on TV for the first time, he exploded with a laughter so contagious, the whole room came to life. Everyone laughed with him. He could not stop. To this day, whenever I think about the orphanage, I remember this adorable child, and I'm filled with that joyful moment. Even after so many years, there are times I wonder where all these children are and if they are having worthwhile lives.

Memorable photos were taken, some with Boris, some with their caregivers, and some with their friends. One of the pictures has sixteen children in it. Kristina stands in the middle of the group surrounded by her girlfriends. Kristina was reserved and semi-serious in all of these pictures. The other young girls were looking with eyes that were pleading, "Why can't you take me too?" I couldn't take them all. It broke my heart. These young girls did not ask to be born.... now that they were, most had no home to go to. I often think of them.

For Kristina, when the judge asked her if she wanted to come to America and have me as her mama, her yes answer would be the most important life decision she would ever have to make, and she was only thirteen years old. Once in America, a new dawn would begin for Kristina and her brother. A new birth, a new journey with an unknown path . . . overwhelming . . . in some way, terrifying . . . for such a young person.

As I write this chapter, I'm filled with sadness looking at the beautiful, touching pictures taken that day. The young boys, Anton's age, were full of smiles. They were excited. Kristina's friends were older, more somber. Some were looking straight into the lens of the camera. Again, I saw their gloomy, morose eyes, and I heard their hearts screaming, "Please take me with you." How sad it was to be able to take two children but not all of them.

My hope is perhaps, after reading this book, some of you will be inspired to give a future to a child or two or more. These beautiful children, some in just a few years, will be on their own, most with no parents, no aunts and uncles. Their siblings, if younger, will remain in the orphanage. They may never see each other again. As it is in many parts of the world, the mafia and the sex slave markets are very active in Russia. The young girls leaving the orphanage at eighteen are prime targets. My children would be safe with me in America

Kristina had a bad cough that day. It worried me. I decided that as soon as we arrived home, both children would see a pediatrician. Anton was completely shaved, bald, almost like Sir John— at least, Sir John had a ring of hair around his head. Anton was happy with the stuffed monkey I gave him earlier. He carried it around his neck during the whole visit. The new representative from the Ministry of Education arrived. We were introduced. Sergey was a young man in his early twenties with no life experience. Ours would be his first court case. I had a long conversation with him. I tried to convince him I was a responsible person capable of caring for Kristina and Anton.

Sergey shared the following via the translator, "I believe you, but I am overwhelmed with my new job." His comments concerned me as well as it concerned Boris and Tasha. Could the insecurity he felt in his new job sabotage our court day?

It was time to say goodbye. The children seemed hopeful. I was. I wanted to be. There was no room for pessimism.

On our way home, Vera the driver, said, "C.C., there are now one million five hundred thousand orphans in all of Russia."

My heart was weeping at this news. Just think, all these lovely abandoned children . . . not just those in Russia but in all countries around the world . . . . I repeat, these children never asked to be born. That's right. *They never asked to be born.* Most of them face such a bleak future.

Back at the hotel, my new friend, the wonderful hotel receptionist, Olea, who spoke beautiful English, could not understand the difficulties we were facing. She had never seen anything close to our story.

A note was left at the desk. The court hearing was scheduled for Tuesday, April 26. Back in my room, I calmed down. The dark evil cloud hovering over my head in October 2004, seemed to have vanished or at least weakened. My friends back home must be praying very hard. I felt God and my angels were back on duty. My intuition told me, "This time C.C., you will be going home with your children." I was holding on to hope.

This would be a long week! The English C-Span TV programs were no longer offered. All programs were now only in Russian. Such was life for me in Siberia at that moment.

42.

Waiting

Patience is not the ability to wait,
but the ability to keep a good attitude while waiting.
Joyce Meyer[40]

APRIL 21, 2005

My room was on the fourth floor. A restaurant/bar was located at the end of the hallway. As it was on my first visit, the breakfast buffet was huge, even including heavy entries we would consider dinner dishes at home. Most mornings I ate at this restaurant.

At 8:15 a.m., it was generally busy with business patrons. Some were dressed in suits, some in jogging clothes, some in sport clothes and some were obviously working in infrastructure/construction and were dressed accordingly. Very few people, if any, smiled. It's very serious business to have breakfast in Krasnoyarsk.

Similar to what had happened on my first visit last October, all tables were occupied when I arrived. A hostess, maintaining a starchy face, gestured to a table with an empty chair where two man were already sitting. I carried the tray with my breakfast selection of cereal, milk and a cup of coffee. I placed the food on the table, then laid the tray against the wall. Another starched-face hostess picked up the tray immediately, without ever looking at me.

As I started to eat, a semi-attractive red-haired woman returned to her table, now my table. She took her seat across from me. Her plate sat at the end of the table close to mine. She moved it as though I would contaminate it. She never looked at me, never acknowledged my presence and kept her eyes down, raising them only when she spoke to the two young men. The two young men looked at me once, spoke to the red-haired woman, and ignored me as though I was some repulsive creature. They left without ever acknowledging my presence.

Every morning was the same. Voices were low. There was no laughter, no music. The predominant noise was the clinking of the dishes and utensils. The aura, the mood of this environment was so unfriendly, so uncomfortable, so different from where I came from. The whole feel of this room made me want to shout. But what would I gain or change? Perhaps there are cultural reasons for them to behave this way. Perhaps they could be punished for speaking to a stranger. Their behavior didn't change my self-confidence. I felt sadness for them.

On April 22nd, I emailed my Belarus friend in Naples.

Dear Lidia,

The stress continues, but this time there's hope. I was pleasantly surprised at what I observed at the orphanage. It was clean and the children looked relatively happy. Kristina loved the hair decorations you sent her.

Ludmilla and Tasha briefed me on how important it is for Kristina to answer in the following way if the judge asks why she want to come to America. She must say, "Because I love C.C. and C.C. loves Anton and me. I love her and feel comfortable with her."

If the judge asks her, "Do you want C.C. as your mama?" Kristina must say, "Yes." I explained to Kristina and Anton I will never replace their Mama. I will be Mama C.C. Ludmilla said children who are adopted must want to have a new mama. I understand that it will be hard for my children as they are older, and they remember their biological mother. Ludmilla also said the judge may try to discourage Kristina from leaving Russia. Kristina must make it clear to the judge she wants to come with me. I'm sure Ludmilla will prepare the children but to hear it from you, their American, Russian-speaking friend, would be reinforcement.

My dear Lidia, I would so appreciate if you could call the orphanage and discuss the above with Kristina. Much love to you always, C.C.

When hunger came, I was sick in bed with a sore throat and a bad cough. The smoked salmon I had bought with the mushroom cream cheese was appealing. I placed the "vacuum packed smoked salmon" on a plate. It looked much thicker than the smoked salmon available in the U.S., but it was pink and looked delicious enough. I thought, "Here in Siberia, things are different . . . maybe their smoked salmon is just thicker."

I proceeded to open the package. With the help of a fork, I tried to separate the contents . . . It did not separate . . . . "What in the world is this? By God, it's raw salmon . . . ." I was starving. I placed the short cord electric tea kettle on top of the TV. I filled it 3/4 of the way up to avoid the water boiling over and shocking the old-fashioned TV with a shot of salmon bouillon. I remembered so vividly the incident when the TV was killed by a shot of chicken bouillon last October. In addition, salmon bouillon would stink up my room with a fishy smell.

I baptized this recipe "Salmon à la Siberia" boiled for one minute, then held in the hot water for four minutes. The salmon skin was still attached, helping the flesh to stay firm. One slice of brown bread, mushroom cream cheese and salmon should make a good sandwich . . . until I tasted it. The salmon was extremely salty . . . really uneatable . . . but I was hungry. What was left of the salmon went into the garbage.

Sunday, April 24
I wrote a short email to Sir John.

Court day is scheduled for Tuesday, April 26. Once my petition to adopt Kristina and Anton is granted, we will be able to fly back to Moscow on April 30th. Another three days will be needed to complete the paperwork with the American Consulate. We could probably fly home on May 4th, but it's probably safer to confirm our flights for May 5th. It would be a great help if you could make the reservations for the three of us for May 5th.

Earlier that day, as I walked out of the hotel, festive sounds coming from the other side of city hall attracted me. Halfway up the beautiful stone stairs, I saw a wonderful scene on the street below. A crowd of perhaps two thousand young students was preparing to start a 5K run. The lively music sounded patriotic, almost military. All were responding to the commentator with enthusiasm.

The following is what I observed from where I stood. A total of five groups, divided by age, lined up behind their respective ropes waiting for their signal to start. Each group, beginning with the older ones, began their run at three to four-minute intervals.

All were well dressed in colorful jackets, red caps, jeans, some in name brand jogging suits, fleece, etc. The participants could have been from anywhere in the West. The crowd was well behaved. A man with a rickety, home-made, low-flying, motorized tricycle with large fixed wings passed by several times, entertaining the crowd. People in wheelchairs enjoyed the festivities. Teenage girls grouped together, some dancing to the music. Some young couples walked hand-in-hand, stealing a kiss or two. Balloons were flying. Commentators rallied the crowd with their words and patriotic music. It was clear spring had arrived. The large tree in front of me was already budding. If it were not for the language, it felt as if I was somewhere in North America. When the five groups had departed, the street cleaners immediately started picking up the very little trash left on the street. This was a happy, invigorating experience.

While this joyful event gave me hope for the future of the Russian people, an incident in the stairway took away that hope. While I was savoring this whole ambience, two old *babushkas* came down the stairs slowly and with difficulty. They stopped next to me to look down where this excitement was taking place. They were both very old looking, deeply wrinkled, almost toothless. Both were wearing worn out blue coats. One covered her head with a pointed orange-colored headscarf tied below her chin. The other wore a blue wool bonnet. They looked at me with questioning eyes. I smiled. They smiled back. I so wanted to speak with them, ask them about their lives, their age, their challenges and their hopes.

At that moment, a policewoman followed by a policeman came down the stairs, said a few words to the old *babushkas*, then she shooed them away with her hands. As they prepared to leave, they both looked at me, their eyes saying, "Why can you stay, and we cannot." They obeyed and left. My eyes connected with the policewoman. I stared into her eyes. I wanted to say, "These two ladies are not hurting or disturbing anyone. Couldn't you let them enjoy this little bit of pleasure for a short moment?" Without being able to communicate in Russian and wanting to avoid anything that could jeopardize the outcome of the adoption, I chose to stay silent. Staying silent in the face of unfairness is not my style. This time, I swallowed my words.

So it was, in the heart of Siberia, toward the end of April 2005.

43.

Court Day April 26, 2005

Never lose hope. Storms make people
stronger and never last forever.
Roy T. Bennett[41]

ONE DAY BEFORE THE court hearing, Ludmilla, Tasha and I met one more time to discuss the court's procedures.

"C.C., just answer the questions. Do not give extra details. Speak in short sentences. Your papers were reviewed, they were cleared by the court. We will pick you up at 9 a.m. Judge Alexandra N. will hear your case at 9:30. Some of the questions will be similar to the first hearing, but it may be helpful to prepare answers for the following questions."

"OK. Let's practice. I'm ready."

"Why Russian children?"

"Your Honor, in August 2003, I met a couple who adopted seven-year-old twins from Russia. They were my inspiration. Working with their adoption agency, I registered to host two older children with the intent of adopting them if the children and I bonded."

"Why do you want to adopt two children?"

"Because of my age, Your Honor, I felt I should adopt two children so that when I'm gone, they will have each other."

"Please explain the kind of work you did."

"Your Honor, I worked for a medical supply company as a sales/marketing representative. I travelled in eastern Québec and in the four Atlantic Provinces of Canada. After three years of service, I was promoted and transferred to Toronto to take responsibility for sales in all of Canada. Three years later, I was offered a transfer to Boston, Massachusetts. I worked for another twelve years then retired."

"Why did you not marry? Are you a feminist?"

"Your Honor, although I was asked to marry several times, I chose to stay single. I never considered myself a feminist. I believe there is a place for men and a place for women in our society. I enjoy the company of men. I loved my father and I was raised with four brothers with whom I have a very close relationship."

Ludmilla, who had been listening, said a few words to Tasha and left. For the next hour, Tasha and I sat across from each other, she on the couch, me on a straight chair. We continued to review more answers to possible questions from the judge or from the prosecutor. Then, Tasha asked, "C.C., can we discuss your financial report?"

How can one explain annuities, dividends, interest, portfolios, securities, real estate investments when the person seeking to understand does not have the simplest comprehension of these terms? I recalled the conversation we had the previous October when I had asked Tasha if she had a bank account. Her answer then was, "No, I hide my money because I don't trust the government."

Very slowly, using the simplest explanations, we reviewed the various financial terms starting with interest and dividends. Tasha left saying, "I hope there will not be too many questions about your finances."

The next day, April 26, we arrived at the courthouse early in the morning. That afternoon, as soon as I returned to the hotel, I went to the business center to write the following email to explain what had happened at the court that day.

Dear Family and Friends,

We waited for the children in the lobby. They arrived at 9:15 a.m. We exchanged a few hugs. Kristina appeared stressed. She left the court building with her hands in the pockets of the blue jacket I gave her in October 2004. She walked outside to the edge of the short wall beside the courthouse. Anton followed her. She seemed lost in her thoughts. She kept her body facing the horizon, away from the building. For sure this was the biggest decision she'd ever have to make. Was it the right decision? Not able to speak her language was so frustrating. How could I reassure her?

The court started at 9:45 a.m. It ended at 12:30 p.m. The questions were gruesome, similar to the ones of October 2004. Kristina was brought in. She stood behind the balustrade facing the judge. I was sitting perhaps fifteen feet behind her on the bench next to Tasha. Both the judge and the prosecutor questioned her for approximately twenty minutes. Tasha translated, whispering the questions and answers in my ears.

"Why do you want to go to America? Do you realized you will never see your friends again? You don't know anyone in the United States. It will be difficult for you and for your brother to go to school; you don't speak English. You don't know C.C. You just met her a few times. She can't speak Russian. How will you communicate with her? You will forget your language, lose all your friends." Similar questions were asked by the prosecutor. I felt the judge and the prosecutor were trying to confuse or discourage her or perhaps, they wanted to be sure Kristina was rational in her choice to come with me. To each question Kristina gave a solid answer.

"I know it will be hard at first, Your Honor, but I love C.C. and I know she loves us. My brother and I want to live in a family."

She stood, looking stoic, answering without hesitation. I was so proud of her. When the questioning of Kristina was over, the judge asked me, "Miss LeBlanc, is there anything you want to ask Kristina?"

While Kristina's gaze was still on the judge, I rose to my feet with the speed of lightning. Tasha followed me. I walked right behind Kristina. I placed my arms around her, held her close to me. Choking, tears filling my eyes, I responded,

"Your Honor, I do not have any questions for Kristina. I fell in love with Kristina and her brother Anton three days after we met at the

end of 2003. I feel they are my children in my heart. I want to love them, take care of them as a mama, give them an opportunity to have a family, go to college and help them develop whatever talents they may have. Your Honor, I ask you and I ask the court to trust me, to believe my intentions to care for Kristina and Anton are honorable. I respectfully ask you to grant my petition to adopt these two beautiful children. Your Honor, I have carried Kristina and Anton in my heart for the last one-and-one half years."

I choked up . . . I couldn't speak. There was total silence in the courtroom. Then I looked up at the judge and said with a broken voice, "Please Your Honor, I beg of you, give them a chance to have a family, to have a better future."

I could not speak anymore. I was choking with emotions, fearing another denial. Tears filled my eyes, now rolling down my cheeks. I was still behind Kristina, holding her with my arms. Hearing the translation of my words into Russian, Kristina turned toward me. Her cheeks were wet with her own tears. We hugged tightly for a several seconds. The silence in the courtroom was sobering. I looked at the judge and the prosecutor. I sensed they were deeply touched by the intimate moment Kristina and I were sharing. Everyone in the courtroom was witnessing the strength of our desire to be together as a family. Kristina turned back toward the judge who softly asked her to wait outside the courtroom.

"The judge called for a ten-minute recess, after which Ludmilla, Tasha, Boris, Sergey and I returned to the court room. The judge started reading her report. Then we heard, "The court is delaying their final decision until the following three documents are received."

Yes, as unbelievable as it may seem to all of you, we have another delay. The court will resume when the requested documents arrive notarized and apostilled. When the judge finished verbalizing her requests, she asked, "Miss LeBlanc, do you have any questions?"

"Your Honor, in three days, April 29, Kristina will celebrate her 13th birthday. What a precious gift it would be, if on that day, you find it in your heart to grant my petition to adopt her and her brother."

The judge did not answer; she left the courtroom. The hearing ended.

When Kristina heard there would be yet another delay, she started crying, sobbing. I held her. I cried with her. I reached out for Anton. The three of us held tight for a few minutes while Tasha was voicing words of hope. (figure 27)

Here are the three additional requests:

First, the prosecutor wants another piece of paper to prove there is a house on lot 28 in Stonebridge, all because my deed shows a legal description but does not show the mailing address of 1925 Winding Oaks Way. The title company provided a letter stipulating the deed is correct and is the actual legal description. I also have a letter from Abe Skinner, the county appraiser, showing the tax record with my name. In addition, Abe Skinner's assistant wrote a description of my property for which the court has pictures. The document has the county's legal seal, is notarized and apostilled. It explains clearly my ownership. I will ask Murray and Valerie to have Jamie, their executive assistant, go to the tax collector, Guy Carlton, to get a receipt which shows that the real estate taxes were paid by me, and fax it to Adoption Over-Seas as quickly as possible.

Second, the prosecutor wants statistics of longevity for women living in Florida. The court will accept a computer copy. Sir John, could you help me with this request? I have seen statistics for the United States, but not precisely for Florida. Could you search Google, find statistics confirming life expectancy from the time a woman reaches sixty years of age. It could be as high as ninety years. Please fax this information directly to my hotel. It doesn't have to be notarized nor apostilled. The Economist statistics booklet of 2004 shows that in the United States, men live to seventy-eight women a little older. Thank you, one more time, for your help, my dearest friend.

The third request is for Boris, the orphanage director. The children's blood test must be updated, as it is over thirty days old.

Boris, Ludmilla, Tasha, the children and I left the courthouse, boarded the van, then drove to a medical clinic for the children's blood test. Once there, Ludmilla took the children to the registration office. Boris waited at the door. I stood with Tasha, the translator, approximately twenty feet away. An old looking woman dressed in a *grey coat with a dark wool bonnet and black winter boots came out from the clinical room and began conversing with Boris. They were looking in my direction.*

I asked Tasha, "Who is this woman?'

"She is a physician here at the clinic. She is finishing her day shift. Boris probably told her you were adopting these children. She's probably curious and is asking about you."

After a few minutes, the woman left. Almost at the same time, Ludmilla and the children returned to the waiting room. Ludmilla informed Boris,

"The children need to go to a different clinic. This clinic works mostly with HIV patients. There is a three-hour wait. Boris will stop at the Kantz clinic on their way back to the orphanage."

We walked out of the clinic. The woman physician with the old gray coat who had just left the clinic heard the chatter as we walked back to the van. She turned around and saw us. She kept her eyes on me . . . . Spontaneously, for no comprehensible reason, I walked toward her . . . . As I approached, she extended both hands toward me. I took them in mine. We held each other's hands for few seconds looking in each other's eyes. We stood there in complete silence. Then, in a totally natural and beautiful way, we hugged for a few seconds. The touching, profound beauty of that moment is indescribable. Two women, unknown to each other, from different lands, different cultures, different languages, were embracing each other without ever exchanging a word. Her love and her heart melted with mine for a moment. This lady doctor knew and understood the adoption of Kristina and Anton would save their lives. There was no need to speak. As I am writing these words, I can still see the woman, in her old grey coat and her dark wool bonnet extending her arms toward me. I so vividly remember the beautiful emotions of this sacred moment.

Back at the van, Kristina was crying as we said one more goodbye. With the help of the translator, I tried to convince her, "This time Kristina, there is real hope. This time my love, God is with us. I'm fighting very hard."

Such is life here in Siberia at the moment. Please, all of you in Canada and in the United States, stay with us, keep praying. The more I am with Kristina and Anton, the more it feels they are my children, the ones I am to care for.

From Russia, always with love,
C.C.

44.

Second Court Hearing, April 29, 2005

Today I pray for you, a heart free of sadness,
a mind free of worries, a life full of gladness, a body free
of illness and a life full of God's blessings.
Mutuyimana David[42]

IT WAS 4 A.M. I was awake, praying, crying, and thinking. What would I say if the judge asked me to address the court? What could I add? I thought of the words First Lady Barbara Bush spoke at the commencement at Wellesley College in Massachusetts in 1990.

"At the end of your life, you will never regret not having passed one more test, not winning one more verdict or not closing one more deal. You will regret time not spent with a husband, a child, a friend or a parent."[43]

Based on those words, I would want to say,

Yes, Your Honor, at the end of my life, I will not be asking how much money I have, nor will I calculate how many black ties or how many cruises I took traveling the world. Instead, I will ask myself what I contributed to make our world a better place.

Your Honor, if with the love I have for Kristina and Anton, if with my determination, my strength, my ability to make things happen, and if with the help of God, I am successful in guiding two children toward a positive future, I will die happy. What is the point of having a comfortable lifestyle, or having a big house, if there is no one to share it with?

I tried to go back to sleep. Half conscious, I started making a movie in my head or was it a dream? The end of my life was near. I was in palliative care. Kristina and Anton were by my side. I was in and out of consciousness. I felt happy. Kristina and Anton both had secure jobs. They both had a family. My eyes teared up, but there was a smile on my lips. *Mission accomplished,* I thought. I opened my eyes, looked at my children,

"My dearest Kristina and my dearest Anton, I thank God and the universe for giving me the opportunity and the privilege to be a passage in your life. I love you today; I have always loved you no matter what. Wherever I'm going, if I can, I will continue to be with you." My eyes closed. I stopped breathing.

The alarm clock rang. I had to get up. Today, the Russian court would decide the fate of Marie Cécile LeBlanc's petition to adopt Kristina and Anton. What emotions! I felt agitated all night long. Not only was today our second court day, it was Kristina's thirteenth birthday. Would it be a happy day? Would the judge grant the adoption? Only the power of God could change what the judge and the prosecutor had already decided.

On our way to the courthouse, I asked Ludmilla, "Did the judge review the life expectancy charts I handed to you two days ago? In Florida, white women live an average of eighty-two years. If I live to that age, Kristina would be twenty-nine, Anton twenty-six."

Ludmilla did not know.

Tasha, Ludmilla and I arrived at the courthouse at 9:15. Boris, Sergey, the representative of the Ministry of Education, Kristina and Anton arrived a few minutes later. We had just enough time to hug and smile. Ludmilla spoke to my children, preparing them as to what to say, in case the judge questioned them.

The children waited in the hallway with Kayla, the driver. We entered the courtroom at 9:30. We sat. Upon hearing the court official's footsteps, we stood up. For the next two-and-one-half hours,

I was again bombarded with questions. They were repeated over and over. The answers were always the same. As I said before, the truth never lies.

Around noon, the judge called for a recess. The officials left the courtroom. I was on pins and needles. Approximately twenty minutes later, the judge returned alone. She gave me a glance as she climbed up to her perch. I detected a faint smile. I filled up with hope but seconds later doubt crept in. What if I misread her smile? Could she be mocking me? *Stop these negative thoughts, Cécile,* I told myself.

The judge looked at us, her eyes stopped on mine for a few seconds. She began to read her long report. Tasha translated. All sounded positive, as it did in October, when the judge denied my petition. All of a sudden, the judge stopped talking.

I stopped breathing. My eyes were focused on the judge's. She looked at me for what seemed an eternity. I perceived kindness in her eyes. I could almost sense an affectionate look on her face. It made me more nervous. The judge continued reading. I held Tasha's arm tightly. Tasha whispered the translation in my ear, "The petition of Marie Cécile LeBlanc to adopt Kristina Bajenova S. and Anton Bajenov S. is granted."

For an instant, my heart stopped. I froze. Did I hear correctly? I glanced around, Boris and Sergey were walking toward me, smiling. I looked at Tasha.

"Did the Judge say *granted*?"

In her stoic, controlled demeanor she answered, "Yes, she did, C.C. You are now the mama of Kristina and Anton. Congratulations!"

They surrounded me with hugs and tears of happiness this time. The judge was watching. I walked toward her. I shook her hand. Thanked her. She smiled. During that time, Tasha was taking pictures with my camera. Ludmilla entered the courtroom with Kristina and Anton. When I turned around my children were standing before me. I knelt down, wrapped my arms around my two beautiful children and said, "We're Going Home." (cover picture)

I'm thankful to have pictures of this glorious moment in the very courtroom where my first petition to adopt was denied but where, on this day, my children were granted their freedom. Kristina appears somewhat somber in the pictures, almost in disbelief that finally, baring no other delays, we were on our way to America. Ludmilla hugged her and whispered,

"Kristina, the judge said YES. No more going back to the orphanage. You're going to America with Mama C.C." What a beautiful gift on Kristina's thirteenth birthday.

45.

Adoption and Kristina's Thirteenth Birthday Celebration

I was chosen, I was wanted, I was cherished,
I grew in her heart, I was the missing piece,
I was loved, I was adopted.
Adoption Magazine[44]

TOGETHER, AND WITH THE help and prayers of so many in Canada and in the United States, we overcame every bump, every hill and every mountain, though at times our own Mount Everest, the KACC mountain, seemed to be impossible to reach. We would never give up. NNNQ was our motto. Today, April 29, 2005, we were rewarded. We were rewarded for our determination, our perseverance, for believing God will ultimately reward a noble cause. The moment the judge said "Granted" we had conquered the peak of our own mountain, the KACC Mountain I drew for my children on a piece of paper last October while they lived at the transitional orphanage. In the next few days, we will fly to Moscow then start our descent all the way to America. Will it be a smooth descent, or will there be more obstacles to overcome?

Holding my children's hands, we left the court room all smiles. On our way to the hotel, I looked up to the sky to thank God and our angels, not only for the gift of my children, but also for the gift of all those who supported us, especially for my most loyal friend Sir John. With the granting of the adoption, Sir John became Grandpa John to my children, his wife, Grandma Laura.

Everyone's face was radiant as we walked out of the courthouse. We were happy, hungry and ready to celebrate the birth of the new LeBlanc family and Kristina's thirteenth birthday. Tasha helped arrange a festive lunch in the beautiful red-walled dining room of our hotel. We sat at a spacious rectangular table. Tasha and Kayla, the driver, sat at one end, I at the other. The children sat next to me, facing each other. Boris sat next to Kristina, Anton across, facing his sister. Sergey sat next to Anton facing Boris.

The menu was the same for everyone. A salad, baked chicken with potatoes and a vegetable, bread and butter, soft drinks and a glass of wine for me. For the first time, I observed two Russians, Boris and Sergey, drink straight shots of pure Vodka the Russian way. A shot glass was placed in front of each man. The hostess brought a carafe filled with undiluted Vodka. She placed it the middle of the table in front the two men. Boris filled both shot glasses to the rim. We raised our glasses to our success. The two men clicked their glasses. The Vodka disappeared in one swallow. "Wow!" I thought, "These are real Russians." Immediately, the shot glasses were filled up again to toast Kristina's birthday. Again, the vodka was gone in one swallow.

Boris and Sergey were talking, laughing and they kept toasting . . . to whatever. I could not understand but I bet they were toasting their own victory in the granting of Kristina and Anton's adoption. I remember so vividly how nervous Sergey was, at my children's orphanage few days ago, about his new role with the Ministry of Education. Our case was Sergey's first time to testify for the recommendation of an adoption. It was his first victory. Every time their shot glasses clicked an ounce of straight Vodka went down their throats. As soon as the carafe was emptied, they ordered another one. I laughed internally, wondering how Boris would survive the five-hour drive back to Dzerzhinsk.

Throughout this day of celebration, my mind was realizing that today was the beginning of the end, or the death of my children's life in Russia in exchange for a rebirth in America. From this day on, by choice, they were letting go of everything they had known since birth, in exchange for a new mama, a new country, a new language, new schools and new friends. It would be years before they would return to their Russia, if ever. I wondered if Kristina, at thirteen years of age, really understood the magnitude of her decision.

Boris and Sergey were still clicking their shot glasses when the server brought the birthday dessert, a decorated plate with seven sweet squares cakes, each topped with a magic lighted candles. We sang "Happy Birthday" in English, Russian and French. Kristina made a wish, blew out the candles . . . . We all clapped. But wait... surprise! Each candle came back to life. Everyone laughed. She blew them out again. Oops, once more, all were reignited! Puzzled, Anton walked next to his sister to assist. They both blew on the candles with all their might. The candles went dark only to light up again a few second later. Boris came to the rescue. Now all three were blowing. The candles had a mind of their own, they would not die. This became the new challenge of the day, albeit one that brought laughter. Every time the candles came back to life, everyone laughed. Kristina threw her arms in the air as if to say, "I don't know what to do." Boris came to the rescue. He put some saliva . . . or was it vodka?... between his thumb and index finger and finally killed the flames. Everyone laughed while Boris and Sergey had yet another shot of vodka to toast the killing of the flames. (figures 30, 31)

Kristina opened her birthday gifts. To her surprise there were many, decorations for her hair, a necklace, an English reading book with pictures, a pink lipstick and a purse. Then, when she saw a CD player with earphones her face lit up. Anton opened his wrapped presents, a Lego kit and a truck.

This happy moment came to an end at 3:30 p.m. Boris, filled to capacity with Vodka but still walking straight, was a bit emotional when he hugged the children one last time. Everyone walked out of the dining room toward the beautiful main door of the hotel. We waved a final goodbye. This time, there were no tears. The children will never return as residents of an orphanage. This time a brand-new LeBlanc family was on its way to America.

Once in our room, Kristina again claimed the couch for her bed. Anton would sleep in the king size bed with me as he did in October. The children unpacked their new clothes from the suitcase one piece at a time, placed them on their shelf in the closet. Kristina looked at me several times with a smile. Anton made sounds of joy at each piece of clothing. He paraded around in his favorite one, pretending to be a model. Later in the afternoon, we walked to the corner grocery store. We bought cooked salmon and potato salad from the deli. Once outside, we visited our favorite fruit lady's table. We added oranges and bananas to our purchases. Again, Anton insisted on carrying the heaviest packages. Back in our room, both children placed the food in the refrigerator.

We looked at each other. What do we do now? We're a family now, but we can't communicate . . . . The video and the still camera saved the day. We filmed and took pictures of each other. We looked at them. We laughed. Anton was forever the comedian. Again, he took different poses pretending he was an actor, then waited for us to laugh. Then he pretended to be a baby wanting to be rocked. Kristina and I obliged. This newfound freedom created lots of joy and excitement. We laughed ourselves silly. When I addressed them in English they repeated after me in a laughing mocking way. I did the same when they spoke in Russian. We ate dinner on the coffee table using a towel for a tablecloth. The children washed and dried the dishes in the bathroom sink.

After showering, Kristina wore her new night gown. As soon as Anton had put on his new pajamas, he started teasing his sister, laughing and running away, hoping she would not catch him.

Kristina threw a pillow at him . . . . A pillow fight started. When peace returned, Kristina spent time listening to her new CD player. Anton played with his Legos. I sat quietly to write my notes. It was time for Anton to go to sleep. After hugging him, I tucked him in on his side of the bed. He got up several times, still playful. Then he would drag me back, wanting to be tucked in once more, knowing that each time he would get a big hug. Kristina and I sat in the living room. She continued to listen to her music, I finished writing my notes. When it was my time to go to bed, Kristina and I hugged. Anton was still awake. After I lay down, I held his hand hoping he would fall asleep.

This beautiful day ended. We went to sleep exhausted but happy. For each one of us, the dawn of a new journey officially began at noon April 29, 2005, on the very day Kristina turned thirteen. Our lives would now be forever interwoven from the moment Judge Alexandra N. of the Krasnoyarsk's court read,

"The petition of Marie Cécile LeBlanc to adopt Kristina Sergeevna Bajenova and Anton Sergeevich Bajenov is granted."

46

The LeBlanc Family's First Week, Easter in Russia.

Happiness... lies in the joy of achievement,
in the thrill of creative efforts.
Franklin D. Roosevelt[45]

APRIL 30, 2005

A snowy, cold and windy morning greeted us. But the weather was secondary to the happiness we felt inside. The children dressed in their new American clothes. Kristina, in her favorite pink sweater and black jeans. Anton paraded his new black jeans and a plaid flannel shirt. These clothes were their very own, not ones from the bins at the orphanage.

We ate our morning meal in the fourth-floor restaurant. As usual, Anton entertained us at the breakfast bar, gesturing and pretending he would eat food from every dish on display. The more we laughed, the more he gestured. He was happy, carefree, totally comfortable with his new mama. Kristina was his protector and as long as she was there, he had no fear. He went along with every decision she and I made. He insisted on opening doors and carrying packages. He was a lovable, rambunctious young boy with a great attitude. When Anton played with his Spider-Man Lego, I was amazed with his creative ability to put the pieces together. When finished with one project, he presented it to Kristina and me with pride. He carefully gathered all his toys, protected them under the desk which he claimed as his toy box.

Later that morning, Kristina had her first professional manicure/pedicure. At first, she was a little timid, but then, she was all smiles as she sat like a grown up, looking at various magazines which included the Cosmopolitan translated in Russian. When it was all done, she showed Anton and me her newly painted nails with pride.

Kristina, now a young lady of thirteen, was more poised, very feminine and beautiful. I sensed she wanted to be part of the decision making, even to be sort of in charge. She was more reserved, more pensive. The decision to be adopted and move to America was hers alone. Only Kristina was interrogated by the judge. A child had to be twelve years old, Anton was only nine. She carried the consequences of her decision on her shoulders. I wondered what was going through her mind. Was there any remorse, any fear? At thirteen years of age, how did she envision her life in America? So many questions . . . with the language barrier, we could not discuss these thoughts.

Every day, for one hour, we studied English. The children first learned to pronounce their new names and their Naples, Florida address in their new language. We studied various English words using a small picture dictionary. Each page had a different topic. For example, a page displayed various fruits or vegetables with the English word printed next to its picture. There were pages on anatomy, tools, cars, etc. When Anton saw the musical instruments page, he pointed to the violin saying, "Me C.C. Me C.C."

"You want to play the violin?"

"*Da*"

"O.K. When we arrive in America you can."

I asked Kristina if she wanted to learn a musical instrument. She said, "*Da*" and pointed to the piano.

I was thrilled with their choices. I had a piano and my dad's violin.

We spent time pronouncing words and numbers. We practiced simple addition and subtraction in English as well as reviewing the multiplication tables. Communication was challenging but we used sign language we made up as we went along. When translation was important and Tasha was not with us, we asked Olea at the front desk to translate. We used gestures to communicate our most basic needs. I asked my children to teach me a few words in Russian. When I repeated the words, they laughed. We smiled a lot, hugged a lot, and we said "I love you" as often as we could. We took lots of pictures. Both children used the video and the still camera whenever they wanted. They were new toys and a learning experience for them.

The strong bond between the children was very noticeable and beautiful to observe. They were very affectionate with each other, and they were both affectionate toward me, Anton more so as he had a more extroverted personality.

Ludmilla and Tasha both suggested, "C.C., I would encourage the children to call you Mama. Every school child has a mama."

Ludmilla explained to Kristina, "C.C. will never replace your biological mama. By granting the adoption, the judge gave you and Anton a second mama, an American mama."

I began referring to myself as "Mama C.C." Both children called me "C.C." the name they knew me as from the time we were introduced at CampKidHope at the end of December 2003. Once in a while, I heard "Mama C.C." from Anton, but Kristina called me "C.C." all the time.

Ludmilla was encouraging when she said, "Don't worry, 'Mama C.C.' will come gradually, then it will be just 'Mama.' "

In the afternoons, we went for long walks. We visited several stores. Kristina asked that I buy her a CD of Russian songs. Kristina had become a little reluctant to study English.

I said, "OK, Mama C.C. buys CD, if Kristina study English."

"Da," she answered.

The children were all smiles when I offered them ice cream cones. This newfound freedom was wonderful for them and for me. Every day, on our return to the hotel, we stopped at the grocery store. We always bought water, some cheese or ready-to-eat chicken. Then we stopped at our favorite fruit lady's table to buy fruit. Each of us had to carry a package or two back to the hotel. Anton insisted on carrying the two large jugs of water. Halfway back to the hotel, he would slow down then stop, drop his load on the street gesturing with a smile what I understood to be, "It's too heavy, I'm tired, could you trade bags with me . . . ." We laughed.

May 1 was the Russian Orthodox Easter Sunday. Early in the morning, Tasha brought a dozen hard boiled eggs, decorated à la Russian for the occasion. The egg was a symbol of rebirth. It was adopted by early Christians as a symbol of the resurrection of Jesus at Easter.

We played the Russian Easter traditional game, egg tapping also known as egg fight, or egg knocking game. The rules of the game are simple. There are two participants. Each one holds an egg between the index finger and thumb. With the pointed part of the eggs facing each other, the participants tap each other's egg with the intention of breaking the shell of the competing player's egg, without breaking one's own. It was quite a fight. The winner? I do not remember, but it was not me. Now you ask what was the breakfast menu? Well, you guessed it, hard boiled eggs, as many as desired.

We walked to the Orthodox Church with Tasha to attend the Easter service. The church was filled to capacity, parents with young children, old wrinkled *babushkas*, wearing old dark grey coats with their heads garnished with semi-colorful scarves. As it was in the previous religious services I attended, the voices of the female choir sounded as if they came straight from heaven. They had the sweetest and purest voices one could ever imagine.

This time, the large table was filled with several festive types of bread and decorated cakes for the occasion. A large tray of candles, some lighted, some waiting to be lighted, was placed next to the bread table. A closed container with a slit on the top was ready to accept donations. Confessions were heard under the priest's shawl. I was still amazed the tea was served in cups everyone drank out of, even young children. Perhaps the thinking was God would never allow the transfer of diseases from one to another within the church walls. My children became restless. At their eye level, much of what they saw were coats from the waist down and beautiful pointed boots or shoes. Anton was a bit agitated. We left before the service ended. Kristina and Anton were able to observe a part of their culture they had never been introduced to.

In the afternoon, we joined Lorette and John from North Carolina, who were in Krasnoyarsk waiting for their court date to adopt a baby girl. Together we went for a walk. We came across an amusement park. Eight rubles per person gave us entrance. Each ride cost an additional 50 to 60 rubles, or about $1.50 to $2. For the Russian budget, it seemed expensive. In one of our many conversations, Tasha admitted that, in some ways, Russia was a third-world country. Looking at the setup of this amusement park, she was right. The rides were so old they looked as though they were repurchased from another third-world country.

The first ride was the Crazy Bus. Kristina and Anton were the drivers. Four steel tubes attached to some sort of a large motorized wheel going up and down, sometimes backward, sometimes forward. Then came the Rocking Tug. Like a tugboat, it went up and down and side to side giving the participant the impression of experiencing a vicious hurricane or typhoon. Kristina went on the small roller coaster. Anton did not meet the required height to join her. The last ride consisted of several seats, each connected to a wheel by a cable. As the wheel accelerated, the chair moved in a circular motion higher and higher as though one was flying. Then the Disney character Goofy came to say hello. All in all, the park created amusement and pleasure for all of us, but it was bitterly cold.

"Do I hear you asking how cold is bitterly cold?"

"Siberia cold, my friends! Coming from Naples Florida, that is colder than the Arctic Ocean, colder than you have ever experienced. We were the only crazy people freezing on the rides!"

Hunger came. What looked like a hot dog came out as a baloney/kielbasa sandwich. And the toilets? That's another story. No toilet paper, no soap, no hand towels. You must bring your own or you ice it out in your undies.

47.

Activities, Monday, Tuesday, Wednesday

Not flesh of my flesh, nor bone of my bone.
But still miraculously my own. Never forget for a single minute,
you didn't grow under my heart but in it.
Fleur Conkling Heyliger [46]

EARLY MONDAY MORNING AND for the next few days, we spent time signing documents for the transfer of responsibility of Kristina and Anton to their new Mama C.C. In each of the government's large ledgers, their Russian name was changed. They became Kristina Cécile and Anton John LeBlanc. My name was added in bold letters in the ledgers where their medical and school records were recorded. Several ledgers had to be signed. With each signature, I looked at my children and smiled. They smiled back. Every time my name was written on the dotted line, the responsibility of the children was gradually being transferred to me. I had definitely reached the point of no return. I loved my children; I fought for them with every fiber of my body. All I wanted to do is shout, "America, we're going home!"

In the afternoon, we visited the small museum across the plaza and down the steps toward the river. I had visited this museum during my October visit. In the basement of the three-level-building, exhibits displayed the history of the Russian aboriginal or indigenous people. Again, the reproduction of a beautiful aboriginal woman, standing in a glass-encased exhibit, caught my attention. I saw some resemblance to Kristina. I took a picture of Kristina standing in front of this lovely reproduction, dressed very much like our Québec First Nation people. Astonishing! How could this be, with so much distance between Québec and Siberia?

In another part of the museum Kristina and Anton were able to experience using electronic equipment and computers for the first in their lives. Their faces showed total amazement.

Tuesday, early morning, Tasha took us to retake the pictures for the children's passports. The passport pictures taken the previous October had expired. It always baffled me why so many documents had to be redone, most, if not all, at additional cost. Knowing several days were needed after the adoption to finalize the transfer of the children, and knowing their passport pictures would expire, why were they taken last October before the final decision of the judge? Was it another way to extract more money?

On our way back to the hotel, Tasha asked, "C.C., to keep the children busy, would you like to visit the Krasnoyarsk Zoo this afternoon?"

I suggested she ask the children. They gladly accepted. The location of the zoo was set high on an elevation and offered a beautiful view of the Yenisei River. The land was vast. If we judged by the extensive construction taking place, it appeared the zoo was expanding. I can still visualize the animals. Perhaps it was the time of the year, but what a pitiful sight! My heart was not only crying for the people of Russia, it was crying for the animals in this Siberian zoo. The large birds, black ravens, owls with ears were pitiful in their large dirty cages. The grizzly bears, brown bears, Siberian tigers, wolves and the Amur leopard looked sad. They were very thin. Their cages were dirty. The polar bear was especially a sad sight. He and his swimming pool were filthy. He looked malnourished, hungry and very angry. I was happy the children enjoyed their visit, but I would have preferred not to have seen the sad living condition of these animals. As I write these words, I can still see them. In my mind these animals were condemned to a sort of Siberian gulag for the rest of their lives. Perhaps the difficult experiences with the court in Krasnoyarsk since October 2004 has contributed to these negative comments.

Wednesday, when we went for our walk, the cloud ceiling was very low. At times, wind gusts whirled dust around, reminding me of mini tornadoes. We could barely breathe. Olea was right when she said, "There is so much dust in this city." One night, the wind was so strong that the thick dust was in a constant whirl; nothing was visible from our room windows. I remembered, in October 2004, a similar powerful windstorm sifted layers of sand into my room through the porous window seals.

That day, as we returned to our hotel, the children asked in sign language if they could spend some time on the plaza to run around. I answered, *"Da"* with a smile. Before the adoption was granted, part of the time, I entertained myself by looking at the beautiful young ladies, with hairdos of reddish, blondish or brownish tones, generally elegantly dressed, wearing the most beautiful winter boots, boots which fascinated me every day I spent in Krasnoyarsk. I sat on a frozen flowerpot and watched the strong determined steps of several ladies passing by, wearing high stiletto boots with pointed toes. Each step they took was hitting the pavement at a fast and determined pace, creating a sort of musical click-clack that could have been part of a concerto. I wondered where they came from and where they were going. I also wondered how many pairs of these expensive looking boots they would wear out during their long cold winters.

Shortly after we returned to our hotel room, Anton complained of a toothache. I remembered visiting the dentist on the fourth floor last October, after finding my eyetooth crown in my sandwich. Anton and I walked down the hallway, knocked on the door. As she opened it, she said *"privet"* and smiled. She remembered me. She invited Anton to sit in her dentist's chair. He turned white and became quite distressed. With Anton's mouth wide open, the dentist explained to me in sign language and gestures what I understood to be his baby tooth, still well in place, had to be removed to allow the permanent tooth to push through. At the pick of the needle, he screamed a little and looked at me with eyes saying, "Please save me from this, Mama C.C." He cringed when the dentist twisted the tooth side to side and back and forth to get it out. That is one moment when the heart of a mother wants to take the pain and the fear away from her child. But that is also a moment for a child to be strong and learn to face the many challenges life will continue to bring. The tooth was removed. All was well. After the children went to sleep, I sat to write my daily notes, knowing that one day, I would write this book.

48.

Bank Account, the First Week Continues . . . .

Earth provides enough to satisfy every man's needs,
but not every man's greed.
Mahatma Gandhi[47]

MAY 3, 2005

Early Thursday morning, after signing one more document, we stood in front of the government building to take pictures. Tasha approached me.

"C.C., each month since the death of your children's father, in May 2002, the Russian government has deposited funds in a bank account for their benefit."

"Really?"

"Yes, the money is held in a Dzerzhinsk bank, under the guardianship of Boris, the orphanage director."

"What will happen with this money, Tasha?"

"The money would have been given to the children at age eighteen, when they moved out of the orphanage. Since you're now the legal guardian of Kristina and Anton, you're the only person who can sign for the release this money."

Tasha stopped talking, giving me time to digest this news.

She continued, "As is customary, and as a gesture of goodwill, I suggest you sign the appropriate papers to donate each account to Boris for the benefit of the orphans left behind."

I looked straight into her eyes, hoping to find the true intent of her words. Then I asked, "What is the approximate value of each account?"

"Probably a little more than $1,000 each."

"Well . . . Tasha . . . this is a difficult decision for me to make. Could Ludmilla explain and ask the children what they would like to do with their money?"

When asked, Kristina timidly shrugged her shoulders and shyly said, "I don't know."

Ludmilla looked at Anton.

"What about you Anton?"

Without hesitation, he blurted, "This is my money, and I want it."

My immediate thought was, "These children have received very little since birth. This money is the only thing they own, the only thing they can take out of Russia." I looked at Tasha.

"Let me think about it, I'll let you know tomorrow."

When we returned to our hotel, I knocked on Gail's door, in the room just next to ours. Gail was an IBM manager, here with her mother. She had just successfully adopted a baby girl. I asked for their opinion regarding the children's money. Her mother, German born, was in the back of the room changing the diapers of her new grandchild. As soon as I finished explaining this bank account situation, without wasting a second, the mother shouted with a strong accent, "This is not your money to give! If it gets in the hands of the orphanage director, who knows where it will end up?"

There was no argument. I could not give away my children's money. I returned to our room.

Friday, April 6, Ludmilla and Tasha picked us up in the early morning for the signing of the last documents. My thoughts were on the children's bank account dilemma. At the first opportunity, I said, "Tasha, regarding the children's bank account, I truly feel uncomfortable giving it away. It is their money. Since I'm their custodian, I'll bring it with me and open a bank account in each of their names in Naples."

Tasha translated to Ludmilla. This is not what they wanted to hear.

"But C.C., this money is in Dzerzhinsk. When will you be back to Krasnoyarsk to close the account?"

I quickly answered, "I will not be back here for a very long time. Let's go to Dzerzhinsk right now."

"Today is not possible. Tomorrow is Saturday. You're flying to Moscow."

I did some quick thinking.

"Ludmilla will be coming to Tampa, Florida in July with a group of children to attend a CampKidHope. How about if I sign a power of attorney to authorize Boris to transfer their bank account assets to Ludmilla. When Ludmilla comes to Tampa this summer, she could carry a cashier's check in U.S. dollars."

We entered the notary public's office. Two women sat at their desks, approximately four feet apart. Light was pouring into their small office through a large window. Both desks were cluttered with papers and file folders three feet high. Having heard our reason to seek her help, it was obvious the notary was not happy about the way this money exchange would take place. She asked, "What if the money gets lost . . . or is stolen . . . who would be responsible?"

The notary suggested Ludmilla close the bank account and that she accept sole responsibility from Boris until the money would be transferred to me during her visit to Tampa. We both signed the agreement. I had to trust it would be done. With the signature transfer of the last documents and the bank account dilemma solved, we returned to our hotel late morning.

The sun came out around 2 p.m. The wonderful receptionist Olea called. She offered to take us for a city tour, "I'll bring my son. He is close in age to your children."

I handed the phone to Kristina, who gladly accepted. All five of us fit well in Olea's large SUV. She drove way up high on a hill to visit the quaint, tiny chapel named Paraskeva Pyatnitsa. The several visitors who walked in engaged in the customary tradition of lighting a candle, saying a prayer and dropping a few rubles in the collection box. Kristina and Anton solemnly chose a candle and proceeded to light it, a first experience for both. As they dropped rubles in the box, they looked at me with proud smiles.

The location of this church offered a magnificent view of the city below. The 2,100-plus mile Yenisei River begins in Mongolia. It is the largest river system flowing to the Arctic Ocean. It flows north to the Yenisei Gulf, then the Kara Sea. The famous Krasnoyarsk giant bridge connects the two banks of the river. The bridge was built around 1895. It is the symbol of the city. It's large size and intricacy were never seen before. Not only was a model of it presented at the Paris Exhibition of 1900, its architect, Lava Proskurvakov, was awarded a gold medal for its design.

As we walked outside the chapel, a young boy was riding a little scooter. Olea's son, Eric, asked the boy if he could borrow it. The boy gladly agreed. First, Eric rode it, taking time to teach Anton how to use it. He then asked Anton to try it. How fun for him to experience his first scooter ride. He struggled a bit and almost fell off, but succeeded in maintaining his balance. A proud Anton asked, "Me C.C.?"

"You want a scooter, Anton?"

"*Da.*"

"OK . . . in America."

Kristina was asked but preferred not to try it. The children were very quiet throughout the visit. I sensed Kristina and Anton felt a shyness *vis-à-vis* Eric, whom they had just met. I wondered if their discomfort was because they were adopted. We returned to our hotel. I invited Olea and her son to spend time with us in our room. The children continued to be uncomfortable with each other. After a while, we hugged and said goodbye.

Late afternoon, Tasha called to inform me the envelope containing the children's documents for the American Embassy would be ready Friday afternoon. She added, "You can make your reservations to fly to Moscow Saturday or Sunday."

"Tasha, do you know if the American Embassy will be open Monday and Tuesday, May 9th and 10th? You know President Putin has called for two days of National Holiday to celebrate the end of WWII."

"I really don't know, C.C."

"Tasha, dignitaries from all over the world, including President Bush, will join Mr. Putin in Red Square."

I vented my frustration.

"Tasha, I need to know. I have to secure a flight to America for all three of us. I need the departure date. Last October, Delta had a seven-day delay to fly to the US."

"There is nothing we can do C.C. you have to call Pyotr."

Whenever Tasha said, "There is nothing we can do," I knew there was no point pressing further. I walked to the business center. The internet did not respond. The telephone lines didn't work. I couldn't make a call to the United States; the Delta airline's office was closed. Their airport telephone number did not answer. I could have screamed. Under my breath I said, "And this country was part of the G8 Nations before the Obama Administration and other leaders kicked them out."

Then I remembered there was a travel office on the third floor of the hotel. I went back to our room and asked the children to follow me. The delightful young lady booked our flight to Moscow for Saturday. Then she dialed Pyotr's telephone number, who assured me we could fly to America on Wednesday the 11th. Next I contacted my dearest friend, Sir John, to ask him to make our flight reservations to America. Kristina and Anton had no idea the struggles that went on behind the scenes.

After we left the travel agent's office, we shopped for dinner at the corner deli. Then we stopped to say goodbye to our favorite fruit lady. After we selected a few fruits, Kristina explained that this was our last visit, that we were flying to Moscow the next day then to America. The fruit lady locked her eyes on mine, walked from around her table, gave me an emotional long hug. She refused to take any money and said, "*Spaciba*." What an emotional moment! Imagine, this wonderful fruit lady would not take our money! It was her way to show her appreciation for adopting these children. She knew they were going toward a better life.

We walked back to our room. The telephone rang. Tasha and Ludmilla asked if the children and I could meet them in the hotel lobby. They came to say goodbye. It was a tender moment. Ludmilla brought a beautiful souvenir book of Krasnoyarsk for the children. With moist eyes, she hugged them for the last time.

For our last dinner, Anton, as usual, was totally silly. Kristina joined in. Anton pretended to be a baby. Kristina fed him like one. The more she fed him the more he laughed. When some food dribbled down his shirt, they laughed and giggled even more. After dinner, we watched a spectacular ballet presentation on the Art Channel. All was well; another day had ended bringing us closer to home.

What a precious day! Together, we had overcome all the obstacles and all the challenges thrown at us so far in our adoption quest. We were near the peak of the KACC mountain. Were there more obstacles waiting for us in Moscow? I trembled at the thought.

49.

Saying Goodbye to Krasnoyarsk

It doesn't matter who you are, where you come from.
The ability to triumph begins with you—always.
Oprah Winfrey[48]

No matter how hard the past is,
you can always begin again.
Jack Kornfield[49]

SATURDAY, MAY 5, 2005

The day before, we had had a mini crisis. We had packed our luggage. We left out only the clothes we would wear to fly to Moscow. We were limited in clean clothes. Kristina insisted on wearing her favorite, heavy cotton sweater, white with black diagonal stripes. We had just washed it. It took more than twenty-four hours to dry. Gesturing, I suggested, "Kristina it would be better for you to wear this white sweatshirt and keep this sweater clean for our visit to the U.S. Consulate."

Communication was not easy. Kristina was not buying it. She had already started to assert her independence. We went to Olea at the reception desk for help. Kristina was not happy. She pouted a little, but in the end, she agreed.

The wake-up call came at 7:45 a.m. We were ready for breakfast at 8:20. We left the hotel at 9:30 with Ramon, a driver, and Kathya, a translator. I made sure Anton wore his sea sickness bracelet.

The ride to the airport was quiet. Ramon did not speak English. I had only met Kathya once. Truthfully, at that moment, my mind was looking forward, anticipating what our few days in Moscow would be like. Kathya stayed with us and guided us until we reached the gate for our flight. As soon as we sat in the waiting area, two drunk men arrived, staggering from side to side, holding on to chairs to keep their balance. What a sight for my children to observe! *Will these drunks be on our flight*, I wondered?

Finally, we boarded the Kras Air, flight direction Moscow. And yes, the two drunks and a few other drunks were on board. Lift off was at 11:30 a.m. We looked out the window for a last glance at the city. The smog was very thick or was it the dust? Who cares? The LeBlanc family was on its way home. Each mile brought us closer to God Bless America.

I sat between my children. Kristina had the window seat. She listened to her CD player. Anton could not sit still. He first made sure his sister and I had our seat belts on. Then he checked every button. When he was satisfied, he walked around looking and observing what was going on. I closed my eyes. My mind turned toward the many Krasnoyarsk people whose passage in my life would be remembered for a long time, some for as long as I live.

In this gray, depressing, far-away place, Ludmilla will be remembered as a kind, loving grandmother type, whom I believed really wanted the adoption to be successful. Tasha, the translator, was more stoic and more detached. But she, too, wanted the adoption to succeed. The two female drivers were very professional, warm and kind.

I remembered fondly the seven or eight caregivers at the transitional orphanage from October 2004. The profound statement of the assistant director of that orphanage will forever live in my mind, "We appreciate the Canadians, the Americans and the Europeans who adopt the children our government cannot take care of." I can still see their faces, and I can still hear the sound of the assistant director's voice.

Nor will I forget the beautiful, tall, and slender Olea, our friendly translator at the reception desk who was so helpful. My mind now travelled to the Dzerzhinsk orphanage and the sight of all the orphans left behind, whose faces, especially their eyes, seemed to be pleading, "Can't you take me too?" The images and the memory of those young girls and boys still brings tears to my eyes.

Then I focused on the lady doctor finishing her shift at the medical clinic, who asked Boris, "Who is this lady adopting these children?" As we left the clinic, I remember so clearly while walking toward the van. She turned around, looked in our direction. I felt a need to walk toward her. Our eyes locked onto each other's as I approached. She tended me her hands then her arms. We embraced for several seconds. We communicated spiritually, with a love language only we could understand. She understood the incredible blessing my children were receiving. A very powerful moment for this *babushka*-looking physician and me. She will live in my heart forever.

How can I not remember the wonderful lady at the fruit stand? On our last day, Kristina thanked her for helping us select the best fruit and told her we were leaving in the morning. Upon hearing the news, she walked around her table, gave me an intense look, her eyes were moist. She then opened her arms and gave me a long Russian hug. She then hugged the children. She refused payment for the fruit. She insisted it was her gift to us. Our fruit lady understood the children were going toward a better life. This emotional precious moment is still present deep in my heart. I can still see her smiling face, her petite body frame covered with a wool bonnet, a winter jacket and winter pants.

I also remembered with sadness the five women who walked away from me as I tried to ask for directions with the note the hotel receptionist had prepared for me. The look on their faces was nothing short of disdain. They were afraid to talk to me, afraid to give me directions, afraid of repercussions for speaking to a stranger, fears left over from the Stalin era. Then, I remembered the two sixteen-year-old girls who could not stop asking questions about Canada and the United States. They had no fear of repercussions from long dead Stalin. They were three or four generations removed from his horrors.

My thoughts travelled to the cheerful concierge lady on the fourth floor who gave us a chocolate bar when we left. Then there was the older concierge lady who never looked at me. I would tend her my key; she would give me the corresponding card without ever raising her eyes. She did the same when I returned the card in exchange for my room key. One day, I held on to the key until she looked up. I smiled and said, "*Spaciba.*" One corner of her mouth moved upward in a half smile and then she immediately looked down again.

But then there were the nasty ones. The spiteful and vicious judge and prosecutor in 2004. The large man in the hotel lobby who yanked the phone out of my hand after giving me a "hockey check" with his large shoulder. I almost flew to the other side of the lobby. Most of the housekeepers on my floor were very unpleasant. They looked at me as if I were contaminated. They seemed so miserable, so unhappy; I felt sad for them.

Wise words were shared with me that we should never let our earlier experiences affect our future. The past cannot be changed, and our present and future life should not be punished because of our past. I hope to share these words of wisdom with my children someday.

Krasnoyarsk is a place I will probably never return to. The only attraction to that city was my children. They are with me now. They are giving me a reason to wake up each morning, a purpose like no other.

I prepared to say a prayer. The thought that one-and-a-half-years ago, a powerful intuition invaded me. Was it from God? Was it from the universe? The message was, "These are your children, and you are to take care of them." *Well God, here I am.*

I have fulfilled your request. Now I need your help. You must send special guides to oversee and direct the mission you placed on my shoulders. My children's new lives in America must be directed for the greater purpose that only You know. I felt such inner happiness. Somehow, their story must be told so that abandoned children all over the world are not left behind to be preyed upon by prostitution rings, slavery, crime or other unsavory elements. I say again, "Children do not ask to be born. Once they are, we must give them a chance."

It was close to noon Moscow time. One hour to go before we were to land. Lunch was served. Hot dogs or fish, peas that had soaked in the cooked rice for hours, salad made of cabbage and corn, ham or salami, two pieces of bread, one cookie, one piece of chocolate, tea, coffee, juices. The food was bad, not very tasty. Even the children who love their kielbasa and salami could not eat it.

The airplane seats had to be the worst in the industry. They were so close together. The seat cushions were so worn out they could not hold the passengers. One slouched down, impossible to sit straight. But the toilets! Oh my God . . . the toilets. One had to really need to go to lock oneself in this small, smelly cubicle. The second time around, there was no soap left. First time there was no toilet paper; I used a paper towel. Airplane toilets in general are not very appealing but these ones were disgusting to the utmost degree. Flying on an American airline home would be a real treat.

We landed safely at the Sheremetyevo International Airport, at 12:30 p.m. Moscow time. Max and a chauffeur were there to greet and drive us to central Moscow. Two hours later, we walked into the twenty-one-story Rossiya Hotel, a three-thousand-room hotel adjacent to Red Square. It towered over the Kremlin walls and the cupolas of Saint Basil's Cathedral. So large was this hotel that it included a two-thousand-five-hundred seat concert hall, a movie theater, and a police station with jail cells behind unmarked black doors.

We were guided to our small suite, a large bedroom with a king-size bed and adjoining small sitting room with a sofa bed.

Kristina again chose the sofa bed. With the four-hour time zone difference, it was close to our bedtime. We had dinner, and soon thereafter, we tucked in for the night.

50.

Moscow, Dr. Gronsky

The repugnant, disgusting, filthy doctor...
touched my daughter... in front of my eyes....
I did not speak... we needed to go home.
C.C. LeBlanc

May 8, 2005

When we checked into the Rossiya Hotel, I had reviewed the reservation fees with the receptionist.

"Yes, Miss LeBlanc, breakfast for you and your children is included with the rate of your room."

This morning, as we finished breakfast, the waitress presented me with a check for 800 rubles, or approximately $28.

I looked at the young lady and softly said, "This bill must be a mistake. Our breakfasts are included."

In a heavy Russian accent, "Nothing can do. Need sign here. Go business office, room 3.088."

The pretty blond lady at the business office looked at our reservations on the computer and said, "Miss LeBlanc, the receptionist you spoke with when you registered made a mistake. Your breakfasts are not included."

"But please, review my hotel reservations. It clearly stipulates, 'Buffet breakfast included.' "

"This is a mistake, Miss LeBlanc. Your breakfasts are not included, according to our papers."

In Russia, one does not pursue nor argue . . . . There is no point. The battle is lost before we can even get started. Thank God, we're only here for a few more days . . . . What's another few $$$!

On a regular day, there would be bumper-to-bumper traffic around the circle outside Red Square. On this day, and for the next two days, only official vehicles and people with passes were allowed near Red Square. Barricades, attended by guards, were everywhere. With our Rossiya Hotel passes, we were able to walk in and out of the area. A large group of military soldiers were lined up to enter Red Square to practice for the parade. We were able to walk near enough to the soldiers to talk to them and make them smile. From the large opening to the square, we could glance at the Kremlin, the famous Gum Department Store, the State History Museum, Lenin's Mausoleum and, of course, Saint Basil's Cathedral, all designed by architects of the 16th century.

After visiting a small museum nearby, Kristina became agitated. She was pulling on my arm.

I asked, "What is it Kristina?"

"CD, please C.C., CD"

We found a music store. She looked on the shelves intently. She then turned toward me holding two CD's, gesturing and saying,

"Please C.C., buy CD, please C.C."

How does one engage in a meaningful conversation when such a language barrier exists? Very slowly and in a pleasant voice, I said, "Kristina, in Krasnoyarsk, Mama C.C. bought two CDs. You promised to study English. But you did not; no more CDs Kristina."

Kristina understood enough English to figure out what I just said. Since the adoption, I sensed she wanted to establish her position with me. It became obvious, at the onset of her teenage years, her position would become one of opposition. I smiled to myself. I fully remembered my own teenage years, "My poor *Maman*." I could already visualize several crises were on their way.

Taking advantage of being in Moscow, I arranged to have a guided tour of the city with Alina, a translator/guide. She met us at the hotel in the early afternoon. With pride, she introduced us to several of the beautiful Metro stations, considered to be a "testament to Stalinism." Stalin's goal was to build an elaborate Metro to show the superiority of socialism over the capitalist world. Construction started in 1931. The first thirteen stations opened in 1935. The artistic design and the beauty of each station was as spectacular as the other. Its construction incorporated high ceilings with materials such as marble walls, stained glass, mosaics, chandeliers, etc. The early subway stations were built by prison camp labor. At the time of our visit, the metro had approximately one-hundred-seventy stations and transported nine million people every day.

We walked to The Bolshoi Theater. Due to renovations, no visitors were allowed inside. We continued walking, visiting several parks before returning to our hotel. This private tour gave my children a chance to experience a little of their native land outside of Siberia.

Late in the afternoon, Max, the adoption agency's representative/translator, called.

"C.C., the children's medical and consulate papers will not be ready by day's end on May 10th. You will not be able to fly to America on the eleventh."

"Max, what do you mean the papers won't be ready in time for our flight?"

"C.C., you know President Putin called for a holiday May 10th and 11th to celebrate the 60th anniversary of Victory Day? Even your President Bush, with your First Lady, along with fifty other dignitaries will attend the celebrations. Everything will be closed. The earliest you could fly to America is May 12th."

"This is very upsetting Max. I called your boss Pyotr, before we left Krasnoyarsk. He assured me all paperwork would be ready in time for our flight May 11th."

At 7:00 p.m., Max called again.

"C.C., Pyotr just told me he only spoke to you once. It was about coming to Moscow on Thursday, doing the medical exams on Friday and flying to America on Saturday."

"Pyotr is correct. He told me Ludmilla could perform miracles. But Vera, Ludmilla's secretary and driver said the papers needed to leave Krasnoyarsk would only be ready on Friday May 6 at 5:45 p.m. Ludmilla said the earliest we could leave Krasnoyarsk was May 7."

"Hmm"

"I tried to call Pyotr back to tell him we couldn't leave Krasnoyarsk until Saturday. He did not answer. I spoke to Nadya, his secretary. She checked with Pyotr. He confirmed the medical clinic and the U.S. Embassy would both be open even if President Putin called for a holiday. Pyotr confirmed the papers would be ready on Tuesday May 10, and that we could leave on Wednesday May 11, as scheduled. Max, hospitals don't close. People get sick on weekends and holidays."

"C.C., the children have a positive TB test. They will require an X-ray."

"Adoption Over-Seas told Pyotr and me that my children's positive TB test was the result of the anti-TB vaccine they received. Max, we need to go home."

Kristina started crying again when she heard there may be more delays. My heart sank to my ankles. *Will we ever get out of here?*

Max called back, "C.C., Dr. Gronsky could come to your room around 9 p.m. to start the medical exit exam. But, understand, if the doctor comes to your room, it will be more money."

"How much more Max?"

"$150 instead of $100. The extra $50 is for the doctor's drive to your hotel."

"Will it be $150 for Kristina and $100 for Anton?"

"That is a good question. I don't know. He probably will charge you $250. You'll have to discuss that with the doctor."

My dear readers, as you continue to read further, follow my words, make a movie in your own mind, walk in my shoes to experience the emotions I felt as a mother.

At 9:35 p.m., there was a knock on the door. Enter the Russian doctor, an unfriendly, overweight, barrel-looking man, with a jet-black, greasy, curly hairdo. After a quick handshake, he asked for the medical papers. I tended the files.

Sitting on the edge of the sofa chair with his head down, looking at the floor, avoiding eye contact, he said, "Monday and Tuesday are declared holidays. Everything will be closed. I cannot do all the work on the same day. Kristina will need a chest X-ray, at an additional cost of $20 and she will need a rubella shot."

"Dr. Gronsky, all hospitals can't be closed. People get sick on holidays. Our flight confirmations are for Wednesday, May 11."

He did not answer. I broke the silence.

"Dr. Gronsky, can you help us?"

The "good doctor" placed the medical files on the table and directed Kristina to the bedroom.

"May I go in doctor?"

He addressed Kristina. I watched her strip to her underwear. He quickly looked in her ears and her mouth. He then grabbed the vanity stool, sat on it. His eyes were level with her very young breasts. As he started the examination of her chest, I wondered why he was holding his stethoscope in a way that his knuckles touched Kristina's skin. He pressed the stethoscope around one breast six times, then around the other breast again six times, touching Kristina's skin and nipples each time he pressed the stethoscope.

He then pressed his stethoscope three more times onto the middle of her breast. When he started the same procedure a second time, exactly the same way, I became very concerned. Could there be something suspicious in her heart? Perhaps her lungs? I worried about Kristina's bad cough. Finally, he stopped, looked up at me. *OMG, something is wrong, how serious is it?* I thought. He looked straight into my eyes, and in a cocky voice he said,

"Miss LeBlanc, the worst problems you'll have with this little girl will be to keep the boys away from her."

What a disgusting, filthy man! Touching my little girl's breasts with his knuckles gave him pleasure, right in front of my eyes . . . with no shame. I wanted to kick him, kick him so hard as to damage his family jewels. What a vulgar man. To think that this physician is under contract with the Unites States government.

He then asked Kristina to lie on the bed. He examined her tummy and then told her to get dressed. I remained silent, fearing further delays.

Anton was invited into the bedroom. I stayed to observe. This time, the good doctor held his stethoscope properly with his fingertips. He only pressed the stethoscope two or three times around Anton's chest, checked his stomach and then asked him to get dressed. He obviously did not have any interest in a nine-and-one half year-old boy. Anton's exam lasted a maximum of three minutes. We returned to the sitting room.

With a defiant look, Dr. Gronsky said, "Miss LeBlanc, it will be $300 for this visit."

God help me. I wanted to give him the knee, hit him so hard as to destroy the most revered part of his body. I have a very strong knee. Had I been able to kick him, he would have left running and crying for his mama. I wanted to scream, "Remember you work for the government of the United States of America." But instead, cowardly, I walked into the bathroom, retrieved $300 from the money bag strapped around my body. We could not sustain another delay. We needed to go home.

51.

Hospital Visit

*Indeed bribery, favoritism and corruption
in a great variety of forms were rampant not only
in politics but in all levels of society.*
David McCullough[50]

MAY 9, 2005

Shortly after Dr. Gronsky left our room, Max called.

"C.C., tomorrow morning we'll meet at 8:30 a.m. at the Metro platform level."

Security was on high alert due to the WWII celebration. We walked out of the hotel lobby and made a right turn. We came face-to-face with the first barricade. A young guard planted himself in front of us. Gently I asked, "Could you please let us through, sir? We're meeting our guide at the Metro platform."

He couldn't understand. Kristina explained. A bilingual guard was called. Fearing they would not let us though, perspiration started running down my face.

"Mr. Officer, my children and I are meeting our guide in the Metro."

I showed him our Rossiya Hotel passes. He looked at them, gazed into my eyes for a few seconds, ordered the barricade to open. *OUF!* Success!

Max was waiting. We boarded the train. We exited at the third station into sort of a circular courtyard with several small stores. Max looked at me.

"C.C., I strongly suggest you buy a bottle of liquor for the doctor."

"What, Max? Buy the doctor a bottle of liquor?"

"C.C., this is the way we do business around here. Today is a holiday and you are expected to bring a bottle. Dr. Gronsky is doing you a very special favor. You're the only family he will see in the hospital today."

While talking, Max led us to the small liquor store located in the courtyard. I was embarrassed, even mortified.

"Max, my children are orphans because their parents, grandparents, and some of their aunts and uncles were alcoholics. You're asking me to offer the good doctor a bribe in the form of liquor while my children are watching? Max, Dr. Gronsky is under contract with my government. Enough! I've already paid him $300."

I felt very ill at ease, sick to my stomach. On one hand, one does not want to be forced to pay a bribe. On the other hand, one doesn't want to alienate the very "good doctor" who would provide the medical papers needed to fly home in two days. If I did not bring a bottle, could Dr. Gronsky sabotage the children's medical records? As much as I wanted to scream and kick, I really did not have a choice. Russians function with bribes. Going home was more important than a bottle of liquor. As we entered the store, I asked, "What kind of liquor Max? A good bottle of wine? A nice bottle of champagne maybe?"

"A bottle of Johnny Walker Black Label will be fine," he replied.

I looked on the shelves.

"Max, I can't see any Black Label on display."

He spoke with the clerk who walked to the back room, returned, placed the Black Label bottle on the counter and looked at me.

"How much?" I asked, looking at the clerk.

Max translated, "2,100 rubles, approximately $77."

"$77 Max? I'm not spending almost $100 for a bottle of liquor. Enough! This doctor was very well paid last night. What about the Red Label?"

We settled for Johnny Walker Red Label for 900 rubles, about $33.

The children were watching in silence. When the transaction was terminated, we started our walk toward the hospital. Anton gestured, wanting to carry the bag. I refused. *My son was not going to carry a "liquor bottle bribe."* I gave it to Max to carry. Dr. Gronsky was waiting in his office. After the usual greetings, we followed Max and the doctor to the clinic. My sense was that Max used this time to inform the "good doctor" about the less pricey bribe he was getting. Both turned around from time to time to check on us. I could tell the good doctor was not happy. I smiled to myself, but I was also concerned that punishments were on the horizon.

We arrived at the clinic. Most of the conversation was in Russian. Communication in English only took place when Max or the doctor addressed me. The children were asked to follow the nurse who led them to the X-ray department. Dr. Gronsky returned to his office to fill out the children's medical report. Max and I filled out the questionnaire required for the American Consulate.

While at the clinic, another American family came in with a Russian interpreter.

"Max, I thought Dr. Gronsky came in today just for us."

He answered, "The interpreter for this couple called Dr. Gronsky who told him since he was already in the office, he would finalize the medical papers for them."

"Really?"

As soon as we finalized filling out the American Embassy papers, Max asked, "C.C., I need $20 for Kristina's X-ray."

Max took the money to the doctor's office. Within seconds, he returned to the waiting room.

"C.C., you need to give me another $40. The X-rays are $30 per child."

At that moment, Dr. Gronsky walked into the waiting room. I looked at him.

"Dr. Gronsky, at the Rossiya Hotel last night, you said the American government requires X-rays on children over age eleven. You added that only Kristina would need one at a cost of $20."

In a very strong voice, he replied, "Last night, I made a mistake."

There was no argument. Like I've been told before, "That's the way the system works. We can't do anything about it." I tended another $40. In addition, Max asked for another 125 rubles to pay for photocopies.

As I anticipated, Max had informed the good doctor, "C.C. refused to buy you the Black Label." The doctor punished me . . . charging me through the nose. Who knows, he may have charged me the same amount had I bought the Black Label. What did I learn? It's impossible to fight against such corruption . . . . For my children's sake, I stayed silent and I paid. . . . Dr. Gronsky will live in my memories as the most disgusting professional person I have ever met.

We returned to our hotel. The sixtieth anniversary celebration of WWII victory over Nazi Germany was in full swing. In Russia and other former Soviet republics, this anniversary is called Victory Day or the celebration of the Great Patriotic War. In Russia, it's the most important holiday after New Year's.

On this day, May 9, 2005, more than fifty dignitaries and world leaders were present, including Chinese President Hu Jintao, French President Jacques Chirac, Indian Prime Minister Manmohan Singh and U.N. Secretary General Kofi Annan. Welcomed as friends were the leaders of World War II's three major Axis powers, German Chancellor Gerhard Schroeder, Japanese Prime Minister Junichiro Koizumi and Italian Prime Minister Silvio Berlusconi. President Bush and our First Lady were given a seat of honor next to President Vladimir Putin.

President Putin paid tribute to the enormous Soviet wartime sacrifice. He vowed his country would never forget the debt owed to the tens of millions of Soviet citizens who died during World War II. On this day, about 2,500 WWII Soviet veterans marched into Red Square. Thousands of others, unable to march, were driven in motor vehicles. As we walked around our hotel before going to dinner, we could observe the activity of the military. Security soldiers were on every corner.

At the end of the festivities, one of Russia's biggest firework displays illuminated the sky for almost one hour. Having a room on the sixteenth floor, with a large, double, screenless French window that opened inward, gave us a terrific view. Not only did we have a good view of the fireworks, but we could also see to the horizon. We became attracted to the happy sounds from the street below. We hung our heads over the windowsill to see what was happening.

What we witnessed were hundreds upon hundreds of happy, crazy, young military men singing Russian patriotic and military songs, marching by group after group, on their way home. The three of us were enjoying it all until, all of a sudden, as I hung my head down, my prescription glasses dropped several stories to crash on the platform below. Anton got very excited. He wanted to go down to retrieve them. Kristina held him back. I called the reception.

"Miss LeBlanc, we send security to room."

When the knock on the door came, the children took over. They directed the gentlemen to the open window and pointed to my glasses, barely visible in the darkness. The security guards said a few words to the children, what I understood to be that they would be back. Shortly thereafter, we saw the two men walking on the platform below, one of them bending to pick up my indispensable glasses. Within a few minutes, a pair of slightly twisted glasses were handed back to me. I was able to see again.

In the distance, smaller fireworks were sprouting up all over town. The happy noises, along with the laughter from the soldiers passing by on the street below, lasted for hours. From time to time, silence returned only to be broken by another group of soldiers.

For my children and me, to be part of these festivities in some small way was an enjoyable surprise to end our day.

52.

American Consulate Visit

We are all in this together, by ourselves.
Lily Tomlin[51]

MAY 10, 2005

Our last day in Russia required a visit to the United States Consulate to complete all of the documents needed for Kristina and Anton to fly out of Russia and enter the United States. We met Max outside the barricade in front of our hotel at 8:30 a.m. As we walked out of the hotel, a young couple was waiting with their newly adopted daughter. They introduced themselves as Amy and Todd. We climbed into the van. I broke the silence by congratulating them on the adoption of their baby girl. Then asked, "Where did your child's medical exam take place?"

"Dr. Gronsky came to our hotel room Sunday night."

"Really! How much did you pay?"

"Dr. Gronsky asked for $150. We were told it was the price for the doctor to come to our hotel room."

WOW! I thought. Dr. Gronsky collected $450 for three exit medical exams. I'm assuming he pocketed the $60 for my children's X-rays, plus a bottle of liquor . . . very lucrative for the "good doctor," in a country that pays their physicians only $100 a month.

On our way to the American Consulate, we stopped at a hotel, approximately two miles from the Rossiya. Another family climbed into the van with their young daughter. They sat on the seat facing me. I smiled, introduced myself then asked, "When did your daughter receive her medical exam?"

"Dr. Gronsky came to our hotel room Sunday night."

The good Dr. Gronsky made $600, a $200 premium over what he would have been paid if the exams had been done in the hospital, plus whatever bribes he received. There was no question in my mind; it was all planned.

First, Max put the fear in each family that our medical reports would not be ready on time because of the two-day holiday. All three families were told Dr. Gronsky was willing to do the medical exit exam in our hotel rooms on Sunday night, as a big favor . . . just for us. These four medical exams, two babies and my two children could have been done at the hospital on Monday. Working for the United States government is quite a lucrative business for the "good doctor."

The van stopped at the main door of the consulate. We followed Max. Many other families were already waiting in the reception room. We stood in line to speak to the representative sitting behind an open window. As each family reached the window, the representative reviewed the contents in the envelopes we each carried for our children. A few additional questions such as name, address, and reason for the adoption were asked. We were told to wait for our name to be called.

I sensed a certain uneasiness or nervous energy in the room. This was the last step for every parent to receive permission to bring his or her adopted children home. Without the precious documents locked inside the brown envelope, the adopted Russian children would not be allowed to board the plane. One at the time, a family was called to the window. The wait was long. The children became jittery. We hugged we smiled, and we waited. Suddenly, there was a voice on the speakers.

"Attention, attention." Everyone stopped talking.

"We are sorry to inform you that due to a computer glitch, we are unable to finalize your documents at this time. Communications with the United States have stopped. We are doing our best to resolve the problem. We suggest you return to your hotel. We will communicate with your representatives as soon as the documents are available. We hope to deliver them to your hotel this evening. We are truly sorry for this inconvenience."

Everyone was stunned. We looked at each other in shock. Someone shouted, "What are we going to do? Our flight is scheduled for early tomorrow morning!"

Max gently suggested, "There is nothing more we can do here. We just have to wait."

We drove back to the hotel in silence. The stress on the other parents' faces was palpable. I looked up at the sky. Silently, "We must get out of this country now, God. We so need to go home. Please, no more delays."

Back in our room, I fell apart. We were so close to going home, yet still so uncertain . . . . Emotionally, with this last hurdle, I had reached my breaking point. I locked myself in the bathroom and cried, sobbed, until there were no tears left. A little voice inside said, "Don't give up C.C. You're almost there."

Hope returned. I regained my composure. I looked up again.

Please God, don't let us stay any longer. Please, we must go home.

The children were hungry. We took the elevator to the hotel lobby and found a restaurant. We were quiet. I smiled as best I could. While waiting for our food, I took a piece of paper, drew a snowman using an orange and a grapefruit for the body, a tomato for the face, a newspaper for the hat, topped with a pound of butter. The children looked intrigued. I stopped for a few second and then continued.

"A cherry for the eyes, a strawberry for the nose, a banana for the mouth, peanuts for the teeth, celery for the arms, carrots for the legs and a little blueberry for the navel."

As I named each item, the children repeated after me. Not only were they learning more English words, they were learning to pronounce the words as well, albeit with a slight French accent. When the snowman was completed, they looked at me. We laughed together. Still waiting for our food, I gave each one a sheet of paper and managed to ask them to draw their own version of a snowman. Communication was still a challenge, but we managed.

With the festivities over and the barricades removed, traffic had resumed around Red Square. We took a short walk and returned to our room. In defiance of the uncertainty of our departure, we finished packing our bags. Around 8 p.m., we went to the money exchange window located in the lobby at the end of a long wall on our right. Halfway along the wall, we passed by an open office door. I glanced in. A negative, queasy feeling overcame my whole being. Four men dressed in black suits and two women dressed in black skirts and white blouses were standing in the doorway.

I continued walking toward the cashier's window, about fifteen feet further, holding tight to my children's hands. The window was in the corner. As I stood, I was almost touching the wall on my right. I moved my body away from the cashier's window to let my children stand securely in front of me for protection. Kristina was doubly protected by the wall. The two women came out of their office and stood on my left. Instinctively, I put my arm on Anton's shoulder and turned around. The two men standing in the doorway were staring at us. I stared at one woman on my left with eyes ready for a fight. She stared back at me for a few seconds. She exchanged a few words with the other woman. They walked back to their office.

When the transfer of currency was completed, I took Kristina's hand with my right hand so she would walk furthest away from the office door. Anton held my left hand. Holding my children's hands as tight as I could, we turned around. The two men were still standing in the doorway watching us as we passed by. That encounter shook me. I felt genuine fear. I wondered if this could be one of the recruiting centers for young girls applying for a "better job abroad," as advertised on billboards. As I heard on the English news on my October 2004 visit, once young girls are lured and cross the threshold of these office doors, they may never be seen again. Unknowingly, they become part of the repulsive sex slave rings.

I assume, when the two women took a look at me, they realized I was much too old for their business, but my little Kristina . . . Just the thought makes me ill.

When we were back in the safety of our room, we watched TV. The phone rang.

"C.C., Max here. I have your envelopes from the United States Consulate. I'm on my way to your room."

53.

We're Going Home

Having a place to go is a Home.
Having someone to love is a Family.
Having both is a Blessing.
Donna Hedges[52]

MAY 11, 2005

"We're going home! Or will we? Please God, no more delays. Please!"

Up at 7:00 a.m. Breakfast at 7:30. We left the hotel at 9:05 with our transportation team, Alina and a driver, for a fee of $50.

While standing at the airport ticket counter, I turned around to peruse our surroundings, still worried that we may be delayed again. Standing a few feet behind us, who was there but Derick, the Eurasia CEO for *Hope for World's Children*, the one who represents this non-profit organization to help in difficult adoptions. He is the one who travels from Russia to Jamaica and to a few other countries on donors' dollars. In a friendly way he said, "I see you were successful in adopting your children?"

"Yes, I was. But it sure was not because of your help."

I turned back to the airline representative. She handed me our tickets. We walked away. Just a few seconds later, I heard, what I thought was my name being called, "Miss LaBlanche, Miss

LaBlanche . . . ." A tap on the shoulder followed. My heart stopped . . . . No, no! Not again... not another delay....

"Tickets wrong, you go Fort Lauderdale. No go Fort Myers . . . ." *God help us, we're still good!*

New tickets were issued. We resumed our walk to the first security zone. In a cool tone, the security agent asked,

"Please open luggage."

Anton watched like a hawk while Kristina stood by me. After several minutes, the officer said, "OK. Go."

Before entering the next security area, we stopped at the restroom. Just my luck . . . I was graced with the last twelve inches of toilet paper. I know you're smiling. You probably think I have an obsession with Russian toilets, but wait, I learned to carry paper napkins in my purse. I felt happy in that cubicle. My spirit was high. *We're going home today!*

As quickly as I thought of America, so quickly doubts returned. *Are there more challenges ahead?* I prayed that we get through all of the checkpoints safely. If only we could be in the air, flying over international waters. If only we could be landing in New York City. What a beautiful day it would be!

At the next security stop, I tended our three passports. With a heavy accent, the guard asked, "Russian Documents please."

I didn't recall anyone informing me that I had to show Russian documents at the Moscow airport. I was given a brown sealed envelope for each child for the immigration officer at our port of entry in the U.S. These two envelopes were sacred. Right now, they were as important as my life itself.

The dark-haired young woman spoke very little English. She continued to say, "Russian documents, Russian documents."

I kept showing her the two brown envelopes. She said, "No. Russian documents."

I suddenly remembered. I had placed all the adoption documents in my carry-on bag, not taking a chance they would get lost in transit. I opened the carry-on bag. The Russian officer pointed to the pink plastic envelope. I handed it to her with a smile. Very seriously, she looked at all the documents. She found the two adoption certificates. She took several minutes to review them. My heart started beating faster. *Pins and needles . . . pins and needles . . . OMG, something's going to happen . . . .* After what seemed an eternity, she looked at us, smiled, "Papers OK. Go."

"*Ouf!*" We are one more step toward freedom. It was now noon. We reached our gate. We sat on a bench.

My children had no idea what kind of house they would be living in. I showed them pictures of the exterior of their new home. Anton exclaimed something in Russian, something that I interpreted to be, "Look Kri, three-car garage."

Looking at the picture, pointing at each garage door, I said, "*Da*, one for Kristina, one for you, Anton, and one for mama." They smiled.

A woman sitting near us asked, "Did you just adopt these children?"

"Yes, we we're going home today."

"Would you like me to translate for you?"

"Yes, it would be very helpful, thank you."

Kristina asked if she had her own bedroom and bathroom.

"*Da*, a beautiful bedroom and bathroom."

Anton asked if there was a pool. I smiled, "*Da*, a pool big enough for Kristina, for you and for me, and . . . you also have your own bedroom and bathroom, Anton."

After living in an orphanage for five years, sharing a room with eight to ten girls, it was perfectly understandable that Kristina, now thirteen, wanted her own space. Anton remembered how he loved going into the pool in Tampa during CampKidHope. Hearing there was a pool made him happy.

At 12:30 p.m., a voice on the speakers announced that our flight was delayed. At this point, after all we went through, a few hours delay would not seem to matter, but I was still nervous. Finally, at 5:00 p.m., we were ready to board. What luck, we had bulkhead seats, 18 C, D, E, with a TV monitor and lots of leg room. Kristina chose the window seat. She was quiet . . . pensive . . . .

I sat in the middle. Anton was beside himself. Within minutes, he had already checked all the buttons. Then he became so very upset when he realized Kristina's seat had a set of earphones, but there were none on his seat nor on mine. He just couldn't wait for the flight attendant to pass by. At that moment, Anton believed, "If the attendant doesn't come to us, I will go to the attendant myself." He got out of his seat, went to the attendant's station, asked for two sets of earphones, one for himself and one for his new mama . . . . He returned with a smile, handing me my earphones with pride.

We strapped ourselves into our seats. The airplane door closed. *Yes, we are going home.* Just then, the door reopened. My heart stopped!

"No, no, no. We're not going back."

A passenger, out of breath, rushed in. The door closed again.

"*Ouf!* We're still safe."

The late passenger will never know he almost gave me a heart attack.

The roar of the plane increased. It pushed back. Yes . . . we're backing up . . . moving forward now . . . yes . . . further from the terminal . . . the plane slowed down . . . it stopped . . . . My heart stopped with it . . . could they still be coming for us?

The pilot announced,

"We're third in line. We will depart shortly."

We're moving forward again . . . faster . . . accelerating . . . faster . . . faster . . . full throttle now . . . . Yes! My body was pressed against the back of the seat. Yes . . . yes . . . yes . . . we're lifting, up . . . up . . . up . . . people are shrinking . . . smaller . . . invisible now . . . thank you, God . . . yes higher . . . further . . . no one can stop us now . . . no one can catch us. . . . We are flying west, far away from Moscow. *We've reached the point of no return! What an incredible feeling! Home! We're going home!*

I closed my eyes to say a prayer of gratitude to God, to my angels, to my family, my friends, those who supported us, especially Sir John who always remained by my side. He was true to his motto, NNNQ, never, never, never quit. He never quit, he never stopped helping us.

Kristina wrapped herself in the airplane's navy-blue blanket listening to her own music. Anton's sea sickness bracelets were doing their job. He had not stopped being excited. Not only did he know how every button worked, he checked how the tables came out of the arm rest. He looked at everything that moved or made noise. Both children look happy and content. Mama C.C. was . . . well, there are no words to express how I felt.

I thought I would cry with joy, but I couldn't, although there was such overwhelming joy in my heart. The airplane reached its cruising altitude. Anton walked to the back of the plane asked the attendant for water. The children occupied themselves watching TV. I closed my eyes. My mind and body were totally at peace for a moment, but it was soon joined by doubts. I thought that when presidents win elections, they must experience doubts and they must ask themselves, "Now that I am the president, where and how do I begin?"

Now that I'm a mama, how do I begin? Will I be able to fulfill my commitment to God, to my children, to myself and to the Russian court?

I leaned back and closed my eyes, only to find myself reliving this beautiful story that started when Sir John introduced me to Valerie and Murray with their adopted children. So many times, I felt thrown against the rocks by waves, which at times became insurmountable surges, only to find myself healing my wounds and continuing to fight. It's a wonder I did not drown. I couldn't drown. God and Sir John would not allow me.

Today, sitting on this flight on our way home, I realized the strength and determination my parents had given me. But perhaps more so, I was gifted with the ability to face challenges head on, the ability to sacrifice what needs to be sacrificed, to achieve or reach the summit of the bigger cause, the ability to survive the bumps on the road in order to reach "The impossible dream." If God has gifted me with these above qualities, he had gifted my parents before me. I inherited these powerful traits from them.

Unlike my mother, I have been able to leave the nest, and like an eagle, soar over the mountains to explore my talents in an unrestricted way. I lived outside the mold imposed by society on women of my mother's age and, in a lesser way, on women of my generation. I was always supposed to be the next one to get married. I was asked to marry so many times. I could never say yes . . . . I was afraid to make a commitment that would trap me inside a box I could not get out of easily or without breaking a sacred vow.

I was able to lead my life outside the structure of marriage, outside the responsibility of a family. Now, at sixty-five and, by my own choice, the enormous responsibility of motherhood had caught up with me. In the end, would all this strength, all this determination and all the love I have to give, be sufficient to guide these two wonderful children to independence and success? I pray it will.

I'll say it again, this awesome mission could not have been possible without the help of my dear and most loyal friend, John Percy Carey Woodhams, the man I refer to as Sir John, Saint John, and now, Grandpa John. Throughout this turmoil, Sir John was my lifeline while in Russia, both in October 2004 and in April 2005. He was the "Grand Central Station" for my family and for all my friends. He is the one who introduced me to Valarie and Murray Wise who became my inspiration to adopt.

Then, there was my very long-time friend (fifty-plus years) Sol M. whose parents were from Russia and who now lives in Birmingham, Alabama. He spent one week during CampKidHope to help with translation. Lidia from Belarus was the Russian voice to my children. She translated my thoughts to Boris, the director of the orphanage, and to Ludmilla, the coordinator in Krasnoyarsk. Polina, a Muscovite, who lived in Naples was my link to Irina, the lawyer in Moscow, and helped me understand the Russian system.

There were prayer groups asking to sustain us through this ordeal. Members of my family in Canada accepted and would welcome my children. My American cousins encouraged me to keep with it. Then I thought of all my other dear friends and close acquaintances who supported me, cried with me, prayed with me and encouraged me. For example, there was Liz Mossman and Trudy Graham who organized the kitchen while I was packing for the first trip to Russia in 2004, and Greta and Miss Fran who organized the baby shower. Then there were the parents of adopted Russian children, "The Russian Connection," who truly understood the challenges I faced, as well as the love we feel for our children.

I couldn't know it at the time, but there would be many more people who would become part of this story. There were the wonderful Stonebridge Golf and Country Club neighbors who received the children with open arms, love, smiles and gifts. My dear friends Mr. John Z., and later, his lovely wife, Phyllis, who took and still have a special interest in Anton; the Carlozzi family, wonderful neighbors whose daughter reached out to Kristina; the Pattons; Mr. Jerry K., Mr. Jeffrey, and so many more. A tsunami of support came our way from so many different directions. I cannot end this paragraph without mentioning one more time the "NNNQ" from Sir John. NNNQ equals: Never, Never, Never Quit. I didn't. With all this support, how could I?

Several hours later, the TV monitor map showed our airplane flying over Newfoundland, Goose Bay, the Gulf of St. Laurence, Seven Islands. . . . My heart started pounding. An incredible excitement overcame me.

"Look children, look . . . this is Canada where I was born. We're almost home! If this flight falls, we'll be rescued in Canada, my homeland. We're going home . . . . Kristina! Anton! Look, we're flying over North America! This is Eastern Canada, where I travelled in my professional life. Kristina! Anton! Look, New York City over there . . . see all the lights? Look! We're landing at Kennedy Airport . . . we're landing in America. This is America! How magnificent!" My words were meaningless to my children, but for sure they felt the excitement in my voice.

We prepared to disembark. Kristina was very responsible. She made sure we didn't forget anything on the plane. We walked to the customs counter. With my children by my side, I handed the officer the three passports. He welcomed us to the United States and then directed us to the immigration office. With nervousness, I handed the officer the two brown envelopes from the Moscow American Consulate. He opened both envelopes. I watched his facial expressions, looking for approval. Anxiously, I asked, "Mr. Officer, when will my children receive their green cards?"

In a serious and cold voice, he replied, "Your children will not receive a green card."

OMG! Another catastrophe . . . . Bewildered, I asked, "What do you mean my children will not receive a green card?"

"Ma'am, your children became Americans the moment the airplane touched the United States soil. They are Americans as we speak." He smiled.

"My children . . . Americans? . . . plane . . . touch . . . U.S. soil? You mean . . . ?" He smiled again,

"Yes, I mean they have been Americans for about half an hour now." He smiled. "You may proceed to your next flight."

54.

America, We Are Here

Winners never quit and quitters never win.
Vince Lombardi[53]

Overcoming every challenge brought us home.
With so much support, we survived it all. Thank you.
C.C. LeBlanc

WE FOLLOWED THE CROWD on our way to the carousel. *Oh!*
The sweet smells of New York City! Today, the ugly New York accent
is music to my ears.

Kristina picked up her bag. Anton would not let me touch
mine. He was the man. Bags rolling, smiles stretching to our ears,
we walked to the gate for our final flight, direction Ft. Lauderdale.
Kristina and I sat quietly in the holding area. Anton noticed the
activities on the tarmac through the ten-foot high glass panel. He
sat on the windowsill watching with amazement the very dense
airplane traffic congestion. Planes were taking off and landing
every few seconds. His fascination with the process lasted until
we boarded our flight.

The cabin door closed. No more fears of delays. We were on
American soil now! Kristina was quiet, sleepy. Anton got really
agitated. He pointed to the information panel, talking up a storm

in Russian. I thought he wanted to adjust the air vent. I pointed to it.

"*Nyet.*"

He got more and more frustrated. I turned on the light.

"*Nyet.*"

He continued pointing. My finger was almost touching the seat belt sign. With a smile he blurted, "*Da! Da!*"

I buckled up . . . . At that, he looked happy. I guessed he did not want to lose his new mama. We landed in Ft. Lauderdale past midnight. We collected our bags and jumped in the hotel van. Bedtime was almost immediate.

Our body clocks did not allow us to sleep in. At 7:00 a.m., the children woke up. Looking through our bedroom window, they noticed the swimming pool below.

"C.C., pool. Please C.C. Go pool, please."

To the pool we went. They played like two baby dolphins. Such a wonderful moment!

After our leisurely breakfast, the Holiday Inn van took us to secure a car for our drive home. The distance between Ft. Lauderdale and Naples is approximately one-and-one-half hours or one-hundred-and-ten miles. Kristina preferred to sit in the back seat and listen to her music. Anton sat in front with me. He looked at every button on the dashboard. He observed how I drove, how I passed other cars, etc. If he thought I did something good, he gave me a thumbs-up with a smile.

Whatever clean clothes Kristina and Anton had in their luggage were for a winter climate. The month of May in Florida is already warmer than any summer day in Siberia. On our way home, to the delight of the children, we stopped at a department store. Kristina perused the clothes in the teenage department. I wondered if she noticed the quality of the clothes at Dillard's were a notch or two higher than the Tampa store we had shopped at in December 2003. Anton followed his sister from rack to rack. He even helped her select a pretty pink T-shirt to match the white jeans she had chosen.

We walked to the boy's department to find Anton a new outfit. This time Kristina was the helper. Lightweight khaki and a black T-shirt were the choices. The children were speaking in their native language when I approach the cashier's desk. The women asked in a strong accent, "Did you just adopt these children from Russia?"

"Yes, we arrived in Fort Lauderdale late last night. We're on our way home now."

She walked around to the customer's side of her desk, took me in her arms and whispered, "Thank you for taking these children out of Russia."

We both became emotional. She introduced herself as Katarina. We spoke for a few minutes and exchanged phone numbers. She offered her help to translate or to babysit whenever needed. Later, Katarina, a very attractive, educated and refined woman and I would develop a friendship. She shared how she came to America.

"Some fifteen years ago, I was so desperate to leave Russia that I put my name in a magazine to find an American man who would have me. My now husband and I started communicating via a translator. In one of his letters, he wrote, 'If you marry me, I will take you to America.' I agreed. My dream to immigrate to the United States was granted."

With their new clothes, my children looked like long time Floridians. We drove the last few miles to our new home on Winding Oaks Way. A welcoming celebration arranged by a group of friends, awaited our arrival. My heart was racing as we turned the corner to enter the Stonebridge security gate. The guard greeted us with a smile. I introduced my children. The gate opened. We drove along the golf course and the beautiful homes.

Attached to our mailbox were balloons floating and bouncing in the wind. It was the first welcoming sign of our memorable arrival home. The helium-filled balloons displayed "Welcome Home," the American flag, happy faces, red hearts and red roses. Sir John and Laura, now Grandpa John and Grandma Laura, were away traveling, but they had made sure their presence would be with us.

I pointed toward our house.

"This is your home, Kristina and Anton. This is where you will live."

Their eyes were wide open. The three-car garage, the elegant palm trees, colorful flowers, green grass and their beautiful new home stood right in front of their eyes. The main door opened. Twelve friends greeted us with smiles, hugs and gifts. The children were overwhelmed.

Almost immediately after we entered, I took Kristina to her room. Anton followed. The room contained a single bed, a dresser with a mirror, a round table with a chair, a custom closet, her own bathroom and a beautiful six-foot diameter Alpaca rug in off-white and light brown. In her closet, Kristina saw several feminine products, a purse and a collectible teddy bear gifted by the previous owners. She looked at me with a beautiful smile of approval.

Next, we walked to Anton's room via the kitchen. This time, Kristina followed. His room had a single bed, a dresser, some games, roller blades left by the previous owner, my old desk and his own custom-made closet. His bathroom was just outside his room. From there we walked into the green room or the family room. We then joined the rest of the group in the living room. That's when Anton noticed the pool. I heard him say in Russian, what I understood to be, "Look Kri, a swimming pool!"

"Yes, a swimming pool Anton, are you happy?"

"*Da.*"

The children noticed the beautiful tray of fresh fruits on the coffee table. They started nibbling. Just as the pizzas were delivered, Lidia arrived with a beautiful tray of *petit fours* and chocolate-dipped strawberries. The children ran to hug her. They remembered her from their visit during CampKidHope. She was the Russian voice on the phone calls from America during the long delays of their adoption.

While all were busy enjoying Lidia's Russian conversation with the children, I looked around to observe everyone's faces. Finally, the very children they had cheered and prayed for, for so long, were now here. Everyone was smiling except for one guest. I felt her sadness. She was very quiet and stood sort of removed from the group. Her moist eyes turned to a few tears, which she wiped away immediately. I wondered if it was because my children reminded her of the grandchildren she never had.

In the middle of this brouhaha, Grandpa John called. He asked about the children then, "C.C., did you check your refrigerator?"

"Not yet Grandpa John."

"You will find milk, bread, cheese, eggs, fruit, peanut butter and cereal in your pantry."

"You are the best Sir John. You so often said, 'C.C., you must bring these children to America.' We're here Grandpa John, and it's because of you. Thank you for all your help."

The adults shared a glass of wine or two. The children were offered a variety of juices. Before we ate, I openly thanked God for giving me such wonderful supportive friends, for giving me the privilege to be Kristina and Anton's second mama, and for giving my children the chance to have a better life in America. After our joyful dinner, the guests hugged the children as they said good night. Lidia stayed to help explain a few things.

Knowing how Anton loved to press every button in his path, Lidia explained to him what to touch, how to touch it and what not to touch. The pool control thermostat was off limits. She explained what the security system touchscreen pad was for and how to use the one for the garage entrance. An adult had to be present if they wanted to swim. My office was out of bounds. The entrance doors had to be locked at all times. Our wonderful Lidia from Belarus gave us big, loving hugs and left.

Finally, it was just us. Just the three of us in our permanent home. How did I feel? Overwhelmed, nervous! One set of challenges was over, but the onset of the real work was just beginning. Yes, it was a frightening thought. But, if others did it, so could I.

I'll do the best I know how. Will it be good enough? I was apprehensive about the beginning of Kristina's teenage years. I remembered my own, poor mama! *She got through it, so will I.*

The sun had gone to sleep. Our eyes were spiritless. It was time to go to sleep. We exchanged several bear hugs, and we said, "Good night" and "I love you." I tucked them both in their beds.

As I closed my eyes, the long-awaited vision of C.C. LeBlanc accepting the responsibility of first-time mama, after receiving her first social security check was now so real. She challenged herself, she never gave up on her mission. Her determination has now borne fruit. Her dear children will have a chance for a better life and a better future in America.

Should you, dear reader, choose the path of adopting a child, the joy in your heart will surpass any and all the challenges this enormous human gift of love and generosity will bring you.

I remember the words of the welcome letter I receive the day I became a United States citizen. They so vividly reflect the essence of what came to pass. A woman of French-Canadian blood, birth and soil became an American citizen to adopt two children of Russian blood, birth and soil. All three have moved beyond their backgrounds and have become an integral part of the American fabric. How beautiful!

Epilogue

THIS BOOK WAS WRITTEN from notes, pictures and videos I took throughout the adoption process and from the truth of my heart and of my soul. The words reflect the profound love I have for my children, the unflinching determination to bring them to America for their chance to live a better life, and it describes the challenges we had to face during the adoption process. This story reflects what I saw, what I experienced, what I felt. I have no other agenda.

We all have stories to tell. Now, you know my most significant one. Would it be reasonable to think that in making the decision to adopt I was in need of finding a meaningful purpose for my life? Was there an important missing or essential need that drove me to change direction? Did I sense an emptiness deep down in my soul as I returned home alone after various social activities? What I know now is the adoption of my children, Kristina and Anton, has filled my life in a positive way more than I had imagined.

On April 29, 2021, we celebrated our sixteenth anniversary as a family. I can still hear Tasha translating the judge's words in my left ear on that very special day, "The petition of Marie Cécile LeBlanc to adopt Kristina Sergeevna B. and Anton Sergeevich B. is granted."

My daughter was thirteen years old that very day, her brother nine-and-one-half. This was a ready-made family. No diaper changes nor the challenges of the *terrible twos,* but we were at the onset of the formidable teenage years.

Kristina had become Anton's second mama from the time he was born. She was already mature at her young age. At thirteen, I believe she felt she did not need a new mama. About eight months after we arrived home, while having breakfast at the kitchen bar, she said,

"Mama, when we were still in Russia and you were trying to adopt us, I thought I was coming to America to an old stupid woman."

Her comment caught me by surprise. I burst out laughing and could not stop. When finally I asked her why she thought that way, she answered,

"Because in Russia mama, everybody over sixty is old and stupid.

At that time, life expectancy in Russia was between the ages of sixty-one and sixty-three. In Kristina's mind, I was an old woman at age sixty-five. I should have been floating somewhere with angels. I suspect that she created a movie in her mind that once in America, she would be in charge.

Within just a few days following the adoption, Kristina started to slowly establish or try to establish control. She gradually rejected my parental authority. Needless to say, we had some serious and stormy moments. Kristina eventually lived with the family of her best friend for a while, then transferred to a boarding school to complete her high school education. During that time, she met her future husband, Jesse.

She and Jesse live in Colorado. Together they are raising two wonderful daughters and Jesse's son from a previous relationship. All the turmoil and pain Kristina and I experienced with each other at the onset have disappeared. We now enjoy a wonderful mother/daughter relationship. I am very proud of my daughter. She is a happy, loving, strong, determined and a hard-working young woman. She and her husband live for their children within the embrace of Jesse's extended family. During this last year, Kristina surprised me by sharing that she had started to take on-line classes to prepare for a career in nursing. I'm very happy with her decision.

In contrast, Anton at nine-and-one-half wanted and needed a mama from the onset. He enjoyed everything he was introduced to. I believe life was more difficult for him in the orphanage. He was hyperactive. Often times, in the orphanage, the punishment was doing sit-ups and push-ups. A few months after he started school in the United States, he returned home and, with his limited English knowledge said the following,

"Mama, me no understand. Boy here do fifty sit and fifty push. Me do two hundred sit and two hundred push. I strong mama, I fast."

No wonder his upper body was so strong.

Another time when I asked him what happened to the brown teddy bear I had given him in Siberia. With sadness in his face, he answered, "Gave it teacher mama."

"Why did you give it to your teacher? Was she a nice teacher?"

"Teacher take me home play with son."

He looked at the floor for a few seconds, then looked at me, "Before you come mama, nobody want me."

After his seventh grade, Anton chose to attend a five-week military summer camp. He loved it. I offered and he accepted to return for his eighth grade. When I picked him up at the end of the school year, he made the decision to go back for his ninth grade. He continued to return to the Academy to complete his four years of high school. He proudly graduated captain/company commander. I was the proudest mama on campus that day.

Anton attended college for one semester. When he returned home for Christmas, he decided to take some time off from school. That's when he started his challenging, rebellious years. As of this writing, he works for a very good company. He is an excellent employee. He is never late for work. To my delight, he and his sister continue to have a close relationship. With the ease of technology, they communicate often via FaceTime. Anton took a little longer to find his niche, but he is on his way. He recently married a wonderful young lady who has just received a bachelor's degree in criminal justice. They live about one hour from Naples. I'm very proud of my son. Knowing and understanding the life both of my children experienced from birth to the time of the adoption, I feel all of the efforts and challenges we faced were not in vain. They have adjusted well and are both good and productive citizens of this country.

Life's journey surprises each of us in different ways. In my case, I became a first-time mother at the age of sixty-five and a first-time grandmother at seventy-two. I will be eighty-two years old toward the end of 2021. . . . I'm still feisty and full of projects. I hope to reach one hundred. Will I make it? My mind is still sharp, but my body "talks to me" from time to time.

Grandpa John and Laura left us in 2010 and 2012 respectively. The Wise family and I remain the best of friends. Their adopted Russian children Diana and David are close friends with Anton. In fact, David and Anton are like brothers. Our dear Lidia who had returned to Belarus passed away mid-September 2021. Emails kept us in touch. This book honors our friendship. I love and will miss you Lidia. My oldest friend Sol (we met when we were both 28) and I are still in touch. One close friend and neighbor we call Mr. John Z. and later his wife, Phyllis, played and continue to play an important role in Anton's life. My younger and dear friend Johanne Couture knows my children well. She has been a great support from the beginning. Dr. Renate is always willing to guide me with medical questions. My special niece, Sylvie, from Québec City and her two sons, the ages of my children, have spent wonderful vacations with us. Her young son Simon and his lady friend just spent a week with us this summer. Life takes away old friends but rewards us with new ones. My significant other Mel has been a constant help in the editing and preparation of this manuscript.

I'm grateful to have had the opportunity and the honor to spend the senior years of my life as the mother of two beautiful children, children I love and call my own. It is said that Motherhood has no age!

Why did I write this book you may ask? First, I wanted my children to know the true story of their adoption process, the story of their birth and of their roots in the United States of America. I wanted to put in writing the challenges and obstacles we faced during the adoption process. Because of their young age and because of the language barrier, they could not understand and remember all the unbelievable situations we had to face. Second, I wanted to convey to my children and to whomever read this book, that by constantly reminding ourselves of the NNNQ, we can overcome most if not all our challenges. By never giving up, by not abandoning our goal, we succeeded to reach our dream of coming to America as a family. Third, perhaps for those of you who are on the fence as to whether or not you should adopt a child, I wanted to share this beautiful story and share the deep joy that follows once you fall in love with your chosen child or children. Once you move forward with the adoption, there is no going back.

Perhaps there is a fourth purpose.... Adopting one, two or more children is a very serious and bold decision. It requires a tremendous amount of love, patience, hard work and the desire to overcome all challenges. If the inspiration to adopt or foster a child comes your way, trust yourself. If I did it, so can you. The love you will give and receive, the joy you will have for sharing your home with a child, a child who longs for love, for hope and for a safe place to grow will be immeasurable. The rewards from such a commitment will be tucked into yours and their hearts and souls forever. May I add, not every adoption is as difficult as this one.

As demanding and challenging as it has been, I'm profoundly thankful and proud to have pursued the adoption of my cherished children Kristina and Anton. Not only has my life been enriched by the experience it has been my proudest accomplishment, one I would do all over again if I could. As a bonus, I now have grandchildren and a beautiful story to share with you.

The profound pain a child suffers by having been abandoned by a parent is real. To know they were *chosen* by you, the adoptive parents, can lighten the pain and give them a sense of worth.

Children do not ask to be born. When they are, it is our responsibility as a society, to give them the tools to reach their full potential.

Mama C.C.

To each there comes in their lifetime a special moment when they are figuratively tapped on the shoulder and offered the chance to do a very special thing, unique to them and fitted to their talents. What a tragedy if that moment finds them unprepared or unqualified [and may I add, unwilling] for that which could have been their finest hour.

Sir Winston Churchill[54]

Notes

1. Adapted from a 1777 quote by author Horace Walpole.
2. Kalam, A and Tiwari, A (1999). *Wings of Fire: An Autobiography of A P J Abdul Kalam*. Sangam Books Ltd.
3. Brown, L (1992). *Live Your Dreams*. William Morrow and Company. Retrieved from https://quoteinvestigator. com/2017/09/08/new-dream/.
4. Hill, N. (2007). *Think and Grow Rich*. Wilder Publications.
5. Hill, N. (2005). *The Law of Success*. Tarcher Perigee.
6. Pavao, J. (1998). *The Family of Adoption*. Retrieved from https:// www.quotemaster.org/author/Joyce+Maguire+Pavao.
7. Retrieved from https://www.proudmummy.com/memes/1177254/ the-day-you-came-into-my-life-i-knew-what-my-purpose-was-to.
8. Obama, B. (2013). *Father's Day speech* (Apostolic Church of God, Chicago).
9. Retrieved from https://obamawhitehouse. archives.gov/the-press-office/2013/02/15/ remarks-president-strengthening-economy-middle-class.
10. Kane, T. (2019). *AllGreatQuotes*. Retrieved from https://www.all-greatquotes.com/ in-loving-memory-cards-i-hide-my-tears-when-i-say-your-name/.
11. Jain, A. (2019). *YourQuotes*. Retrieved from https://www. yourquote.in/aanchal-jain-bpq6q/quotes.
12. Walter Elliot Quotes. (n.d.). *BrainyQuote.com*. Retrieved from https://www.brainyquote.com/quotes/walter_elliot_190719.
13. Douglass, F. (1857). *"West India Emancipation" speech*, Canandaigua, August 3 1857. Retrieved from https://www.blackpast.org/african-american-history/1857-frederick-douglass-if-there-no-struggle-there-no-progress/.
14. Vince Lombardi Quotes. (n.d.). BrainyQuote.com. Retrieved from https://www.brainyquote.com/quotes/vince_lombardi_127517.
15. Winfrey, O. (2002). *O Magazine*, October 2002.

16. Stookey, P. (1893). *The Irish Blessing.* Retrieved from https://digitalcommons.library.umaine.edu/mmb-me/398/
17. Sophia Loren Quotes. (n.d.). *BrainyQuote.com.* Retrieved from https://www.brainyquote.com/quotes/sophia_loren_106851.
18. Winfrey, O. (2002). *O Magazine,* September 2002.
19. Maraboli, S. (2009). *Life, the Truth, and Being Free.* Today Publishing
20. Peter, L.J. (1969). *The Peter Principle.* William Morris.
21. Benny, J. (1974). *QuoteInvestigator.* Retrieved from https://quoteinvestigator.com/2012/12/18/age-mind/.
22. Dean, J. (n.d.). BrainyQuote.com. Retrieved from https://www.brainyquote.com/quotes/jimmy_dean_131287.
23. Newood, F. (n.d.). 100 Heartwarming Adoption Quotes (by Maryn Liles). Retrieved from https://parade.com/989645/marynliles/adoption-quotes/.
24. Tew, Robert (n.d.). *Quotespedia.com.* Retrieved from https://www.quotespedia.org/quotes/authors/r/robert-tew/.
25. Ingersoll, R. (1907). *The Works of Robert Ingersoll* (Daved Widger, ed.). Centenial Oration, July 4, 1876.
26. Gibran, K. (1895). Quoted in *Dictionary of Burning Words of Brilliant Writers* (p. 565) by Edwin Hubbell Chapin.Neal, A. (n.d.) Prayer. Retrieved from https://www.wow4u.com/power-prayerquotes/.
27. Henry Ford Quotes. (n.d.). *BrainyQuote.com.* Retrieved from https://www.brainyquote.com/quotes/henry_ford_132651.
28. Martin Luther King, Jr. Quotes. (n.d.). *BrainyQuote.com.* Retrieved from https://www.brainyquote.com/quotes/martin_luther_king_jr_297522.
29. Ziglar, Z. (n.d.) *GoodReads.com.* Retrieved from https://www.goodreads.com/quotes/976049-f-e-a-r-has-two-meanings-forget-everything-and-run-or-face.
30. Tilton, G.F. (1948). *Forbes Magazine.* Retrieved from https://quoteinvestigator.com/2013/09/03/success-final/
31. Watkins, J. (n.d.). Retrieved from. https://www.goodreads.com/quotes/9603610-a-river-cuts-through-rock-not-because-of-its-power.
32. Lee, J. (n.d.) *Passiton.com.* Retrieved from https://www.passiton.com/inspirational-quotes/7773-be-fearless-in-the-pursuit-of-what-sets-your.

33. Buffet, W. (n.d.). *Warren Buffett Quotes*. Retrieved from https://quotefancy.com/warren-buffett-quotes.

34. Simon S. (2010). *Baby, We Were Meant for Each Other: In Praise of Adoption*. Random House.

35. Napoleon Hill Quotes. (n.d.). *BrainyQuote.com*. Retrieved from https://www.brainyquote.com/quotes/napoleon_hill_152875.

36. Dickens C. (1838-1849). *Nicholas Nickleby* (original serialization). Retrieved from https://www.charlesdickensinfo.com/quotes/hope-to-the-last-said/.

37. Maya Angelou Quotes. (n.d.). *BrainyQuote.com*. Retrieved from https://www.brainyquote.com/quotes/maya_angelou_165173.

38. Simon Sinek Quotes. (n.d.). *BrainyQuote.com*. Retrieved from https://www.brainyquote.com/quotes/simon_sinek_568159.

39. Napoleon Hill Quotes. (n.d.). *BrainyQuote.com*. Retrieved from https://www.brainyquote.com/quotes/napoleon_hill_121336.

40. Meyer, J. (2002). *Battlefield of the Mind: Winning the Battle in Your Mind* (Revised edition). Warner Faith.

41. Bennet R.T. (2020). *The Light in the Heart*. Retrieved from https://quotecatalog.com/quote/roy-t-bennett-never-lose-hope-w7g6ZG1.

42. Mutuyimana David (n.d.). Retrieved from https://www.yourquote.in/david-mutuyimana-vnme/quotes/today-i-pray-you-heart-free-sadness-mind-free-worries-life-hvmmk.

43. Barabara Bush in the Commencement Address, Wellesley College, Wellesley, MA, 1990. https://www.wellesley.edu/events/commencement/archives/1990commencement/commencementaddress.

44. *Adoption Magazine*. Retrieved from https://adoptionmagazine.com/15-popular-adoption-quotes/.

45. Roosevelts, F.D. (1933). *First Inaugural Address*. Retrieved from https://www.brainyquote.com/quotes/franklin_d_roosevelt_124526.

46. Heyliger, F.C. (n.d.). Retrieved from https://www. Scrapbook.com/poems.doc/5561.html.

47. Mahatma Gandhi (n.d.). Retrieved in https://www.goodreads.com/quotes/30431-earth-provides-enough-to-satisfy-every-man-s-needs-but-not.

48. Retrieved from https://www.goodreads.com/quotes/178086-it-doesn-t-matter-who-you-are-where-you-come-from.

49. Kornfield, J. (1994). *Buddha's Little Instruction Book*. Bantam.

50. McCullough, M. (2005). *1776*. Simon and Schuster.

51. Lily Tomlin (n.d.). Retrieved from https://www.brainyquote.com/authors/lily-tomlin-quotes.

52. Donna Hedges Quotes. (n.d.). *Quotes.net*. Retrieved from https://www.quotes.net/authors/Donna+Hedges+Quotes.

53. Vince Lombardi Quotes (nd). *BrainyQuote.com*. Retrieved from www.brainyquotes.com/quotes/vince _lombardi_122285.

54. Churchill, W. (n.d.). Retrieved from https://www.goodread.com/quotes/67420-to-each-there-comes-in-their-lifetime-a-special-moment.